Fire in North American
Tallgrass Prairies

Fire in North American Tallgrass Prairies

Edited by Scott L. Collins and Linda L. Wallace

University of Oklahoma Press : Norman and London

Publication of this volume is made possible in part through the generous support of the University of Oklahoma Foundation.

Data from the Konza Prairie Research Natural Area (a preserve owned by The Nature Conservancy and managed by the Division of Biology, Kansas State University) were collected as part of the Konza Prairie LTER program (NSF grants DEB-8012166 and BSR-8514327). Data and supporting documentation are stored in the Konza Prairie Research Natural Area LTER data bank. Inquiries about the availability and use of such data should be sent to: Data Manager, Div. of Biology, Kansas State University, Manhattan, KS 66506.

Library of Congress Cataloging-in-Publication Data

Fire in North American tallgrass prairies / edited by Scott L. Collins and Linda L. Wallace.
    p. cm.
    "The papers in this volume were derived from a symposium 'Fire in North American Grasslands.' held on 13 August 1987 at the annual meetings of the American Institute of Biological Sciences in Columbus . . . sponsored by the Ecological Society of America and the Botanical Society of America"—Pref.
    Includes bibliographical references.
    ISBN 0-8061-2281-1 (alk. paper)
    1. Prairie ecology—North America—Congresses. 2. Grassland fires—Environmental aspects—North America—Congresses. 3. Fire ecology—North America—Congresses. I. Collins, Scott L. (Scott Lathrop), 1952– . II. Wallace, Linda L., 1951– . III. American Institute of Biological Sciences. IV. Ecological Society of America. V. Botanical Society of America. VI. Title: Tallgrass prairies.
QK110.F53 1990
575.5'2643—dc20   90-12044
                                                                   CIP

The paper in this book meets the guidelines for permanence and durability of the Committee on Production Guidelines for Book Longevity of the Council on Library Resources, Inc. ∞

Contents

Preface   xi
1. Introduction: Fire as a Natural Disturbance in Tall-
   grass Prairie Ecosystems, by Scott L. Collins   3
2. The Historic Role of Fire in the North American
   Grassland, by Roger C. Anderson   8
3. Response of *Andropogon gerardii* to Fire in the
   Tallgrass Prairie, by T. J. Svejcar   19
4. Fire in Central North American Grasslands: Vegetative Reproduction, Seed Germination, and
   Seedling Establishment, by David C. Glenn-
   Lewin, Louise A. Johnson, Thomas W. Jurik,
   Ann Akey, Mark Leoschke, and Tom Rosburg   28
5. Small Mammals and Grassland Fires, by Donald
   W. Kaufman, Elmer J. Finck, and Glennis A.
   Kaufman   46
6. Effects of Fire on Community Structure in Tall-
   grass and Mixed-Grass Prairie, by Scott L. Col-
   lins and David J. Gibson   81
7. The Influence of Fire on Belowground Processes of
   Tallgrass Prairie, by T. R. Seastedt and
   R. A. Ramundo   99
8. Simulated Impacts of Annual Burning on Prairie
   Ecosystems, by Dennis S. Ojima, W. J. Parton,
   D. S. Schimel, and C. E. Owensby   118
9. Landscape Processes and the Vegetation of the
   North American Grassland, by Paul G. Risser   133
10. Epilogue: A Search for Paradigms, by Linda L.
    Wallace   147
Literature Cited   153
The Contributors   171
Index   173

Illustrations

1.1 Conceptual model of the periodic and average response of grasslands to the fire regime. 6

2.1 Diagram of grass morphology. 10

2.2 Climatic patterns and distribution of major grasslands in North America. 11

2.3 Paleovegetation maps for eastern North America. 13

2.4 Topography and presettlement vegetation in McLean County, Illinois. 15

2.5 Fuel availability across a plant production gradient. 16

3.1 Leaf area index and number of tillers m^{-2} of big bluestem in burned and unburned prairie. 20

3.2 Physiological response of big bluestem under burned and unburned conditions. 24

4.1 Effect of fire at different times of the year on number of flowering culms of big bluestem, Indian grass, and Kentucky bluegrass. 34

4.2 Tiller production by big bluestem over 2 years following fire at different times of the year. 40

4.3 Tiller production by Indian grass over 2 years following fire at different times of the year. 41

4.4 Tiller production by Kentucky bluegrass over 2 years following fire at different times of the year. 42

5.1 Relative density of all small mammals in burned and unburned areas on Konza Prairie. 58

5.2 Number of mammal species trapped on a watershed in burned and unburned areas at Konza Prairie. 63

5.3 Hypothetical patterns of change in population density of small mammals with time since fire. 70

5.4 Hypothetical patterns of change in population density of small mammals in grasslands experiencing recurring fire. 74

6.1 Schematic diagram showing the matrix structure of

grasslands and the impact of fire, grazing, and small-
scale disturbances. 84

6.2 Species richness on several watersheds subjected to different fire frequencies at Konza Prairie. 86

6.3 Changes in species diversity during postfire succession
at Konza Prairie. 89

6.4 Effects of fire on patch size in May, July, and September on burned and unburned tallgrass prairie. 91

6.5 Ordination of vegetation samples from inside and outside buffalo wallows on burned and unburned mixed-
grass prairie. 93

6.6 Changes in richness and cover of big bluestem over
2 years on artificial soil disturbances in burned and
unburned tallgrass prairie. 95

6.7 Changes in richness and cover of big bluestem on
artificial soil disturbances on burned and unburned
areas at Konza Prairie. 96

7.1 Aerial photograph of the original Konza Prairie Research Natural Area. 100

7.2 Photograph of grazed prairie with and without burning. 101

7.3 Conceptual model of tallgrass prairie emphasizing the
roles of biotic and abiotic components. 102

7.4 Root lengths, production, and turnover with and without litter. 108

7.5 Foliage and root decay rates. 111

7.6 Amounts of N and P in foliage and roots. 112

7.7 Nitrogen budget for tallgrass prairie. 115

8.1 Conceptual flow diagram of annual burning effects on
tallgrass prairie. 124

8.2 Flow diagrams for C, N, and P submodels in the CEN-
TURY model. 126

8.3 Simulated impact of unburned vs. annually burned
treatments on aboveground and belowground
production. 127

8.4 Simulated effect of annual burning on soil C and N. 128

8.5 Simulated impact of annual burning on total system and
belowground net N mineralization. 130

8.6 Simulation of effects of annual burning on microbial
C and N. 131

9.1 Conceptual model of grassland responses to weather
and grazing conditions. 143

9.2 Diagram of grassland responses to drought, grazing,
and burning. 144

Tables

4.1 Grass species that show increase or decrease in flowering following spring fire. 30

4.2 Forb species that show increase or decrease in flowering following spring fire. 31

4.3 Variation in flowering response of 4 grass species according to habitat, following spring fire, Minnesota. 31

4.4 Increases in flowering of *Bouteloua curtipendula* following 2 spring fires in 2 habitats. 32

4.5 Percentage of adult *Dodecatheon meadia* plants that flowered following spring fire at 2 Iowa sites. 35

4.6 Flowering and seed production in Kansas prairie populations of *Vernonia baldwinii* burned annually, and 1, 2, 4, or 10 years after burning. 35

4.7 Least square means of seeds per inflorescence in 3 grasses following fire at different times of the year, Iowa. 36

4.8 Flowering response of *Dodecatheon meadia* in a northeast Iowa prairie to spring fire. 37

4.9 Total number of warm season grass seedlings and dicots in 6 m² according to time of fire, central Iowa. 38

5.1 Scientific names of small mammals discussed in text. 50

5.2 General population responses of small mammals to fires in North American grasslands. 54

5.3 Average relative density of common small mammals in burned and unburned prairie on Konza Prairie. 57

5.4 Average percentage abundance of common small mammals in burned and unburned prairie on Konza Prairie. 62

5.5 Percentage abundance of western harvest mice and deer mice in burned and unburned prairie on Konza Prairie. 64

5.6 Percentage abundance of Elliot's short-tailed shrews and deer mice in burned and unburned prairie on Konza Prairie. 64

5.7 Changes in relative density of the 3 common small mammals with time since fire on Konza Prairie. 72

6.1 General characteristics of the disturbance regime in North American grasslands. 82

6.2 Average values of diversity, evenness, and richness for plant species in 4 disturbance treatments in tallgrass prairie in central Oklahoma. 93

6.3 Total number of all seedlings and grass seedlings found throughout growing season on control plots and artificial soil disturbances in annually burned and unburned grasslands at Konza Prairie. 97

7.1 Nitrogen concentrations of bulk precipitation, soil water, and streams of annually burned and unburned tallgrass prairie. 105

7.2 Comparison of root and rhizome mass of burned and unburned tallgrass prairie. 107

7.3 Soil characteristics of annually burned and unburned tallgrass prairie. 110

7.4 Plant biomass and soil water inorganic N response to fixed C and N additions. 113

8.1 Short- and long-term observed effect of fire on microbial C and N, belowground net N mineralization, labile P, inorganic N, live root and shoot biomass, and live root and shoot N concentration. 121

9.1 Ammonium captured by undisturbed and mown grasslands in the Netherlands. 145

Preface

On 22 April 1889, the official settlement of Indian Territory, known today as Oklahoma, was initiated through the first Oklahoma land run. This historic event of over one hundred years ago began the widespread settlement by whites of much of the southern Great Plains, a vast region of tallgrass and mixed-grass prairie, oak savannah, and cross-timbers forests. The ecological consequences of this settlement were enormous. Perhaps one of the most significant effects of this mass colonization on the vegetation was the disruption of the natural disturbance regime that previously characterized grassland environments. In particular, the large herds of native grazers were replaced by domestic cattle. Fires, a vital component of grassland ecosystems, were viewed as detrimental and thus were suppressed whenever possible. In an ecosystem maintained by natural disturbances, the settlement and subsequent increase in human population led to a rapid deterioration of the grassland environment. Only small patches of native prairie remain today, and the continued existence of these patches is constantly threatened by development and/or poor management practices.

The role of fire in grasslands has been and still remains controversial from both an ecological and a management perspective. How often did fires occur? Were they started more often by Indians or by natural causes, such as lightning strikes? At what time of year did the grasslands normally burn? How does one use fire as a management tool? What is a proper prescribed burning regime with and without grazing? To a large extent, these questions still remain unanswered. The purpose of this book is to draw together research on many aspects of fire ecology in grassland ecosystems, to indicate where further research on fire ecology is needed, and to stimulate an interest in using grasslands as a natural laboratory for the study of ecological processes.

The papers in this volume were derived from a symposium, "Fire in North American Grasslands," held on 13 August 1987 at the annual meetings of the American Institute of Biological Sciences in Columbus, Ohio. The symposium was sponsored by the Ecological Society of America and the Botanical Society of America. We are grateful for the financial support for publication costs provided by the NSF-funded Long-Term Ecological Research Program at Konza Prairie Research Natural Area and by the University of Oklahoma Foundation. We thank Tom Radko and Patty Dornbusch of the University of Oklahoma Press for their managerial and editorial help on this project. Finally, we especially thank the contributors for their willingness to participate in the symposium, and for their patience and cooperation during the editing of the book.

SCOTT L. COLLINS

Norman, Oklahoma   LINDA L. WALLACE

Fire in North American
Tallgrass Prairies

1
Introduction: Fire as a Natural Disturbance in Tallgrass Prairie Ecosystems

By Scott L. Collins

Fire has played a significant role in the development of vegetation in North America (Kozlowski and Ahlgren 1974, Wright and Bailey 1982) and elsewhere (de Van Booysen and Tainton 1984, Trabaud 1987). The role of fire is especially important in North American grasslands where periodic droughts, high temperatures, and strong winds provide an ideal environment for ignition and perpetuation of fire (Borchert 1950, Sauer 1950, R. C. Anderson 1982). Bragg (1982) noted that prairie fires could occur at any time during the year, but fuel conditions and weather patterns lead to peak fire probabilities in July/August and secondarily during late spring. Although the use of fire by American Indians in the eastern forests is a controversial issue (Russell 1983), most evidence suggests that Indians frequently started grassland fires to modify habitat and either drive or attract wild game (Pyne 1982).

A significant interest in grassland ecology was stimulated by the pioneering American ecologist Frederick Clements and his student John Weaver (Tobey 1981). Weaver, in particular (Weaver 1954, 1968, Weaver and Fitzpatrick 1934, Weaver and Albertson 1936, 1956), provided detailed descriptions of grassland vegetation in response to grazing and drought. Because much of his work focused on the effects of drought during the 1930s, Weaver treated fire as a rare and detrimental component of the grassland environment. Fire suppression, therefore, became a primary management concern. Tobey (1981) suggested that the ecological response of grassland vegetation during the drought contributed to the demise of the Clementsian paradigm of community structure.

Prairies continued to burn periodically, however, and research by Aldous (1934), Kelting (1957), and K. L. Anderson, Smith, and Owensby (1970), among others, provided evidence that fires were not deleterious during times of average to above-average precipitation. Early spring burning actually enhanced growth, tillering, and flowering stem density by the dominant C_4 grasses, especially big bluestem (*Andropogon gerardii*). Additional observations on the invasion of unburned mesic prairie by woody vegetation (e.g., Bragg and Hulbert 1976) provided further support for the notion that fires, caused by human activity or otherwise, were historically a frequent component of the disturbance regime in grasslands (see also Axelrod 1985).

Given that fires are a natural component of the grassland ecosystem, ecologists have often debated the question whether fire is a disturbance in grassland communities. Groups are polarized around two simple answers, yes and no. The "no" group argues that if fire is a natural and predictable component of the system, and if grassland species exhibit characteristics that have been shaped by fire as an agent of natural selection, then *lack* of fire is a disturbance in grasslands. The "yes" group views fire as a significant, even if natural, event. To some extent, answers to this question are exacerbated by terminological baggage in which the word *disturbance* has strictly negative connotations.

In this book, we subscribe to the idea that fire *is* a disturbance in grassland ecosystems. Admittedly, such a statement would not be completely accepted even by the different authors of the chapters in this book. Nevertheless, we feel that this volume provides an important forum not only for reviewing the role of fire in grasslands at different hierarchical levels but also for contributing to theories regarding disturbance in ecological systems (Sousa 1984, Rykiel 1985, Pickett and White 1985).

Pickett et al. (1989) provide an outline for a definition of disturbance that transcends all levels in the ecological hierarchy. Essentially, a system such as a grassland contains structure, which is represented by the presence of, and interaction between, lower level units. For example, a grassland contains a primary producer component that is made up of patches of vegetation. A system derives structure through organization, which is represented by interactions within and among the lower level units. An example would be the dispersal of deer mice from one patch to another within a watershed. A disturbance is an exogenous force that disrupts or alters this structure. Small mammals alter their activity patterns after a grassland is burned. Thus, fire does constitute a disturbance according to this definition.

The important role of natural disturbance has been described in many communities (see reviews by Sousa [1984] and Pickett and White [1985]). As an example, storms, waves, predation, and physical abrasion disrupt plant and animal assemblages in the rocky intertidal zone. These disturbances create patches which are subsequently colonized by early successional species. Thus, disturbance promotes patch dynamics, which in turn enhances community diversity on a larger spatial scale (Sousa 1985). When disturbance is experimentally prevented, species richness declines as superior competitors occupy the majority of available space (Connell 1978). Thus, patterns of dominance and diversity in the intertidal zone reflect a long history of disturbance acting as an agent of natural selection. To follow the same logic that has been applied to grasslands, *lack* of storms and wave abrasion would be seen as a disturbance in the intertidal zone. Such an inference is clearly invalid because it implies that *nothing* (lack of disturbance) caused *something* (dominance and reduced diversity). The same argument holds for the role of gaps in forest dynamics (e.g., Runkle 1985).

Additional confusion is generated by the failure to separate disturbance as a causal factor from the subsequent changes in the system, which reflect a response to this factor (Rykiel 1985, Pickett et al. 1989). Essentially, the statement that "fire in grasslands is not a disturbance because, in the absence of fire, succession leads to dominance by woody species" in fact confuses disturbance and response. A single fire alters the physiology of an individual grass, the population dynamics of small mammals, species diversity, nutrient dynamics, and so forth. Viewing the system over the long term homogenizes disturbance and response, so that the system appears stable (Fig. 1.1). This does not imply that such studies are invalid. Instead, they address the effects of altering the *disturbance regime*, which includes the frequency, intensity, and magnitude of disturbances. In grassland ecosystems, therefore, the system becomes unstable in the absence of fire because of interactions among the component species (competition, dispersal) which lead to successional change. These changes cannot be attributed to the lack of fire. Thus, even though fires are a natural component of grassland ecosystems, they have dramatic and immediate effects on structural components, ranging from individual plants to landscape processes. The duration of these responses varies from a few days to one to three years. From this we conclude that fire is a disturbance in grassland ecosystems.

Given that fire is a disturbance in grasslands, we can now address the question of how fire affects different components of grassland structure. We have approached this question by analyzing the effects of fire on individuals, populations, communities, ecosystem, and landscape components, primarily of tallgrass prairie. We focus on tallgrass prairie because many of the data in this book were derived from the Long Term Ecological Research studies at Konza Prairie Research Natural Area. However, in addition to discussing current research, the authors of each chapter provide broad reviews of the literature and describe gaps in our knowledge of

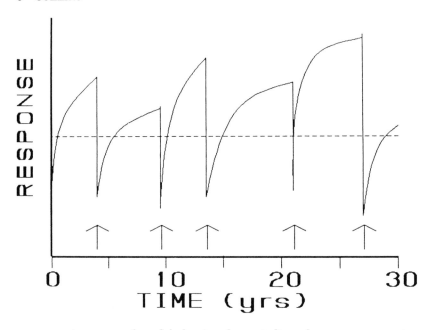

FIG. 1.1 A conceptual model showing the periodic and average community response to fire in grassland ecosystems. The model is designed to show the relationship among disturbance, community response, and disturbance regime. Arrows indicate occurrence of fires. System response could be a variable, such as species diversity, which is decreased by spring burning. Diversity then gradually increases for several years following fire. The dashed line would represent the long-term average species diversity in grasslands given a disturbance regime of 1 fire every 3–5 years. Thus, short-term variation in grasslands is generated by individual fires, but long-term stability is maintained by the disturbance regime, which includes periodic burning plus interactions among species during the time after a burn. (Adapted from Loucks 1970.)

fire effects in grasslands. Some responses to fire have been intensively studied—e.g., increased productivity following spring burning—whereas aspects of physiological and landscape level phenomena are poorly understood. Also, knowledge of the interaction of fire with other disturbances is limited because most studies of fire are short term and are often conducted in grasslands where the large native ungulates have little or no role in disturbing the ecosystem.

The book is organized along a traditional hierarchy from individual to landscape. Roger Anderson (chapter 2) begins the book with a brief historical perspective regarding the climatic conditions and role of fire in the development of North American grasslands. In chapter 3, Tony Svejcar describes the photosynthetic response and water relations of dominant C_4 grasses, especially *Andropogon gerardii,* following spring burning. David Glenn-Lewin and his coauthors (chapter 4) provide a review of the population dynamics of grassland plants, including vegetative reproduction, flower and seed production, and seedling survival, in response to burning during different times of the year. A detailed review of fire effects on population and community dynamics of small mammals is given in chapter 5 by Don Kaufman and colleagues. These authors explain fluctuations in fire-positive and fire-negative species in regard to modification of habitat structure and food availability caused by fires. Scott Collins and David Gibson (chapter 6) describe the effects of fire and fire frequency on plant community structure, diversity, heterogeneity, and dynamics in tallgrass and mixed-grass prairies. Ecosystem dynamics and belowground response are discussed by Tim Seastedt and Rosemary Ramundo (chapter 7), who emphasize the role of the litter layer in controlling ecosystem processes. In chapter 8, Dennis Ojima and his coauthors discuss the use of the CENTURY model for predicting the role of fire in grassland ecosystems. Paul Risser (chapter 9) provides a forum for the development of a conceptual framework on landscape ecology in grassland ecosystems. Because the landscape perspective has developed only recently in North America, this chapter exhibits a wide latitude for speculation and hypothesis generation. In chapter 10, Linda Wallace synthesizes the diverse perspectives of the varied chapters and authors, and suggests important topics for future research.

Admittedly, other topics could have or should have been covered. Studies of birds and large mammals have not been explicitly addressed, nor has the importance of conservation been discussed in detail. We do feel, however, that the material presented in this volume has important implications for the conservation and management of grassland preserves. As Paul Risser (chapter 9) notes, understanding pattern and process at smaller scales will help to predict the impact of human-induced global changes on grassland ecosystems.

Although this book does not constitute a complete documentation of fire effects in tallgrass prairie, it allows readers to synthesize and integrate information gathered from the different perspectives of the various authors. Additionally, this book will provide readers with access to much of the fire literature from little-known sources. Finally, and perhaps most importantly, this book aims to stimulate interest in the ecology of grassland ecosystems. These systems represent an excellent laboratory for addressing ecological concepts and hypotheses. If we accomplish this one goal, we will consider the book to be a success.

2
The Historic Role of Fire in the North American Grassland

By Roger C. Anderson

Various authors have reviewed the literature concerned with the role of fire in grasslands (Daubenmire 1968, Vogl 1974, R. C. Anderson 1982). Recently, Axelrod (1985) suggested that, after climate, fire is the most important determinant in the spread and maintenance of grasslands. While most ecologists would readily accept this as a first approximation to understanding the ecology of grasslands, this simplification does not adequately describe the way in which fire interacts with other factors that influence grasslands and determine vegetational patterns.

The grasslands of North America are a diverse assemblage of vegetation types, ranging from the arid grasslands of the semi-desert Southwest and shortgrass plains, where total annual rainfall may be 25 cm or less, to the eastern tallgrass prairies, which can receive annual precipitation in excess of 100 cm. In North America, grasslands extended from north-central Mexico to several hundred kilometers into the Canadian provinces of Alberta, Saskatchewan, and Manitoba (Risser et al. 1981).

Throughout this area fire was a universal phenomenon (e.g., Humphrey 1958, Curtis 1959, Daubenmire 1968, Vogl 1974, Risser et al. 1981). Yet the historic role of fire and other influences—such as grazing and browsing animals, periodic droughts, topographic relief, and edaphic factors—in maintaining these varied grasslands was not constant in time or space.

The origin of the North American grasslands can be traced to the Miocene-Pliocene transition, perhaps 7–5 million years before present (YBP), associated with the beginning of a drying trend. The increased aridity resulted from the chilling of the ocean as the Antarctic ice sheet spread and from the Miocene uplift of the Rocky Mountains, which served as a partial barrier to moist Pacific air masses. Grasses are generally better adapted to drought than most tree species, and the spread of the grasslands occurred at the expense of forest vegetation. Associated with the expansion of grasslands was a rise in the number of grazing and browsing animals, suggesting that the association of grasses and grazers is an ancient one (Stebbins 1981, Axelrod 1985).

In 1950, the geographer Carl O. Sauer suggested that no single grassland climate could be defined. Instead, unifying characteristics of grasslands included climates with periodic droughts that permit the vegetation to dry, periodic fires, and landscapes that are level to gently rolling, which allows fires to spread across extensive areas. Sauer noted that on a worldwide basis, grasslands subjected to fire suppression rapidly convert to shrublands or forests. To these universal features of grasslands, we can add dominance by grazing animals.

Gleason (1922) proposed that the adaptation that protects grasses from drought was their ability to die down to underground organs, exposing only dead tops aboveground. He noted that the same adaptation that protects grassland plants from drought also affords protection from fire. Grassland fires tend to move rapidly, and although soil surface temperatures can vary from 83 to 680°C (Wright 1974, Rice and Parenti 1978), soil is a good insulator. Thus, there is little penetration of heat more than a centimeter below the soil surface (R. C. Anderson 1982). The adaptation that protects grassland species from fire and drought also prevents mortality of some grassland plants due to grazing. Growing points beneath the soil surface permit regrowth after intensive grazing pressure and protect growing points during dormant seasons, when aboveground palatable tissues are removed (Tainton and Mentis 1984) (Fig. 2.1).

Golley and Golley (1972) indicated that grasses produce more biomass than can be decomposed; this excess herbage production was probably a response to grazing. They also noted that productivity of grassland systems declines if this excess biomass is not removed by grazing or periodic fires. Supporting this view are the results of numerous studies demonstrating that productivity of grasslands is enhanced through litter removal by burning or artificial raking or through moderate levels of grazing (e.g., Old 1969, McNaughton 1979, Risser et al. 1981, R. C. Anderson 1982, Dyer et al. 1982, Knapp and Seastedt 1986, chapters 3 and 7 of this volume).

Studies by several workers indicate that grasses are adapted to grazing and that a symbiotic relationship may have developed between grassland plants and their herbivores (McNaughton 1979, NcNaughton et al. 1982, Dyer et al. 1982, McNaughton 1985). Although grazing, like burning, enhances the rate of nutrient cycling in grasslands, McNaughton (1985) has

GRASS GROWTH FORM ADAPTATION

Protection of perennating organs beneath
the soil surface

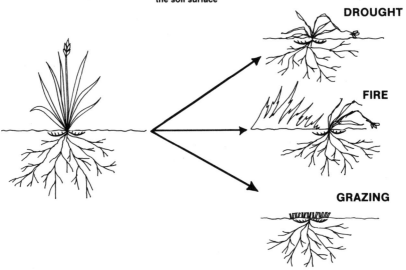

FIG. 2.1   The relationship between the location of perennating organs below the surface of the soil and protection from drought, fire, and grazing animals.

proposed that the relationship between grasses and grazers is not mutualistic. The silicification of grassland plants, which increases following grazing, probably represents a herbivore defense mechanism against grazing. Also, grazing can reduce flowering (and thus fitness), so grazing is not necessarily beneficial.

In this chapter, I focus on the central grassland of North America. This was a large triangular grassland with the base of the triangle running along the foothills of the Rocky Mountains from the Canadian provinces of Alberta and Saskatchewan to southeast Texas and the point of the triangle extending as far east as Indiana, with scattered outliers in southern Michigan, Ohio, and Kentucky. To understand the ecology of the central grassland, it is important to review temporal and spatial variations in climatic patterns in this region, the differential effects of fire on woody plants and grassland species, the role of topography in influencing fire frequency, and the importance of the North American Indians in determining historical patterns of fire.

Three primary air mass systems influence the central grassland climate: the Polar, Gulf, and Mountain Pacific air masses. Of these three, the most important for this discussion are the Gulf and Mountain Pacific air masses.

The Gulf air mass is a humid air mass originating in the Gulf of Mexico, which spreads high humidity and often triggers precipitation as it moves northward. The Pacific air mass also originates as a humid air mass which passes over several mountain ranges and gives up much of its moisture. Thus, the western grasslands in the Great Plains are strongly influenced by the rainshadow of the Rocky Mountains (Fig. 2.2).

Within the central grassland, the frequency of the Pacific air mass decreases from west to east and the frequency of the Gulf air mass increases. Associated with these changes in air mass frequencies are an increase in precipitation and a decrease in periodic droughts and periods of low humidity during the summer from west to east within the central grassland (Transeau 1935, Borchert 1950, Risser et al. 1981). In response to this cli-

FIG. 2.2   The major grasslands of North America and the air masses influencing the climate of the central grassland. (Adapted from Risser et al. 1981.)

matic gradient across the central grassland, there is also a change in species composition and height of the native grasses. Ecologists traditionally have divided this grassland into an arid western shortgrass prairie, a central mid- or mixed-grass prairie, and the eastern tallgrass prairie (Risser et al. 1981). North-south variations in climate and vegetational patterns also occur within each of these divisions (Diamond and Smeins 1988, Kebart and Anderson 1987). Also, snow cover during winter becomes more continuous, and temperature gradients exist from north to south within this grassland (Risser et al. 1981).

The eastern sector of the central grassland, the prairie peninsula (Transeau 1935), has historically fluctuated between a climate capable of supporting grassland and one supporting forest. Paleovegetation maps prepared by Delcourt and Delcourt (1981) illustrate shifts in vegetational patterns in this region from the time of the Wisconsinan glacial maximum of 200 YBP (Fig. 2.3). Spruce and jack pine covered most of the area of the central grassland 18,000 YBP. By 10,000 YBP, there was an eastward migration of grassland vegetation, but most of the prairie peninsula was occupied by oak-hickory forest. Near the peak of the hypsithermal, about 7,000–8,000 YBP, grass-dominated vegetation had extended into a large portion of the Midwest under climatic conditions that had become increasingly warmer and drier following the postglacial pluvial period. From 5,000 to 200 YBP there was a cooling trend and a concominant shrinking of prairie vegetation (King and Allen 1977, Delcourt and Delcourt 1981, King 1981). Brown and Gersmehl (1985) proposed that for the mid-continent plains, some plant species are still migrating in delayed response to postglacial climatic changes. Perhaps a similar conclusion could be reached for the plant species of the eastern tallgrass prairie. Unfortunately, grass pollen cannot be separated beyond the family level in many cases, making it difficult to determine when various species migrated into an area; such determinations have been made for many tree species (Davis 1976, Delcourt and Delcourt 1981).

The recent climate of the prairie peninsula on average should be capable of supporting forest rather than grasslands. Transeau (1935) emphasized that to understand the distribution of grassland in this region the extremes of climate must be considered, and not the average. This area has periodic droughts, and during these times the forest retreated and the grasslands advanced or were maintained. In support of this view is the documentation of the loss of trees from upland sites and their restriction to sheltered locations adjacent to streams during the droughts of the 1930s (Transeau 1935).

Britton and Messenger (1970) proposed that droughts most detrimental to woody species are those that do not permit deep recharge of soil mois-

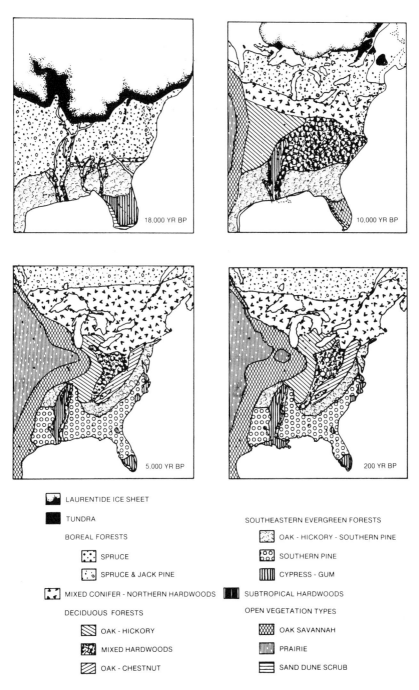

LAURENTIDE ICE SHEET

TUNDRA

BOREAL FORESTS

SPRUCE

SPRUCE & JACK PINE

MIXED CONIFER - NORTHERN HARDWOODS

DECIDUOUS FORESTS

OAK - HICKORY

MIXED HARDWOODS

OAK - CHESTNUT

SOUTHEASTERN EVERGREEN FORESTS

OAK - HICKORY - SOUTHERN PINE

SOUTHERN PINE

CYPRESS - GUM

SUBTROPICAL HARDWOODS

OPEN VEGETATION TYPES

OAK SAVANNAH

PRAIRIE

SAND DUNE SCRUB

FIG. 2.3   Paleovegetation maps for eastern North America. (Adapted from Delcourt and Delcourt 1981.)

ture during the winter. Deep-rooted trees rely on this deep soil moisture during summer, whereas the more shallowly rooted grasses are not dependent on it. Interestingly, they present data showing that areas of the Middle West that did not experience deep soil recharge during the winter 1933–34 correspond to the prairie peninsula.

Today, most ecologists recognize the role of climate, and especially of periodic drought, in maintaining grasslands in the prairie peninsula. Most believe, however, that for the last 5,000 years prairie vegetation in the eastern United States would have mostly disappeared if it had not been for the nearly annual burning of these grasslands by the North American Indians. The extent of these fires and the reasons they were set by the Indians have been discussed by numerous authors (Stewart 1951, 1956, Curtis 1959, Pyne 1983).

The regional effect of fire on vegetation was influenced by a variety of factors, including precipitation patterns before and after the burn, the composition of the vegetation, topography, and the time of the burn (Daubenmire 1968, Vogl 1974, Bragg 1982, R. C. Anderson 1983, James 1985; chapter 6). As previously noted, grassland plants are protected from fires because their growing points are located beneath the soil surface. In contrast, woody plants have exposed growing points, and fires can either kill woody plants outright or reduce their competitiveness if they are top-killed and resprout. Also, after resprouting, woody plant susceptibility to browsing animals, such as deer and elk, is increased (R. C. Anderson 1982, 1983).

In presettlement times, the vegetation of the prairie peninsula was most likely a shifting mosaic of grassland, forest, and savannah that was determined by fire frequency under a climatic regime capable of supporting any of these vegetation types. Frequency of fires in historic times was largely determined by topographic relief and the distribution of fire-breaks, such as waterways. Fires carry easily across level to rolling topography, but dissected landscapes do not readily promote the spread of fires (Gleason 1913, 1922, Wells 1970a, 1970b, R. C. Anderson 1983, Grimm 1984).

The role of topography in influencing vegetational patterns is illustrated by the presettlement distribution of prairie and forest in many parts of the Midwest (Gleason 1913, R. C. Anderson and M. Anderson 1975, Rodgers and Anderson 1979, Grimm 1984). For example, McLean County, Illinois, had presettlement vegetational patterns that were typical of the Wisconsinan glaciated landscape of the Grand Prairie of Illinois (Schwegman 1973), with 90 percent of the county as tallgrass prairie. Fire frequency was determined by the roughness of landscape surfaces. Consequently,

Vegetation of McLean County
Presettlement (1820)

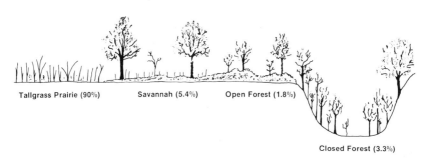

Tallgrass Prairie (90%)   Savannah (5.4%)   Open Forest (1.8%)

Closed Forest (3.3%)

FIG. 2.4   The relationship between presettlement vegetational patterns and topography in McLean County, Illinois, in 1820.

savannah and open forests, dominated by relatively shade-intolerant, but moderately fire-resistant, oak and hickories, occurred on slopes of glacial moraines. These vegetation types were presumably subjected to occasional fires, but less frequently than prairies. Closed forest occurred in stream valleys and protected areas adjacent to waterways and contained mesophytic, shade-tolerant, and fire-susceptible species, such as elms, ashes, and maples (Rodgers and Anderson 1979) (Fig. 2.4). Historically, periodic fires prevented these species from invading the upland forests. In the past 150 years, however, fire prevention has allowed closed oak-hickory forest to develop on upland sites; in most of these, the shade-tolerant, mesophytic trees are replacing the fire-resistant but less competitive oaks (R. C. Anderson and Adams 1978, Adams and Anderson 1980).

Fire can act as a stabilizing or destabilizing factor in vegetation, depending upon fuel availability and quality and species composition. R. C. Anderson and Brown (1983, 1986) examined the role of fire in maintaining the mosaic of prairie, savannah, and forest occurring on sand deposits along the Illinois River in central Illinois. On this site, fire acted as a factor to maintain sand prairies, savannahs, and open forests, but it destabilized closed oak forest. These differential responses to fire are related to the species composition in these varied vegetation types and to the availability of fuels.

Following a fire, patterns of fuel consumption around isolated blackjack oak savannah trees showed that fire never reached the tree bases. When these trees reach sufficient size, they reduce grass growth under their crowns, and wind action sweeps away litter. This reduces fuel availability near their trunks and prevents fires from reaching the tree base (R. C. Anderson and Brown 1983).

Fuel availability also influences the role of fire in maintaining open forests and destabilizing closed forests. Available fuel increased along a gradient from sand prairie, through a prairie–forest transition, and into a closed forest (Fig. 2.5). Over a five-year period following a single burn, tree mortality (stems > 9 cm diameter at breast height [dbh]) was high in the closed forest (a decrease from 630 to 310 trees/ha), whereas in the open forest (forest-edge) tree density increased slightly following the burn (from 117 to 172 trees/ha). Thus, as closed forests develop in areas susceptible to burning, there is a buildup of fuels, so fires of sufficient intensity to kill trees are possible. This converts these forests to open woodlands, with less fuel and potentially less intense fires than those occurring in closed forest. Under these conditions, periodic fires that reduce fuel loads would probably maintain open forests (R. C. Anderson and Brown 1986).

Oaks are relatively fire-resistant, and it seems likely that on some sites fire alone, and even repeated fires, may not eliminate oaks (Cottam 1949). Fire can reduce their density and maintain them as sprouts, but other factors, such as browsing animals or fungal disease (e.g., oak wilt), may be necessary to remove them from some sites (R. C. Anderson 1983, Kline 1983).

Drought can interact with fire to influence vegetation in several ways. Drought patterns can determine the amount of fuel available to carry fires, influence the postburn response of vegetation to burning, and de-

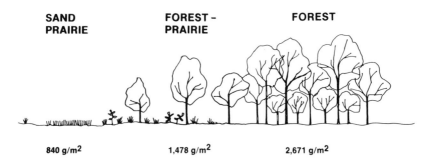

ESTIMATED FUEL IN VARIOUS VEGETATION TYPES

SAND PRAIRIE **FOREST – PRAIRIE** **FOREST**

840 g/m^2 1,478 g/m^2 2,671 g/m^2

FIG. 2.5 Availability of fuel across a vegetational gradient from sand prairie to closed oak-hickory forest in central Illinois.

termine when grassland fires are possible. Grasslands will burn anytime they are dry—including mid-summer, when they support green biomass (R. C. Anderson 1972b). Also, historical records provide accounts of fires set by Indians or lightning during the growing season (Bragg 1982).

It is of interest that, at least in the tallgrass prairie, plants will regrow during the same growing season following mid- to early summer burns. In southern Illinois, following a burn of a prairie along a railroad right-of-way during a summer drought in July, prairie vegetation began to regrow in a matter of a few days, even though no rain was received after the burn. Many forbs resprouted and flowered in a period of four–six weeks following the burn, and by the end of the growing season more than 80 percent of the site was covered with vegetation (R. C. Anderson 1972b).

Based on the response of the tree species and shrubs to this summer burn, I proposed that woody vegetation would be more damaged by a growing season burn than a dormant season burn. Historically, therefore, elimination of woody plants from some sites might have occurred because of fires during periods of active growth. In the summer of 1978, we examined the response of woody plants to summer and dormant season burns (late winter) in south-central Oklahoma. However, the data collected provided no evidence that the summer burn was more detrimental to woody plants than the dormant season burn. The similarity in response of woody plants to summer and dormant season burns was attributed to an extreme drought during the spring following the dormant season burn. We reasoned that because vegetation had become reestablished on the summer-burned site, it had a protective litter surface, and this tended to retard loss of soil moisture. However, on the spring-burned site the absence of a litter layer permitted it to dry more than the summer-burned site. This reduced the vigor of woody plants on the dormant season burn site more than on the summer burn site (Adams et al. 1982).

For the purpose of this chapter, I have focused on the eastern tallgrass prairie, but fire has been an essential ingredient in the origin and maintenance of grassland systems worldwide (e.g., Looman 1983, de Van Booysen and Tainton 1984). Nevertheless, the relative importance of fire as an ecological factor varies in time and space. To understand the composition and dynamics of grasslands it is necessary to consider simultaneously the influences of climate, fire, grazing and browsing animals, topographic relief, and other factors (R. C. Anderson 1982, Looman 1983).

Thus, across the diverse grassland of North America, there is no single prescription that describes the historical role of fire in these ecosystems. For example, while the arid shortgrass prairies and semidesert shrub grasslands were historically subjected to periodic fire (Humphrey 1949, 1958, Cable 1967, Wright 1980), the role of fire in preventing invasion of woody species into these grasslands was complemented by the activities of browsing animals—especially lagomorphs, such as jackrabbits. The recent expansion of trees and shrubs into some of these grasslands may in part be the result of overgrazing by domestic cattle and the associated reduced competitiveness of the grasses, as well as fire suppression (Humphrey 1958, Wright 1980, Archer et al. 1988).

In contrast, in the eastern tallgrass prairie, fire played a more important role in grassland maintenance than it did in the arid western grasslands (Curtis 1959, Vogl 1964, Abrams 1986). In spite of this, the role of fire in any grassland system must be evaluated in terms of other influences. The specific response of vegetation to a fire will vary as a function of species composition, season of the burn, fluctuating climatic cycles, and the complementary actions of other organisms, including grazing and browsing animals.

3

Response of
Andropogon gerardii
to Fire
in the
Tallgrass Prairie

By T. J. Svejcar

The tallgrass or "true" prairie is an ecosystem that has received a good deal of attention in the literature. Risser et al. (1981) have summarized much of the flora, fauna, and climate of the tallgrass prairie. A substantial portion of the tallgrass prairie research has focused on the effects of fire on this system. From the pioneering work of Aldous (1934) to a recent synthesis by Knapp and Seastedt (1986), there has been a continued increase in the understanding of fire effects on the tallgrass prairie. The 56 consecutive years of burning data presented by Towne and Owensby (1984) must be among the most extensive vegetation trend data sets available. However, the literature still shows contradictory results for parameters as straightforward as aboveground biomass. Only recently have the physiological mechanisms responsible for the fire response received much attention. In this chapter, I will focus on the growth response of the tallgrass dominant, big bluestem (*Andropogon gerardii*), to fire, and briefly describe some of the mechanisms that may account for the response.

GROWTH PATTERN

Growth of grasses can be expressed in a number of ways. Generally, the tiller or shoot is considered the basic unit of grass growth, and subsequent productivity is influenced by the ability of a grass to initiate tillers (Laude 1972). In the case of burning on the tallgrass prairie, results from several studies (Svejcar and Browning 1988, Knapp 1984b, Hulbert 1969) indicate that burning nearly doubles peak tiller numbers of big bluestem compared to unburned conditions. On unburned prairie, tiller numbers re-

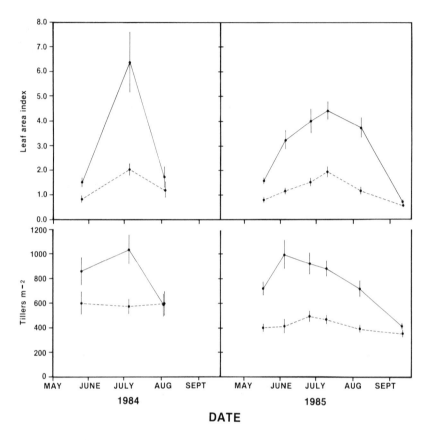

FIG. 3.1 Leaf area index and tillers m^{-2} of big bluestem under burned (solid lines) and unburned (dashed lines) conditions. Vertical lines are plus or minus 1 standard error of the mean (n = 12 in 1984, n = 18 in 1985). (From Svejcar and Browning 1988.)

main relatively constant over the growing season, whereas there is a definite seasonal peak in burned prairie (Fig. 3.1). Burning initially stimulated tiller production, but tiller mortality during the summer drought period reduced tiller number to levels comparable to unburned prairie. On burned tallgrass prairie, I measured light levels of only 50 μ Einsteins m^{-2} s^{-1} at crown level when leaf area indices reached 4.0 or more. Thus, any tillers initiated after mid-June would have little chance of survival even if water were not limiting.

In addition to stimulating tiller production, burning tends to encourage earlier growth and more rapid phenological development (Hadley and Kieckhefer 1963, Kucera and Ehrenreich 1962). Soil temperature is often listed as a major factor limiting early season growth (Rice and Parenti 1978, Peet et al. 1975, Hulbert 1969, Kucera and Ehrenreich 1962, Ehrenreich 1959). However, the importance of soil temperature in response to fire may depend on time of burning and weather conditions after a burn. Kucera and Ehrenreich (1962) found that burning increased surface soil temperatures by 2 to 10°C depending on cloudiness and weather conditions. In central Oklahoma I found that over a two-year period there was seldom more than a 1°C difference between burned and unburned plots at the 5 or 10 cm depths (unpublished data). However, in this instance, burning was conducted after soil temperatures had reached levels sufficient for growth of the tallgrasses, and complete canopy coverage of the soil was attained within two weeks of burning. The stimulation of tillering under burned conditions may be a result of soil surface temperatures immediately after burning or perhaps temperature fluctuation. In Kansas, Knapp (1984b) indicated that soil surface temperatures may be 17°C higher in burned compared to unburned prairie. Presumably, the removal of insulating litter by burning would also increase soil temperature fluctuations, particularly in climates with cool nights.

Increased light reaching emerging shoots may also be of importance in explaining the fire response of tallgrass prairie (Knapp 1984b, Peet et al. 1975, Hulbert 1969). Knapp (1984b) found that burning increased the amount of photosynthetically active radiation (PAR) reaching emerging shoots by nearly 60 percent compared to unburned controls. Deregibus et al. (1985) have shown that increased red light at crown level can increase tillering through an effect on PAR or effects on specific portions of the spectrum. Additionally, nitrogen (N) nutrition can influence pattern of tillering (Langer 1963), and burning typically increases N concentration in big bluestem leaf tissue (Svejcar and Browning 1988, Hayes 1985, Knapp 1985). Thus, burning will generally increase tillering rates in tallgrass prairie, but as Knapp and Seastedt (1986) have pointed out, knowledge of the mechanisms controlling tillering in undisturbed prairie is limited.

ABOVEGROUND BIOMASS

Many studies of fire effects on the tallgrass prairie have considered only total production of prairie vegetation, rather than production by individual species, and results have not been entirely consistent. In sown swards of big bluestem and Indian grass in Illinois, Hadley and Kieckhefer (1963) found that burning increased peak standing crop three to four times that of unburned controls. In Wisconsin (Peet et al. 1975), Missouri (Kucera and Ehrenreich 1962), Kansas (Knapp 1984b, 1985), Illinois (Old 1969), and Oklahoma (Svejcar and Browning 1988), burning of tallgrass prairie dominated by big bluestem resulted in about a doubling of standing crop compared to controls. In Kansas, Towne and Owensby (1984) reported results from long-term burning trials. Over a 10-year period, the optimum burning treatment increased total standing crop by only 15–20 percent. However, the site on which the burning was conducted contained only 17 percent big bluestem at the initiation of the burning. Over 56 years of continuous burning, big bluestem nearly doubled in percent composition, whereas little bluestem declined in composition. Rice and Parenti (1978) found that burning in Oklahoma stimulated total tallgrass prairie production, but depressed big bluestem production. However, they burned the third week in March, which is probably earlier than optimum for big bluestem. In general, Hulbert (1969) was correct in concluding that removal of litter accumulation by either burning or clipping will increase big bluestem production.

Several important factors must be considered in evaluating results of burning research in the tallgrass prairie and elsewhere. Certainly, species composition of the community under study is of vital importance, as is geographical location. As mentioned previously, big bluestem generally responds positively to late spring burns in the tallgrass prairie, whereas little bluestem responds in a negative manner. Thus, the relative proportions of these and other species will determine whole community response. In addition, a given species may not respond consistently across its geographical range. For example, Gartner and White (1986) concluded that big bluestem production is unaffected by fire in the mixed prairie of South Dakota.

A second variable to consider in evaluation of burning research is timing of the burn. In many studies the time of burning is considered only in terms of season of the year, i.e., spring, summer. However, such a gross level of resolution leaves a great deal of room for variation. In addition, seldom is there any mention of the growth stage of species within the community at the time of burning. Towne and Owensby (1984) summarized 56 years of annual burning in the Kansas Flint Hills, and concluded that a difference of only three weeks in time of spring burning had a major effect on vegetation response. Prescribed burning should be scheduled to coincide with a given phenological stage of particular key species. For example, in central Oklahoma, I chose big bluestem as the key species and burned the grassland when big bluestem leaves reached 2–4 cm in length. There was also some growth of little bluestem (*Andropogon scoparius*) and Indian grass (*Sorghastrum nutans*), and both western ragweed (*Ambrosia psilostachya*) and Louisiana sagewort (*Artemesia ludo-*

viciana) had been actively growing for four to six weeks. My choice of burning time greatly altered the competitive relationships among species.

BELOWGROUND BIOMASS

Clearly, there has been a good deal of research into the aboveground response of tallgrass prairie to fire; however, belowground responses have received relatively little attention. The excellent descriptive work of John Weaver (e.g., Weaver 1961) provides a good starting point in understanding prairie root systems. But to my knowledge, Weaver did not study belowground responses to fire.

Total belowground biomass in the tallgrass prairie is generally two to four times greater than aboveground biomass (Risser et al. 1981). For central Oklahoma, these authors gave belowground biomass values ranging from 900 to 1,600 g m^{-2} for unburned tallgrass sites. In terms of fire response, Hadley and Kieckhefer (1963) found that belowground biomass was 900 and 1,300 g m^{-2} in unburned and recently burned prairie, respectively. They suggested that the belowground increase may be a result of higher photosynthetic leaf area resulting from burning. Similarly, Kucera and Dahlman (1968) measured 39 percent more belowground biomass in burned relative to unburned plots. They also measured a large increase in rhizome density as a result of burning. But, as with aboveground response to fire, the results are not entirely consistent. Old (1969) found that fire did not influence belowground biomass, even though she measured an increase in aboveground biomass with burning. Thus, from the limited data available, it appears that fire has a relatively greater effect on aboveground compared to belowground biomass, since reports of a doubling of aboveground biomass are common, whereas root biomass increased by less than 50 percent as a result of burning.

CARBON UPTAKE AND WATER RELATIONS

There is ample evidence that burning alters the carbon uptake patterns of big bluestem. Peet et al. (1975) suggested that increased production of big bluestem after burning can be attributed primarily to higher C uptake during early growth. Knapp (1984b) found that standing dead vegetation in unburned tallgrass prairie reduced photosynthetically active radiation reaching emerging shoots by nearly 60 percent relative to burned prairie during the first 30 days of growth. Standing crop production was reduced a similar amount (54 percent), which led Knapp to conclude that reduced light intensities reaching emerging shoots accounted for reduced production on unburned prairie.

The results of Knapp (1985) and Svejcar and Browning (1988) (Fig. 3.2)

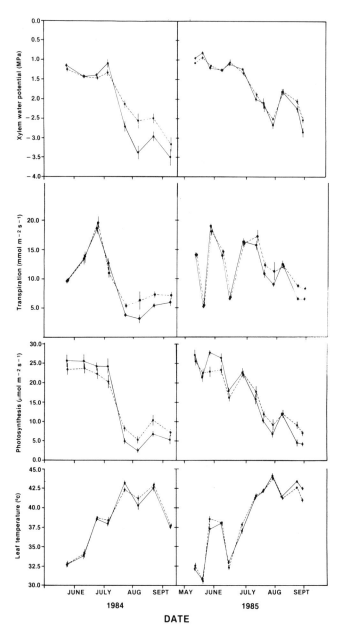

FIG. 3.2 Physiological responses of big bluestem under burned (solid lines) and unburned (dashed lines) conditions. Measurements were taken during below-average (1984) and above-average (1985) rainfall years. Vertical lines are plus or minus 1 standard error of the mean (n = 12). (From Svejcar and Browning 1988.)

show that the early season photosynthetic rate of big bluestem is stimulated by burning. However, the increase in photosynthetic rate per unit leaf area is not sufficient to explain the increase in aboveground biomass, and leaf area indices (LAI) of the burned and unburned canopies must also be considered. The combination of photosynthetic rate per unit leaf area and LAI provides an indication of potential whole canopy photosynthesis. From data presented in Figs. 3.1 and 3.2, the following estimates of C uptake per unit area can be made for late May 1984: for burned plots, 25.0 μmole CO_2 m^{-2} s^{-1} × 1.5 m^2 leaf area per m^2 ground area = 37.5 μmole CO_2 per m^{-2} ground area per second; for unburned plots, 22.5 μmole CO_2 m^{-2} s^{-1} × 0.8 m^2 leaf area per m^2 ground area = 18.0 μmole CO_2 per m^{-2} ground area s^{-1}. At these relatively low leaf area indices, self-shading would probably not greatly influence the calculation; however, such a calculation would probably not be accurate at the high leaf area values measured later in the season (Fig. 3.1). The estimate of big bluestem C uptake per unit ground area is double in burned relative to unburned prairie, which compares nicely with the increase in aboveground biomass mentioned earlier. Knapp (1984b) and Peet et al. (1975) have suggested that improved environmental conditions during early growth are critical in explaining big bluestem response to fire. This tends to support Knight's (1973) contention that leaf area is most important during the early part of the growing season, when LAI is low and soil moisture is available.

Leaf area dynamics have not been studied extensively in native communities, in spite of the importance of this parameter to C uptake and water use. Conant and Risser (1974) reported a peak LAI of only 1.3 on ungrazed and unburned tallgrass prairie, whereas Knapp (1985) measured peak values of 4.2 and 2.8 for burned and unburned prairie, respectively. Values of LAI in unburned prairie were surprisingly similar during two contrasting years in central Oklahoma (Fig. 3.1). Trends are not as comparable over two years for burned prairie, because 1984 was the first year of burning, and 1985 the second year, after at least 15 years without fire. Thus, the high peak LAI in 1984 (the drier of the two years) may represent an initial stimulation by burning, which declines when a second consecutive year of treatment is applied; or the reduced response to fire the second year may be a result of an environmental variable other than rainfall. The second suggestion seems rather unlikely. Regardless of the yearly variation, it is clear that burning stimulates leaf area production of tallgrass prairie.

Leaf area can also have a major impact on seasonal trends in plant-water relations. Burned tallgrass prairie generally achieves lower seasonal minimum xylem potentials (ψ) than unburned prairie (Knapp 1984b, 1985)

(Fig. 3.2). Results from Kansas (Knapp 1984b, 1985) and Oklahoma (Svejcar and Browning 1988) reveal that the differences between burned and unburned prairie are greater during a dry year than during a wet year. These results can probably be explained by treatment differences and prevailing climatic regime in much of the tallgrass prairie region. LAI is typically higher on burned, compared to unburned, prairie whereas at least in the Oklahoma study transpiration per unit leaf area was similar among the two treatments during the first half of the growing season (Fig. 3.2); thus we would expect a higher transpirational demand on the burned prairie and consequently lower soil moisture compared to unburned prairie. Knapp (1985) reached the same conclusion from his research in Kansas. Reduced soil moisture as a result of burning has been demonstrated previously (Hanks and Anderson 1957, K. L. Anderson 1965).

The reduction in soil moisture should be viewed in relation to the climate typical of the central and southern Great Plains. Generally, there is sufficient spring rainfall to allow extensive leaf area development of big bluestem, but by mid- to late June, summer drought begins limiting growth. The high transpirational demand during early growth reduces soil moisture and causes the decline in ψ associated with burning. However, during a wet year—as occurred in central Oklahoma in 1985—soil moisture is not as limiting. Thus, differences in ψ between burned and unburned prairie are less pronounced (Fig. 3.2).

CONCLUSION

Burning generally stimulates aboveground production of big bluestem specifically and the tallgrass prairie as a whole. However, factors such as species composition, geographical location, and timing of burning must be considered in interpreting burning response. There appears to be relatively less belowground, compared to aboveground, response to fire. The increase in total production appears to be a direct result of increased tiller—and thus leaf area—production and slightly higher photosynthetic rates. The pattern of biomass production is also altered by burning, with earlier growth and earlier senescence on burned compared to unburned prairie. The earlier senescence is probably related to the more rapid soil moisture depletion by burned compared to unburned prairie.

RECOMMENDATIONS FOR FUTURE RESEARCH

The majority of tallgrass prairie research has focused on end-of-season yield as influenced by climate or management practices. However, data on response mechanisms and seasonal trends are generally lacking. What are the temperature requirements for growth of the various tallgrass species? How do competitive relationships alter growth and physiology of the dominant species? Dahlman and Kucera (1965) provided initial information on C flows in the tallgrass prairie, but I am not aware of any such studies since that point. Seasonal trends in C flow and how flows are influenced by management should receive attention. A related subject, timing and distribution of root growth, has also not received adequate attention. A detailed study of plant water use and moisture and nutrient extraction from various depths in the soil profile would also aid in our understanding of the tallgrass prairie ecosystem.

4
Fire in Central North American Grasslands: Vegetative Reproduction, Seed Germination, and Seedling Establishment

By David C. Glenn-Lewin
Louise A. Johnson
Thomas W. Jurik
Ann Akey
Mark Leoschke
Tom Rosburg

It is generally acknowledged that fires, at least spring fires, provide a stimulus to grassland production in the tallgrass prairie region. Often, this stimulation disappears in one or occasionally two years, unless the grassland is burned again. So it seems that the effect of fires on prairie ecosystem function is transitory. Of course, prairie fires reduce or eliminate woody plants, and in this way fire serves as an important means of maintaining grassland vegetation in the face of forest encroachment.

If prairie fire has a long-term effect on the composition of grasslands, it must be mediated through plant reproduction, either sexual or vegetative. Furthermore, if fire has played an evolutionary role in prairies, it must have acted through effects on sexual reproduction. In this chapter, we examine the state of knowledge about the effect of prairie fire on plant reproduction, both sexual and vegetative. We do this by combining a review of the literature with some data from recent and active field studies in the Iowa State University plant ecology group.

The literature on prairie fire is replete with reports about the apparent influence of fire on plant reproduction. However, this literature varies greatly in approach to the subject, quality of the data, and adequacy of the experimental design. When a reasonable standard is applied to this literature, the reliability of a substantial portion is doubtful. In what follows, we used literature that provided individual species data and described a design in sufficient detail for the reliability of the data to be assessed. We have also restricted our discussion to primarily tallgrass and mixed-grass North American prairies. We will first address sexual reproduction (flowering, seed production per inflorescence, and total seed production), followed by seedling establishment and vegetative propagation. We will end with a discussion of the methodological problems that we have identified during our review and our own field studies.

SEXUAL REPRODUCTION

Sexual reproduction is a function of the amount of flowering and the number of seeds produced per inflorescence. We examine each of these in turn.

Flowering

The General Pattern after Spring Fire. The flowering response of tallgrass prairie plants to fire has been most commonly studied in conjunction with spring fires. Species of grasses that generally demonstrate an increase in flowering after a spring fire are all warm season (mainly C_4) grasses (Table 4.1). Except in a few cases, all show an increase to varying degrees, with quite spectacular increases in some cases.

Grasses whose flowering generally decreases after a spring fire are usually early season (C_3) species (Table 4.1). The data are fewer than for increasers, except for *Poa pratensis*, and so the generality is less certain. Indeed, a few instances of increase have been reported; one, for *P. pratensis*, was quite large.

The response of forbs after a spring fire is less well known than that of grasses. Some reported increases in forb flowering after spring fire are listed in Table 4.2. Pemble et al. (1981) reported that many species increased following burning, e.g., *Phlox pilosa*, *Rudbeckia hirta*, but they used chi-square values to illustrate this, so these species are not included in Table 4.2. Although the forbs in Table 4.2 are not early season species, neither are they all late season, such as the grasses in Table 4.1. All use the C_3 photosynthetic pathway.

Other forb species have been reported to decrease after a spring fire (Table 4.2); for additional species see Pemble et al. (1981). A number of forb species have variable responses to spring fire. For instance, *Ratibida pinnata*, which is shown as an increaser in Iowa (Table 4.2), had no response to fire in Minnesota (Davis et al. 1987).

TABLE 4.1   Grass species that generally show an increase or decrease in flowering following a spring (or winter) fire

Species	Location	Degree of Difference (%)	References
Increasers			
Andropogon gerardii[a]	WI, IL, IA, MO, KS, MN	54–3,700	1, 3, 4, 5, 6, 8, 10, 11, 12, 13
A. scoparius[b]	WI, IL, IA	50–1,200	1, 2, 5, 6, 7
Bouteloua curtipendula	WI	60–600	5, 9
Muhlenbergia racemosa	IA	—[e]	7
P. virgatum	IA	150	13
Sorghastrum nutans[c]	WI, IL, IA, MO	−79–+663	1, 2, 5, 6, 7, 8, 10, 12
Sporobolus heterolepis[d]	WI, IA	1,000–2,900	1, 5, 6, 7, 13
Decreasers			
Agrostis alba	IA	−100–+20	7, 13
Panicum lanuginosum	IL	−94	2
Phleum pratense	IA	−67–+60	7, 13
Poa pratensis	WI, IA	−70–−20[f]	3, 7, 9, 10, 13

References: (1) Aikman 1955, (2) R. C. Anderson and Van Valkenberg 1977, (3) Curtis and Partch 1948, 1950, (4) Davis et al. 1987, (5) Dix and Butler 1954, (6) Ehrenreich and Aikman 1957, (7) Ehrenreich and Aikman 1963, (8) Hadley and Kieckhefer 1963, (9) Henderson et al. 1983, (10) Johnson 1987, (11) Knapp and Hulbert 1986, (12) Kucera and Ehrenreich 1962, (13) Richards and Landers 1973.
[a] No change in 1 case, most instances 100–500%.
[b] No change in 1 case.
[c] No change in 2 cases, 1 decrease.
[d] In 3 of 4 cases > 1,000% increase.
[e] No plants in unburned plots; cannot be calculated.
[f] In 1 case (Zedler and Loucks 1969), an incease of 450% after a very early spring fire.

Variation in Flowering of Grasses. The influence of spring fire on flowering varies according to habitat (Tables 4.3, 4.4). In one case (Minnesota, see Table 4.3), the effects of fire on several important grasses seem to be most obvious at the extremes of the moisture gradient. In Wisconsin, however, *Bouteloua curtipendula* showed a greater increase in flowering in the somewhat moister environment than at the dry extreme (Table 4.4).

TABLE 4.2   Forb species that show an increase or decrease in flowering following a spring fire

Species	Location	Degree of Difference (%)	Refer- ences
Increasers:			
Amorpha canescens	IA	100	3
Coreopsis palmata	IA	2,000	2
Ratibida pinnata	IA, MN	0–33	1, 3
Solidago canadensis	IA	73	3
Decreasers:			
Dodecatheon media[a]	IA	−186 to −20	5
Helianthus grosseserratus	IA	−300	3
Monarda fistulosa	MN	−86	1
Petalostemum spp.	IA	−33	3
Vernonia baldwinii	KS	−55[b]	4

References: (1) Davis et al. 1987, (2) Ehrenreich and Aikman 1963, (3) Richards
and Landers 1973, (4) Knapp 1984a, (5) Leoschke 1986.
[a] Showed an increase in WI, when litter was very heavy on unburned plots
(Pauly 1984).
[b] Compares plants burned 0 or 1 year previous with those unburned for 2 or
more years.

TABLE 4.3   Variation in flowering response of 4 grass species according to habitat, following a spring fire, Minnesota (Key: +, stimulation; + +, great stimulation; –, inhibition; —, great inhibition; 0, no effect)

Species	Moisture Gradient[a]					
	Dry 1	2	3	4	5	Wet 6
Andropogon gerardii	+ +	+	0	0	0	+ +
A. scoparius	+ +		0	+ +	+ +	+
Bouteloua curtipendula	+ +		–	0		
Poa sp.	—	+ +	+	0	+ +	+

[a] Topographic gradient from a dry-mesic, south-facing slope to a wet swale. Habitats 2 and 5 were also disturbed sites.
Source: Adapted from Pemble et al. 1981.

TABLE 4.4 Increases in flowering of *Bouteloua curti-pendula* following 2 different spring fires, in 2 habitats

	Habitat	
Time of Fire	Dry	Dry/Mesic
Early spring	60%	250%
Late spring	150%	600%

Source: Henderson et al. 1983

In the Minnesota study (Pemble et al. 1981), seven grass species (four of which are included in Table 4.3) showed significant changes in flowering in more than one habitat following a spring fire. When the changes were significant, four of these species always increased: *Sporobolus heterolepis* (significant increases in three of four habitats, one habitat had no change), *Andropogon gerardii* (three of six), *A. scoparius* (four of six), and *Calamagrostis inexpansa* (two of two). No grass species always decreased. Three other species had mixed responses: *Agrostis stolonifera* increased in one habitat out of three and decreased in one out of three; *B. curtipendula* also increased in one of three and decreased in one of three, and *Poa* sp. increased four out of six times and decreased in one of six.

Table 4.4 also shows the effect of burning at different times in spring. In Wisconsin, a late spring burn enhanced *B. curtipendula* flowering more than did an early spring fire. The variation in cool season species shown in Table 4.1 also probably depends upon the differences in timing of the fire. For instance, the large increase of *P. pratensis* occurred after a very early spring fire (Zedler and Loucks 1969). However, the flowering of cool season species is likely more sensitive even to small differences in the timing of spring fires than is that of the warm season species.

Fire frequency affects sexual reproduction in prairie plants. In Kansas, flower production was greatest in annually burned sites (Knapp and Hulbert 1986). In addition, habitat (moisture) variation seemed to interact with year-to-year differences in climate.

Johnson (1987) has examined year-to-year differences, species differences, and the effect of the seasonal timing of fire on flowering of *A. gerardii*, *S. nutans*, and *P. pratensis* in Iowa over a two-year period. Flowering densities of *A. gerardii* and *S. nutans* were measured in September of each year; *P. pratensis* was counted in late May and June. For *A. gerardii*, there was a substantial increase in flowering stalk density after both May and June fires in 1985 (Fig. 4.1,A). (The plants flowered much later after the June fire.) However, this was not the case in 1986, a much wetter year. There was an inhibition or suppression of *A. gerardii* flowering by summer (July/August) burns. A fall (November) burn produced an effect similar to that of the spring fire, at least in this one case. The enhancement of *A. gerardii* following the May 1985 burn was reversed the next year: the May 1985 burn in 1986 had a lower flower stalk density than did the no burn (not shown).

At the same time and under identical conditions. *S. nutans* did not show an increase in flowering after a spring fire (in either year), or after the late fall fire, but it did show a depression after a June, July, or August fire (Fig. 4.1,B). (Flowering in *S. nutans* seems to vary a good deal in its response to spring fire; see Table 4.1.) As was true for *A. gerardii*, 1986 was a better year for *S. nutans* flowering than was 1985.

There was no *Poa pratensis* flowering in 1985, the dry year. *P. pratensis* did not flower in 1986 following a spring burn (Fig. 4.1,C). However, *P. pratensis* did exhibit a second-year stimulus by the summer 1985 (August) fire, and second-year inhibition by the fall 1985 fire (Fig. 4.1,C), the latter presumably because of the fall period of active growth in this species.

Variation in Flowering of Forbs. Variation in forb flowering is less well studied, but it appears that the sources of variation are much the same as for grasses. Flowering of the early spring plant *Dodecatheon meadia* in Iowa showed a general pattern of inhibition by fire, but it also exhibited variation by site (compare Clay Prairie with Hayden Prairie, Table 4.5) and, at Hayden Prairie, by year (Table 4.5). Lovell et al. (1983) showed that the timing of fire differentially affects the flowering of forbs. The data of Knapp (1984a) indicate that fire frequency affected flowering and seed production in *Vernonia baldwinii* in Kansas (Table 4.6). This case has an interesting contrast in the report by Pemble et al. (1981) that flowering of *V. fasciculata* in Minnesota was not affected by fire.

The results of Pemble et al. (1981) show that the habitat variation in flowering by prairie forbs is analogous to that described for grasses. In their data, 14 species showed significant differences in flowering following fire in more than one habitat. In seven species, the significant changes were always increases: *Medicago lupulina, Petalostemum purpureum, Prenanthes racemosa, Psoralea argophylla, Sisyrinchium angustifolium, Galium boreale,* and *Hypoxis hirsuta.* One species, *Pycnanthemum virginianum,* uniformly decreased. Six species had both significant increases and decreases, depending upon the habitat: *Anemone cylindrica, Aster ericoides, A. laevis, Helianthus maximilliani, Solidago canadensis,* and *Verbena hastata.* Pemble et al. (1981) recorded postfire flowering of 196 individual species/habitat instances, out of 90 species in 6 habitats. Of the

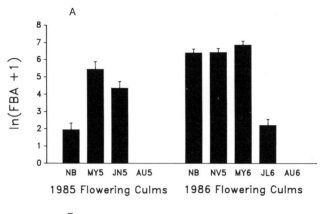

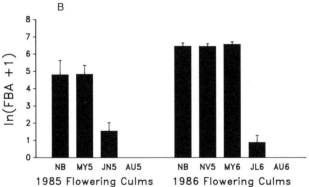

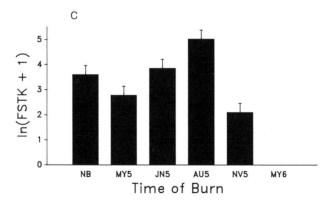

FIG. 4.1 The effect of fire at different times of the year on the number of flowering culms of (A) *Andropogon gerardii*, (B) *Sorghastrum nutans*, and (C) *Poa pratensis* in 1985 and 1986, central Iowa. NB is No Burn; others symbols are months and years. FBA is flowering culms per basal area. FSTK is the number of flower stalks m^{-2}. Error bars indicate standard error of the mean.

TABLE 4.5   Percentage of adult *Dodecatheon meadia* plants that flowered following spring fire, at 2 Iowa sites

	Clay Prairie site		Hayden Prairie site	
Year	Unburned	Burned	Unburned	Burned
1982	20	7	39	33
1983	21	8	64	46

Source: Leoschke 1986.

TABLE 4.6   Flowering and seed production in Kansas prairie populations of *Vernonia baldwinii* burned annually, and 1, 2, 4, or 10 years after burning (Means $+/-$ S.E.; letters indicate statistical differences [$p < 0.05$])

Growing Seasons since Fire	Capita per Plant	Seeds per Head
Annual burn	48.5 ± 7.8^a	20.4 ± 0.4^a
1	50.8 ± 6.2^a	21.8 ± 0.3^b
2	72.9 ± 8.7^b	22.3 ± 0.2^b
4	78.4 ± 10.3^b	22.3 ± 0.3^b
10	78.2 ± 7.4^b	22.0 ± 0.2^b

Source: Knapp 1984a.

196 combinations, 68 showed a significant increase in flowering, and 18 had significant decreases. In the other 110 cases, or 56 percent, fire had no effect on flowering.

Conclusions about Flowering. We draw six conclusions from this review of flowering patterns of prairie plants after fire:

1. Species differ in their responses to fire, even among C_4 grasses.
2. There is significant habitat variation in the effects of fire on flowering.
3. There are significant year-to-year differences in the effect of a fire on flowering.
4. The timing of the burn has an important influence on the degree of subsequent flowering.
5. Fire frequency may be an important factor affecting prairie plant flowering.
6. A second-year effect seems to occur in some cases.

SEED PRODUCTION

Given the significant effects of fire on flowering, we then ask if fire also affects the number of seeds produced per flower and per plant.

Production per Inflorescence

Johnson (1987) measured seed production per inflorescence for *Andropogon gerardii*, *Sorghastrum nutans*, and *Poa pratensis* in 1985 and 1986. Except in one case (*A. gerardii*, 1985), there were no differences in the number of caryopses per inflorescence according to the time of the burn (Table 4.7). However, seed production in 1986 (the wet year) was uniformly higher than in 1985 (dry). That is, there was more year-to-year, and block (that is, habitat), variation in seeds per inflorescence due to amount of moisture than due to burning treatments. We did not find that seed production per flower in *Dodecatheon meadia* was affected by spring fire (Table 4.8), nor did Davis et al. (1987) in *Monarda fistulosa* and *Ratibida pinnata* in Minnesota. However, seed production per capita decreased in *Vernonia baldwinii* (Knapp 1984a) following spring burning (Table 4.6).

Total Seed Production

Most of the available data seem to indicate that changes in total seed production in a population of prairie plants following a fire are due primarily

TABLE 4.7 Least square means of seeds (caryopses) per inflorescence in 3 grasses following fire at different times of the year, in Iowa.

Time of Burn	Andropogon gerardii		Sorghastrum nutans		Poa pratensis
	1985[a]	1986	1985	1986	1986
No Burn	13	60	51	106	183
May 1985	4	46	27	111	198
June 1985	2	46	12	86	178
August 1985		79		79	186
November 1985		56		86	250
May 1986		56		92	

[a] The only significant difference for treatments was that No Burn was greater than other 1985 treatments for *A. gerardii*.
Source: Johnson 1987.

TABLE 4.8   Flowering response of *Dodecatheon meadia* in a northeast Iowa prairie to a spring fire (1983)

	Unburned	Burned
Percent of adults that flowered	21	8
Mean flowers per flowering plant[a]	11.2 ± .2	12.4 ± .4
Percent fruit formation	82	88
Mean number of mature seeds per capsule	120 ± 8	121 ± 9

[a] In 1982, unburned sites had 8.6 ± .2 flowers per plant, burned sites 12.3 ± .3.
Source: Leoschke 1986.

to changes in the number of inflorescences, and especially in the number of flowering stems, rather than the number of seeds per inflorescence. We accept this as a generality, although there are exceptions (e.g., Knapp 1984a).

SEEDLING ESTABLISHMENT

We will now discuss the effects of fire on seedling density, survivorship, and establishment in prairies.

Seasonal and Yearly Patterns

We have followed seedling establishment in a small central Iowa prairie over a two-year period, after fire at different times of the year (Table 4.9). In Table 4.9, the differences between dicots in the no burn treatment in 1985 and 1986 were due entirely to a high seedling count in one block— i.e., there is no evidence that it is a general pattern. However, the differences between spring and summer 1985 and spring and summer 1986 burn plots apply across all blocks. In general, then, 1986 had more seedlings, presumably for weather-related reasons (cf. Rapp and Rabinowitz 1985).

Seedlings of dicots in 1985 no burn plots were more numerous than in the fire treatments; fire in the dry year inhibited seedling development. On the other hand, there were no differences between no burn and 1986 burn treatments in 1986. That is, fire did not inhibit seedlings in the wet year.

The 1985 burn treatments exhibited very high seedling numbers in 1986, indicating that there was a second-year effect on seedling development (see also chapter 6). Rapp and Rabinowitz (1985) stated that seedling

TABLE 4.9   Total number of warm season grass seedlings and dicots in 6 m²
according to time of fire, central Iowa[a]

Seedlings Counted in	Time of Burn	Monocots	Dicots
Fall 1985	No Burn	7	237
	May 1985	9	39
	June 1985	12	27
	August 1985	6	10
Fall 1986	No Burn	5	316
	May 1985	26	876
	June 1985	30	988
	August 1985	63	668
	November 1985	60	518
	May 1986	49	394
	July 1986	23	94
	August 1986	19	282

[a] Totals per 6 m² are reported because the numbers per plot were small and
varied greatly; there was a large number of plots with no warm season grass
seedlings, and therefore the distributions are highly skewed.
Source: Johnson 1987.

recruitment comes largely from currently dispersing seed. Perhaps increases in flowering after fire in 1985—at least by some species in some
plots—account for part of the increased number of seedlings in 1986.
However, many of the dicot seedlings in 1986 were of species whose
flowering normally would be inhibited by fire (e.g., *Melilotus alba*, *Medicago lupulina*). The high 1986 seedling densities of such species imply a
real physiological response.

In 1986, certain species germinated only or mainly in plots burned in
1986: *Oxalis stricta*, *Panicum scribnerianum*, *Verbena stricta*, and *Cirsium* sp. Other species germinated in 1986 mainly on unburned plots, or
on plots burned in 1985: *Aster azureus*, *Daucus carota*, *Lactuca seriola*,
Medicago lupulina, *Melilotus alba*, *Pastinaca sativa*, *Poa pratensis*, *Trifolium repens* and *Viola pedatifida*.

Seedling Densities and Survival

Of the 1986 monocot seedlings, 42 (of the 275 total) were warm season
grasses, or 0.9 warm season grass seedlings per square meter. Blake
(1935), Steiger (1930), Clements and Weaver (1924), and Goldberg and

Werner (1983) all have emphasized the low numbers of seedlings found in undisturbed prairie. Only when openings are created or maintained do significant numbers of seedlings emerge and become established (Clements and Weaver 1924, Platt 1975, Goldberg and Werner 1983, Rabinowitz and Rapp 1985).

Our germination rate is much lower than that reported by Curtis and Partch (1948), who recorded rates as high as 76.1 seedlings m^{-2} of *Andropogon gerardii* alone, on a planted site that was burned annually for five years. The biennially burned sites of Curtis and Partch (1948) had a density of 29.7 *A. gerardii* seedlings m^{-2}, and they found no *A. gerardii* seedlings in unburned plots. It is hard to believe that geography (Iowa versus Wisconsin) accounts for the large differences between our results and those of Curtis and Partch (1948). It seems more likely that the nature of the sites—especially the fact that the Wisconsin site was a planted one—differences in seed bank composition and seed immigration sources, and the more frequent burning of the Wisconsin site explain the discrepancy.

In September 1986, 17 of 29 warm season grass seedlings marked in 1985 were still alive, a 59 percent survival rate. If this is representative, then 59 percent of 0.9 m^{-2} = 0.5 m^{-2}. That is, about 0.5 warm season grass seedlings became established per square meter per year (defining establishment as survival into the next growing season). This extrapolation may well be inaccurate because of the differences in weather between 1985 and 1986, but perhaps it gives an indication of the magnitude of seedling establishment in natural or semi-natural tallgrass prairie. Overall, the seedlings were too sparse to distinguish fire treatment effects (i.e., burning at different times of the year) on establishment, defined in this way.

The data of Rabinowitz and Rapp (1985) indicate that about 16 percent of the seedlings in their study were alive at the end, summed over one, two, three, and four years. Thus, they had lower survival, and their data imply that the seedlings in our plots will continue to experience significant mortality. Indeed, in 1987, the surviving seedlings were still very small. The higher survivorship in our study might also be due to the larger scale of disturbance in our fire plots than in their experiments. It might also reflect the extremely favorable growing season of 1986.

Continuing mortality in our plots could reduce the density of new recruits well below the 0.5 plants m^{-2} calculated here, but given normal densities of warm season grasses and the presumed long lives of these grasses, continuing regeneration seems to occur. Rabinowitz and Rapp (1985) stated: "Turnovers of large numbers of tiny plants occur annually and inconspicuously in many native grasslands and other herbaceous communities." Their data and ours imply an occasional exception of a long-surviving genet, which appears to account for most regeneration of the warm season grasses.

VEGETATIVE PROPAGATION

Concurrently with our studies of flowering, seed production, and seedling establishment, we have been interested in vegetative propagation following fire. In the experiment set up by Johnson (1987), spring fire did not lead to a significantly increased tiller production in *A. gerardii* (Fig. 4.2,A). (In this case the data were analyzed by covariance analysis.) Summer fire, though, reduced the density of tillers of *A. gerardii*. This effect was still noticeable in the beginning of the following growing season, but disappeared by its end (Fig. 4.2,B). In general, fire does not appear to have a long-lasting effect on tillering by this species.

Hulbert (1969) reported that *A. gerardii* tillers increased approximately 2.5 times following a spring fire. Svejcar also found increased tillering by *A. gerardii* following spring burning (see chapter 3). Our data, although perhaps suggestive, do not show this. The apparent contradiction could be due to the fact that the prairies in Hulbert's (1969) and Svejcar's studies had not been burned for 10 years and therefore must have had a deep thatch, or to the fact that their sites were strongly dominated by *A. gerardii*. Hulbert (1969) did not follow the population to see if the effect lasted or not. Dokken and Hulbert (1978) reported a habitat difference in *A. gerardii* tiller responses following fire, but their comparison had no replication.

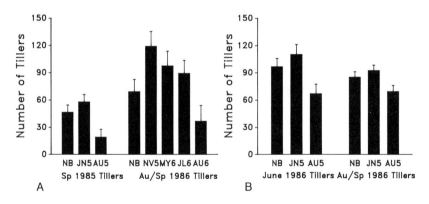

FIG. 4.2   Tiller production (i.e., vegetative propagation) in 1985 and 1986 by *Andropogon gerardii* following fire at different times of the year, central Iowa. NB is No Burn; Au is Autumn; Sp is Spring; other symbols are months and years. Error bars indicate standard error of the mean. (A) Tiller response in the year of the burn, (B) tiller response of 1985 burns in early or late summer 1986.

Similarly, the variability in tillering by *Sorghastrum nutans* makes it impossible to distinguish clear responses to fire by this species (Fig. 4.3,A). Even the suggestion of a response seemed to have disappeared in the next year (Fig. 4.3,B), as was true for *A. gerardii*.

In a dry year (1985, *Poa pratensis* exhibited no response of tiller number to fire (Fig. 4.4,A), but a comparison of these same plots in 1986 (Fig. 4.4,B) shows that the unburned plots had a higher tiller density than did the June 1985 burn plots. There seemed to be a second-year tiller suppression effect in this species. In the wet year (1986), spring and summer burns did depress *Poa* tiller production (Fig. 4.4,A).

Zedler and Loucks (1969) described a habitat difference in the response of *Poa pratensis* vegetative propagation to spring fire. Since we found no block differences in *Poa* tiller production, our data fail to confirm this. The difference between the two results may be accounted for by the extremely high density of *P. pratensis* in the study site of Zedler and Loucks (1969), a situation that may also have influenced flower production in their study (Henderson et al. 1983).

We draw three conclusions from our discussion of vegetative propagation by prairie species in response to fire:

1. Because the results of various studies show mixed responses, it is difficult to make assertions about the response of tillering of even one species to fire at any time of the year.

2. At least for the two warm season grasses we studied, there are

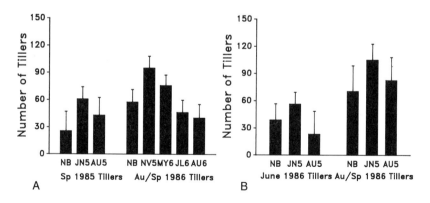

FIG. 4.3 Tiller production (i.e., vegetative propagation) in 1985 and 1986 by *Sorghastrum nutans* following fire at different times of the year, central Iowa. NB is No Burn; Au is Autumn; Sp is Spring; other symbols are months and years. Error bars indicate standard error of the mean. (A) Tiller response in the year of the burn, (B) tiller response of 1985 burns in early or late summer 1986.

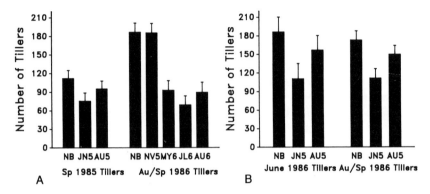

FIG. 4.4   Tiller production (i.e., vegetative propagation) in 1985 and 1986 by *Poa pratensis* following fire at different times of the year, central Iowa. NB is No Burn; Au is Autumn; Sp is Spring; other symbols are months and years. Error bars indicate standard error of the mean. (A) Tiller response in the year of the burn, (B) tiller response of 1985 burns in early or late summer 1986.

greater year-to-year responses of tiller production to weather than to fire.

3. There does not appear to be a long-lasting effect of fire on vegetative propagation. However, our studies followed the plants after only one fire. If in natural systems fire frequency was high, then the short-term effects of fire on vegetative reproduction may accumulate (or have accumulated) over a long period.

The data of Rapp and Rabinowitz (1985) indicate that tillering of graminoids increases as the plants invade small disturbance sites. The disturbances that Rapp and Rabinowitz created were small-scale removals of existing soil and replacement with clean, sterile soil—i.e., small-scale "virgin territory." Fire, however, does not remove underground plant parts, so changes in tillering following fire would reflect stimulation or inhibition of rhizome bud formation or growth. It seems reasonable that changes due to such stimulation or inhibition would be relatively short-lived.

METHODOLOGICAL CONSIDERATIONS

The study of prairie plant population responses to fire is fraught with numerous methodological problems. These include problems of experimental design, the highly variable characteristics of fire, and difficulties of data analysis.

Some literature sources failed to mention a control, or described an inadequate control. Some studies in the fire literature were based on measurements made after an unexpected wildfire. Other studies may have included a "control," but failed to measure the initial state of both the control and experimental units. Thus, one cannot tell whether the reported differences were due to the fire or to initial differences. Indeed, the nature of the "control" in these studies is problematical. A "control" plot has a history; not burning such a plot may be as much of a "treatment" as a burn, since the change in history (or disturbance regime, or management) does not have a neutral effect. Fire studies may best be thought of as comparisons across treatments, rather than as comparisons of treatments with a neutral unit.

A proper statistical design for population or reproduction studies would call for burning individual plants, or burning small plots and then selecting at random one plant within the plot for measurement. However, there are practical difficulties of burning large numbers of individual plants or small plots. This is a time-consuming project, the burns will be highly variable in their environmental characteristics, and the characteristics of the burns (at the individual plant) will likely be dissimilar to those of fires that cover a broad area (i.e., the usual way a fire progresses). Furthermore, since many prairie fire studies are done in conjunction with management burns, which typically cover a large portion of a prairie reserve, the ecologist may not even have the luxury of a choice in design. The alternative to a design based on individual plants, though, presents the analytical dangers of burning two (or more) large areas and calling them different treatments. The differences could well be due to site or area differences, rather than to the fire treatment. We faced this problem in one study (that of *Dodecatheon meadia*), and chose to do the analysis conservatively (i.e., to use large areas as experimental units, so the degrees of freedom were very low), but also to report the means and standard errors calculated over individual plants within a treatment. Furthermore, we alternated the treatments (burned and not burned) between years, to see if the different areas still responded in the same direction. Another possible solution to this problem would be to remove statistically the spatial autocorrelation between individuals in large plots and then to examine the residual variation for differences.

The third design difficulty is inherent in the variability caused by the patch structure in vegetation, the different growth forms of the plants, and the differences in fire characteristics due to variation in fuel load, fuel moisture content, slope, and a number of other factors. This degree of variation means that large sample sizes are required. We have faced this problem several times, finding "trends" that certainly appear to be fire effects, but which, due to their inherent variation, cannot be established by statistical means.

We are concerned about the realism of fires in small plots, compared to fires that sweep across landscapes and are presumably more natural in their behavior and effects. In our studies of grass tillering, flowering, and seedling establishment, we used enclosures to control the fire. One effect of this was that all of the fires were complete and were quite similar in efficacy of thatch removal. The enclosures seemed to have decreased the variation that would be due to differential fire behavior. However, the fires seemed to be hotter, and thatch removal more thorough, than is the case following most open fires. We included a buffer zone around each treatment plot to avoid edge effects caused by different fire characteristics at the enclosure wall, but nevertheless it may not be strictly legitimate to extrapolate fire effects from small enclosures to large prairies.

We have run into several problems of measurement and data analysis in our fire research. For example, when should one count grass tillers in conjunction with fire treatment(s)? We counted them in both the year of the fire and the following year, but we chose to emphasize the latter, since we are most interested in the long-term population effects of fire. Further, we are impressed by the number of second-year effects that we observed. These and the observations that others are making in long-term studies (e.g., at Konza Prairie Research Natural Area) should warn prairie ecologists that interpretations of fire effects based on a one-year analysis may be quite misleading.

Statistical analysis of plant responses to fire can be challenging. For instance, one wishes to account for the initial condition of a plot, before comparing across treatments. Unfortunately, if one uses simple ratios (after over before), small denominators sometimes produce huge (unrealistic) ratios. Furthermore, there are almost always different amounts of the species in each plot. It becomes necessary (and useful) to employ covariance analysis to handle these problems. For related reasons, least square means of seeds per inflorescence were reported in Table 4.7. A third statistical problem arose with the highly skewed distribution of seedlings, their low numbers, and their spatial patchiness. This situation does not seem amenable to statistical analysis, and we have chosen simply to describe the patterns.

Some of these methodological problems are not unique to fire studies, of course; perhaps none are. Nor is our list here an exhaustive one. Nevertheless, research on prairie plant population responses to prairie fire will continue to face these and related difficulties. We hope that our experience will help others in designing their studies, and that they may find some of our analytical solutions helpful.

CONCLUSION

Reproductive responses of tallgrass prairie plants to fire vary by species, timing of fire, and year. Cool season and warm season species exhibit different vegetative responses. Seed germination and seedling establishment are higher in biennials and short-lived perennials than in warm season perennials. Nevertheless, even though the absolute numbers of warm season perennial seedlings are low, they seem to be significant in relation to the life spans of the species. There are often second-year responses of tiller production and seed germination to a fire in the previous year. Fires at different times of the year have clear effects, and fire at the same time of year may produce different results in different years, depending upon the phenological state of the plants at the time of fire. Methodological problems abound in this field of endeavor.

ACKNOWLEDGMENTS

We wish to thank Elmer Paul, on whose land some of our field work was conducted. C. Brubaker, H. Zhang, C. Johnson, J. Lewin, J. Finegan, J. Pleasants, J. Shearer, and E. Ugarte helped with field burns. W. Akey, S. Johnson, and E. Schweiger helped with data collection, and P. Hinz helped with statistical analyses. Our research was supported in part by Sigma Xi and the U.S. Soil Conservation Service through the Southern Iowa Agricultural Boosters.

5

Small Mammals
and Grassland Fires

Donald W. Kaufman,
Elmer J. Finck,
and Glennis A. Kaufman

The classical view of North American grassland ecosystems was that the structure and composition of vegetation were primarily determined by climate and soil. More recently, however, the importance of fire and grazing as determinants of structure and composition of vegetation has been recognized (R. C. Anderson 1982, Axelrod 1985, Dyer et al. 1982; chapter 2). Lightning was the major cause of grassland fires, although the use and misuse of fire by aboriginal humans would have been common (Hulbert 1973, Bragg 1982, Pyne 1986). Fires not only altered average vegetation conditions, but also altered patch structure due to the heterogeneous distribution of occurrence and intensity of fires (see chapter 6). Types of grazers, grazing patterns, and extreme weather conditions, as well as underlying spatial variation in soils and topographic features, would further have enhanced the complexity and richness of the mosaic of grassland vegetation. These mosaics would have also been temporally dynamic due to the unpredictable nature of recurring physical and biological events—such as fires, heavy grazing, and storms—that reset or changed the structure and composition of the vegetation.

At microgeographic to mesogeographic scales, spatial variation in vegetation, soils, and topographic features would have produced a rich mosaic of habitat patches of varying sizes to be used or avoided by prairie animals. Therefore, animals should be adapted to subsets of habitat patches in native grassland types with adaptation now reflected in nonrandom use of patches. Differences in habitat adaptations would undoubtedly occur in animals due to differences in vagility. For example, large mammals are able to move among patches over a large spatial area, whereas small mammals range over small areas and must, therefore, live within large patches or at the interface of two or more small patches.

For study of fire effects, the general null hypothesis is that fire will have no impact on the population density of individual animal species. Any species that fails to change numerically due to fire would be classified as a fire-neutral species. Alternatively, a population could exhibit either a positive or negative numerical response to fire. Such species we classify as fire-positive and fire-negative species, respectively. Most early work on animals and fire was aimed at describing these general population responses. However, understanding the structure and function of grasslands demands that we know patterns of population changes from prefire through a multiyear, postfire period, rather than simply ascertaining whether species are fire-positive, fire-negative, or fire-neutral over a short postfire period.

Population responses are the result of direct and indirect effects of fire on individual animals. Direct effects, which are caused by fire itself, include increased mortality, forced emigration, and reduced reproductive effort. In contrast, indirect effects are mediated through environmental changes caused by fire. Such indirect effects include changes in patterns of mortality, reproductive effort and timing, and movements, including emigration from and immigration into the burned site.

Direct causes of mortality of small mammals include burns, heat stress, asphyxiation as carbon dioxide flows into occupied burrows, physiological stress as mammals overexert themselves to escape, trampling as large mammals stampede, and predation as small mammals flee from fire. Forced emigration occurs when individuals escape fire by running ahead of it, but do not return to their home sites after fire. Direct reduction in reproductive output could occur by complete or partial abortion of litters or by the abandonment of dependent young induced by physiological stresses due to burns, heat, or physical exertion during excape from fire.

Indirect effects may be the result of changes in quantity and quality of food, availability of nest sites, predation pressure, incidence of parasitism and disease, intensity of competitive interactions, and patterns of social interactions. In addition to shifts in litter size at conception and numbers of litters produced due to quantity and quality of food and shelter, changes in reproductive effort could include partial or complete abortion of litters due to decreased physiological condition of females and reduced likelihood of females finding a suitable mate. Shifts in birth rates, death rates, and patterns of movement in mammalian populations would ultimately be caused by fire-induced alterations of vegetation and physical features. In any burned grassland, for example, the removal of litter and standing dead vegetation will have dramatic effects on small mammals immediately after a fire. Fire and the recovery from fire then lead to temporal changes in plant species composition, primary production, amount of standing vegetation, litter depth, and soil moisture and temperature

(Hulbert 1986). Such changes in primary production can directly alter food availability to both folivorous and granivorous rodents, and secondarily to omnivorous/carnivorous rodents and shrews. In light of dietary, nutritional, and physical requirements of small mammals, survival, reproductive capability, and likelihood of emigration or immigration can be greatly reduced or enhanced by the occurrence of fire. Ultimately, direct and indirect impacts of fire on individuals lead to shifts in population density and assemblage composition, followed by succession/recovery through time as environmental conditions recover to their prefire status in the absence of further fire.

Our goal is to review and summarize what is presently known about the responses of small mammals (rodents and shrews) to grassland fires. To do this, we review published material on the responses of small mammals to grassland fires. We also present data from our work on small mammals on Konza Prairie Research Natural Area that bear on understanding patterns and possible causes of the responses to and recovery from grassland fire. Also, initial responses of small mammals are discussed relative to their food and habitat requirements and environmental changes caused by grassland fire, whereas temporal changes in populations of small mammals are considered in terms of changes in food and habitat resources as a grassland recovers from fire.

GENERAL RESPONSES OF SMALL MAMMALS TO FIRE

During the past 30 years, investigators have examined the effects of fires on small mammals in a number of North American grasslands and savannahs. Given the roles and importance of fire in grasslands, it is interesting to note the relatively recent initiation of the study of fire impacts on grassland mammals. Most studies have been focused on demonstrating strong numerical responses to fire rather than on examining the details of such responses, e.g., causes and temporal patterns of shifts in density, immigration-emigration, and reproduction, or repeatability of positive, negative, and neutral responses. Most studies have compared small mammal densities between a single burned site and a single unburned site. In these cases, the statistical approach was to test for nonrandom habitat selection between burned and unburned sites, but it has often been difficult to reject the null hypothesis of fire-neutrality (lack of habitat selection related to fire) because of small sample sizes.

Some studies of mammalian responses to fire have used a single site with surveys of mammals before and after fire. When the number of individuals within a species declines to low levels immediately after the fire, the population response seems obviously negative, whereas a dramatic increase in numbers of individuals within a species after a fire suggests a positive response to fire. Without comparative sites in unburned habitats, however, the validity of such conclusions must be questioned. Finally, analyses in some studies have incorrectly used total captures rather than number of different individuals as the response variable. Caution needs to be used in interpreting the validity of these "supposed" responses to fire, both because multiple captures of a single individual are not independent observations and because differences in the number of recaptures per individual between sites can create apparent differences in population size, when in fact the numbers of individuals are small and similar on burned and unburned sites.

Documentation of nonneutral responses of small mammals is complicated by changes in population size that are unrelated to fire or recovery from fire. Others factors that impinge on small mammal densities are climatic conditions, intensity of grazing, fire history of study sites, general habitat conditions, and size/shape of burn and the associated edge effect. In the following section, we review in chronological order what is known of general population responses of small mammals to grassland fires based on published studies. Species are not included in this review of the individual studies when numbers were too few for any analysis. Results of statistical tests presented in the text are those conducted by us rather than the author(s) of original papers. Table 5.1 gives the scientific names of the rodents and shrews referred to in the studies.

Published Studies

Cook (1959) examined the effects of an October 1953 wildfire on small mammals in an annual grassland in California. No surveys were made before the wildfire caused by lightning; however, based on a G-test (Zar 1974) surveys made three weeks after fire indicated fire-negative responses for the California vole (0 individuals on burned plot, 26 on unburned plot; $G = 36.04$, $d.f. = 1$; $P < 0.001$) and the western harvest mouse (0 on burned plot, 20 on unburned plot; $G = 27.73$, $d.f. = 1$, $P < 0.001$).

During 1957–59, Tester and Marshall (1961) examined the effects of fire on plants and animals in a Minnesota tallgrass prairie burned in October 1957 and April 1958. A negative response was evident for the meadow vole (May 1958: 7 individuals from 3 census lines in burned sites versus 11 from 2 census lines in unburned sites, $G = 3.25$, $d.f. = 1$, $P < 0.08$; September 1958: 7 in burned sites versus 19 in unburned sites, $G = 11.68$, $d.f. = 1$, $P < 0.001$). A positive response was shown for deer mice (May 1958: 17 in burned sites versus 1 in unburned sites, $G = 11.48$, $d.f. = 1$, $P < 0.001$; September 1958: 14 in burned sites versus 0 in unburned

TABLE 5.1   Scientific names of small mammals discussed in text

Common Names	Scientific Names
California vole	*Microtus californicus*
Deer mouse	*Peromyscus maniculatus*
Elliot's short-tailed shrew	*Blarina hylophaga*
Hispid cotton rat	*Sigmodon hispidus*
Hispid pocket mouse	*Chaetodipus hispidus*[a]
Masked shrew	*Sorex cinereus*
Meadow jumping mouse	*Zapus hudsonius*
Meadow vole	*Microtus pennsylvanicus*
Merriam's kangaroo rat	*Dipodomys merriami*
Northern short-tailed shrew	*Blarina brevicauda*
Plains pocket gopher	*Geomys bursarius*
Prairie vole	*Microtus ochrogaster*
Southern bog lemming	*Synaptomys cooperi*
Southern grasshopper mouse	*Onychomys torridus*
Tawny cotton rat	*Sigmodon fulviventer*[b]
Thirteen-lined ground squirrel	*Spermophilus tridecemlineatus*
Western harvest mouse	*Reithrodontomys megalotis*
White-footed mouse	*Peromyscus leucopus*
White-throated woodrat	*Neotoma albigula*

[a]Formerly *Perognathus hispidus*.
[b]Given as *Sigmodon minimus* in J. H. Bock et al. (1976).

sites, $G = 14.30$, $d.f. = 1$, $P < 0.001$). The masked shrew had a neutral response (September 1958: 22 in burned sites versus 19 in unburned sites, $G = 0.68$, $d.f. = 1$, $P >> 0.10$).

From live trap censuses in a Minnesota oak savannah, Tester (1965) found that combined numbers of deer mice and white-footed mice increased dramatically following fire (49 mice, 35–40 days after fire) as compared to numbers before fire (4 individuals, 7–12 days before fire). This dramatic change suggests a positive response to fire; however, without a control for changes in numbers of mice in unburned oak savannah, the direction of the response is uncertain. Additionally, species-specific responses are not discernible because numbers of individuals of both species were combined.

Schramm (1970) censused small mammals in a 2.8 ha restored tallgrass prairie in Illinois that was burned in late March 1966. Meadow voles and prairie voles were present at high densities before fire, but their numbers dropped to zero a few days after the fire. These changes suggested a fire-negative response by both species; however, no comparisons were made to populations of microtines in unburned prairie, so the specific response remains unknown. Densities in burned (April 1968) and unburned portions of the prairie in 1968 suggested fire-negative responses by meadow voles and northern short-tailed shrews and a fire-positive response by the meadow jumping mouse. Unfortunately, no statistical analyses were done, and absolute densities are hard to interpret and analyze since they were calculated using estimates of numbers from mark-recapture techniques divided by only the area encompassed by small grids—a technique that ignores edge effect.

Small mammals were censused on three small study sites (0.16 ha) in a restored tallgrass prairie in Illinois during the summer of 1970 (Springer and Schramm 1972). Analysis of total numbers of individuals for the summer revealed a negative effect of fire on northern short-tailed shrews (9, 30, and 34 individuals on sites burned earlier that year, burned 2+ years earlier, and burned 4+ years earlier, respectively; $G = 17.40$, $d.f. = 2$, $P < 0.001$) and a positive effect on white-footed mice (12, 5, and 0 individuals; $G = 16.76$, $d.f. = 2$, $P < 0.001$), but no fire effect on meadow jumping mice (4, 7, and 7 individuals; $G = 1.07$, $d.f. = 2$, $P >> 0.10$).

Beck and Vogl (1972) surveyed populations of small mammals in August 1967 in two brush prairie savannah habitats in Wisconsin after both were burned that spring. One site, burned 4 times during the previous 15 years, yielded 0 deer mice, 20 thirteen-lined ground squirrels, and 18 white-footed mice, whereas the second site, burned 11 times in 15 years, yielded 59 deer mice, 12 thirteen-lined ground squirrels, and 0 white-footed mice. The impact of these spring fires on deer mice, white-footed mice, and thirteen-lined ground squirrels cannot be assessed since no control sites in unburned savannah were used. However, the absence of deer mice at site one was undoubtedly due to the presence of woody vegetation resulting from an average fire frequency of three to four years and not due to the recent fire. Supporting this suggestion was the abundance of white-footed mice at site one and the absence of white-footed mice at site two where fire occurred almost on an annual basis.

Moreth and Schramm (1973) censused small mammal populations in a number of plots planted to different grass and grass-forb mixtures. The plots were small but no size was given. In a plot dominated by native tallgrasses, meadow voles were similar in number on each half of the plot before fire (8 and 8 individuals on the burned and unburned portions, respectively). Meadow voles dropped to 0 on the burned area, but increased to 11 individuals on the unburned area after the prescribed fire. This fire-negative response was significant ($G = 15.25$, $d.f. = 1$, $P <$

0.001). The authors also suggested that deer mice and white-footed mice responded positively to fire. However, their data do not justify such a conclusion both because the increase was not consistent on all three small plots and because no unburned control areas planted to the same kinds of grasses and forbs were studied to show that the increases from spring to summer for these two species were due to fire effects.

Small mammals were studied in burned and unburned desert grassland (fire in April 1974) and burned and unburned oak savannah (fire in February 1974) habitats in Arizona (J. H. Bock et al. 1976). From July 1974 to August 1975, patterns of total postfire captures (not numbers of individuals because animals were not marked for identification) in the burned and unburned sites suggested fire-negative responses for white-throated woodrats in both desert grassland and oak savannah; tawny cotton rats in both habitats; and hispid pocket mice in oak savannah but not desert grassland. However, species-specific responses were unclear due to the use of captures rather than number of individuals. Data were combined for captures of deer mice and white-footed mice so that suggested responses of individual species were unknown.

C. E. Bock and J. H. Bock (1978) examined the effect of fire on small mammals in ungrazed sacaton grassland in southeastern Arizona using two sites burned in summer (May 1975, June 1976) and one site burned in winter (February 1976). Total captures of rodents (not individuals) during the first year after spring fire relative to captures in unburned controls suggested that fire had a positive impact on hispid pocket mice, Merriam's kangaroo rats, and southern grasshopper mice, and a negative impact on hispid cotton rats. Following a winter fire, total captures on a burned site and an unburned site suggested negative impacts of fire on hispid cotton rats and white-throated woodrats, and a positive impact on hispid pocket mice. Again, responses of small mammals to fire are only suggestive since the number of captures rather than number of individuals was used as the response variable. Captures of deer mice and white-footed mice were combined, which precludes any suggestion of species-specific fire effects.

Responses of rodents and shrews to fire were studied by Schramm and Willcutts (1983) in a restored tallgrass prairie in Illinois. Censuses were made during May–August 1981 on two small grids (0.16 acre) placed in burned prairie and two in unburned prairie. Total numbers of individuals caught during this period demonstrated significant negative effects of fire on meadow voles and northern short-tailed shrews (shrews: one in burned versus seven in unburned; $G = 5.06$, $d.f. = 1$, $P < 0.05$) and positive effects on deer mice, white-footed mice, meadow jumping mice, and prairie voles.

Working on Konza Prairie Research Natural Area, D. W. Kaufman *et al.* (1983) examined the responses of small mammals to prescribed spring burns in native, ungrazed tallgrass prairie in eastern Kansas. Censuses conducted in July in burned and unburned prairie indicated a significant positive response by deer mice and a significant negative response by western harvest mice to April fires.

In pine savannah in South Dakota, deer mice were studied in burned (October 1979 and April 1980) and paired unburned sites (C. E. Bock and J. H. Bock 1983). Comparison of captures in burned and unburned savannah suggested a positive response of deer mice to the conditions created by fire. However, the analyses were based on˙captures and not individuals and, therefore, suffer from the same statistical weakness already discussed.

Vacanti and Geluso (1985) examined the effects of fire on meadow voles in adjacent burned (May 1979) and unburned tallgrass prairie sites in eastern Nebraska. Although numbers were similar on both areas before fire, voles were absent from the burned prairie for at least three months following fire. During this same time, vole density on the unburned area remained high, as expected.

Consideration of the available information on fire responses of small mammals (summarized in Table 5.2) suggests that most effects of fire are not neutral; rather, rodents and shrews tend to exhibit either fire-positive or fire-negative responses. Fire-negative responses appear typical of rodents and shrews that are associated with plant debris and/or are foliage feeders. Fire-negative mammals include (1) species that forage on invertebrates in the litter layer (northern short-tailed shrew); (2) species that live in relatively dense vegetation and eat plant foliage (California vole, prairie vole, meadow vole, tawny cotton rat, and hispid cotton rat); and (3) species that use, at least partially, aboveground nests of plant debris (California vole, prairie vole, meadow vole, white-throated woodrat, and western harvest mouse). Fire-positive mammals include (1) species that use ambulatory locomotion in microhabitats with a relatively open herbaceous layer and feed on seeds and/or insects (hispid pocket mouse, southern grasshopper mouse, white-footed mouse, deer mouse, and thirteen-lined ground squirrel), and (2) species that use saltatorial locomotion (Merriam's kangaroo rat and meadow jumping mouse).

The cause of the unexpected negative response of hispid pocket mouse to fire in oak savannah (J. H. Bock et al. 1976) was unknown. However, low population densities of fire-positive species following fire, although caused by factors other than fire, appear as discrepancies from the increased density expected from conditions created by fire. In contrast to

TABLE 5.2 General population responses of small mammals to fires in North American grasslands (Key: +, fire-positive response; −, fire-negative response; 0, fire-neutral response; ?, observations suggestive of the listed response, but data available were not or could not be tested statistically)

Mammal	Grassland Type[a]	Response	Reference
Shrews			
Masked shrew	Minnesota tallgrass prairie	0	Tester & Marshall 1961
Northern short-tailed shrew	Illinois tallgrass prairie (restored)	−?[b]	Schramm 1970
	Illinois tallgrass prairie (restored)	−	Springer & Schramm 1972
	Illinois tallgrass prairie (restored)	−	Schramm & Willcutts 1983
Heteromyid rodents			
Hispid pocket mouse	Arizona desert grassland	0?[c]	J. H. Bock et al. 1976
	Arizona sacaton grassland	+?[c]	C. E. Bock & J. H. Bock 1978
	Arizona oak savannah	−?[c]	J. H. Bock et al. 1976
Merriam's kangaroo rat	Arizona sacaton grassland	+?[c]	C. E. Bock & J. H. Bock 1978
Cricetine rodents			
Deer mouse	Minnesota tallgrass prairie	+	Tester & Marshall 1961
	Illinois tallgrass prairie (restored)	+	Schramm & Willcutts 1983
	Kansas tallgrass prairie	+	D. W. Kaufman et al. 1983
	Wisconsin brush prairie savannah	+?[d]	Beck & Vogl 1972
	South Dakota pine savannah	+?[c]	C. E. Bock & J. H. Bock 1983
Hispid cotton rat	Arizona sacaton grassland	−?[c]	C. E. Bock & J. H. Bock 1978
Southern grasshopper mouse	Arizona sacaton grassland	+?[c]	C. E. Bock & J. H. Bock 1978
Tawny cotton rat	Arizona desert grassland	−?[c]	J. H. Bock et al. 1976
	Arizona oak savannah	−?[c]	J. H. Bock et al. 1976
Western harvest mouse	Kansas tallgrass prairie	−	D. W. Kaufman et al. 1983
	California annual grassland	−	Cook 1959
White-footed mouse	Illinois tallgrass prairie (restored)	+	Springer & Schramm 1972
	Illinois tallgrass prairie (restored)	+	Schramm & Willcutts 1983
	Wisconsin brush prairie savannah	+?[d]	Beck & Vogl 1972

TABLE 5.2 *(continued)*

Mammal	Grassland Type[a]	Response	Reference
White-throated woodrat	Arizona desert grassland	−?[c]	J. H. Bock et al. 1976
	Arizona sacaton grassland	−?[c]	C. E. Bock & J. H. Bock 1978
	Arizona oak savannah	−?[c]	J. H. Bock et al. 1976
Microtine rodents			
California vole	California annual grassland	−	Cook 1959
Meadow vole	Minnesota tallgrass prairie	−	Tester & Marshall 1961
	Illinois tallgrass prairie (restored)	−?[b]	Schramm 1970
	Illinois tallgrass prairie (restored)	−?[d]	Schramm 1970
	Illinois tallgrass prairie (restored)	−	Moreth & Schramm 1973
	Illinois tallgrass prairie (restored)	−	Schramm & Willcutts 1983
	Nebraska tallgrass prairie	−	Vacanti & Geluso 1985
Prairie vole	Illinois tallgrass prairie (restored)	−?[d]	Schramm 1970
	Illinois tallgrass prairie (restored)	+	Schramm & Willcutts 1983
Sciurid rodents			
Thirteen-lined ground squirrel	Wisconsin brush prairie savannah	+?[d]	Beck & Vogl 1972
Zapodid rodents			
Meadow jumping mouse	Illinois tallgrass prairie (restored)	+?[b]	Schramm 1970
	Illinois tallgrass prairie (restored)	0	Springer & Schramm 1972
	Illinois tallgrass prairie (restored)	+	Schramm & Willcutts 1983

[a] Study areas for each species are listed from moist to dry grasslands, followed by moist to dry savannahs.

[b] Response pattern only suggestive, since data given as absolute density (individuals/acre) with no statistical analysis and individuals captured on burned and unburned not available to readers.

[c] Response pattern only suggestive, since data given as number of captures rather than number of individuals. Use of captures is flawed by the lack of independence among observations and is possibly biased by differences in trappability between individuals in burned and unburned sites.

[d] Response pattern only suggestive, since data given for burned areas only. Lack of control sites in unburned prairie leaves open the possibility that the supposed response to fire was caused by other factors.

this pattern, low densities of fire-negative species after a fire, although caused by factors other than fire, always enhance the apparent response of fire-negative species. The one positive response to fire, and thus un-expected result, for the prairie vole occurred when the density of the meadow vole, a congener, was high in the unburned sites (Table 5.2). Thus the positive response recorded might be due not to fire but rather to avoidance of competition with its larger congener (Schramm and Willcutts 1983). In all cases with sufficient data to demonstrate fire responses, only two support the occurrence of fire-neutral responses. One is for masked shrews in autumn following a spring fire (Tester and Marshall 1961), the other for meadow jumping mice for total numbers of individuals caught during summer (Springer and Schramm 1972). Masked shrews may have recovered from the effects of spring fire by autumn, although responses by deer mice and meadow voles to fire were still evident in autumn. How-ever, detailed analysis of temporal changes in numbers of the masked shrew from the time of spring fire to the subsequent autumn should be assessed before fire-neutrality of the masked shrew is accepted. In the case of meadow jumping mice, fire-neutrality was not a consistent re-sponse in restored tallgrass prairie, because the other two observations suggest that this species is fire-positive.

Studies from Konza Prairie Research Natural Area

In autumn 1981, we established permanent trap lines in tallgrass prairie habitats on the Konza Prairie Research Natural Area to assess and de-scribe long-term fluctuations in population density and assemblage char-acteristics, as well as to assess and describe seasonal and annual variation in the responses of small mammals to prairie fires. Initially, 2 traplines were set in each of 10 watersheds (G. A. Kaufman et al. 1988), but this effort has been expanded to 2 traplines in each of 14 watersheds. The 14 watersheds represent an array of fire histories and planned regimes of experimental spring fires (unburned, and burned at intervals of 1, 2, 4, and 10 years; Hulbert 1985). Each census line (20 stations at 15 m intervals with 2 live traps per station) was live-trapped for four con-secutive days in spring, summer, and autumn with all small mammals uniquely marked for future identification (details of procedures are given in G. A. Kaufman et al. 1988).

Commonly occurring small mammals in prairie habitats on Konza Prai-rie, in descending order of abundance, were the deer mouse, Elliot's short-tailed shrew, western harvest mouse, white-footed mouse, prairie vole, thirteen-lined ground squirrel, and southern bog lemming. A com-plete list of small mammals occurring on Konza Prairie is given in Finck et al. (1986). From autumn 1981 to autumn 1987, relative densities for each of the common species showed a several-fold range of differences among years for each of the seasons. Since high levels of temporal variation make it difficult to assess fire effects, we tested for constancy of fire-positive and fire-negative patterns for small mammals from autumn 1981 to autumn 1987 using a ranked sign test. Relative density of all small mammals combined was consistently higher in burned than unburned prairie (15 of 19 censuses; Table 5.3). When relative density in unburned areas exceeded that in burned sites, differences in density were small, and relative density in burned prairie fell into the lower portion of the range of recorded values for burned prairie (Fig. 5.1). Differences in numbers of small mammals in burned and unburned prairie depended primarily on number of deer mice in censuses. The four cases (Fig. 5.1) when density of small mammals was greater in unburned than burned prairie occurred during four of the seven times when the relative density of deer mice was low (six or fewer individuals per trapline) and similar in the two habitats.

The deer mouse was the only small mammal that exhibited a strong fire-positive response, with relative densities higher in burned than unburned prairie during 18 of 19 censuses (Table 5.3). The only exception

TABLE 5.3 Average relative density (number of individuals/trapline) of common small mammals (ranked from fire-positive to fire-negative) in burned (B) and unburned (U) prairie from autumn 1981 to autumn 1987 on Konza Prairie, with the number of censuses (19 total) in which this density index was greater in burned than unburned prairie (B > U), was greater in unburned than burned prairie (B < U), and was the same in burned and unburned prairie (B = U; values in parentheses are the number of censuses in which B = U = 0)

	Relative Density					
	B	U	B > U	B < U	B = U	P^a
Deer mouse	7.7	3.1	18	0	1 (0)	<0.001
Small mammals	12.5	9.3	15	4	0 (0)	<0.01
13-lined ground squirrel	0.5	0.3	12	5	2 (1)	<0.09
White-footed mouse	1.1	0.8	10	8	1 (0)	<0.20
Prairie vole	0.5	0.6	5	11	3 (2)	<0.15
Western harvest mouse	0.9	2.3	4	13	2 (2)	<0.05
Elliot's short-tailed shrew	1.2	2.0	2	15	2 (2)	<0.001
Southern bog lemming	0.04	0.15	1	11	7 (7)	<0.01

[a] Probability values are for ranked sign tests in which the ratio of B > U to B < U was tested against a 1:1 ratio.

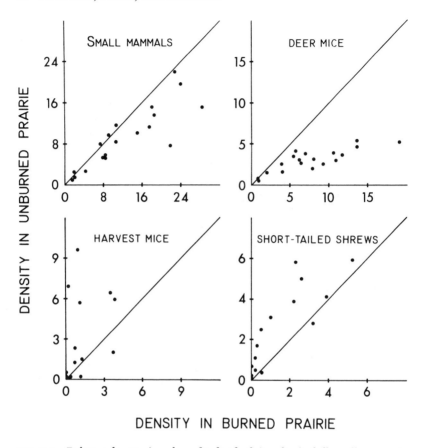

FIG. 5.1   Relative density (number of individuals/trapline) of all small mammals, deer mice, western harvest mice, and Elliot's short-tailed shrews in burned and unburned areas on Konza Prairie. Values plotted are for each of the 19 censuses made from autumn 1981 to autumn 1987, except for censuses in which no captures were made. Censuses in which densities in burned and unburned prairie are equal would fall on the diagonal lines.

occurred in spring 1985 when densities were extremely low and similar in both habitats (0.8 individuals/trapline). This fire-positive response for the deer mouse was consistent with reported patterns (Table 5.2), and likely depends on an increased availability of seeds on the soil surface as the result of the removal of plant litter and standing dead vegetation by fire. In laboratory trials, deer mice selectively foraged in microhabitats with sparse litter rather than in microhabitat patches with moderate to heavy litter (D. W. Kaufman and G. A. Kaufman, unpublished).

The fire-positive pattern of deer mice as illustrated in Fig. 5.1 indicates that relative densities in burned and unburned tallgrass prairie approach each other when relative density in burned prairie is low (< 3 individuals/trapline). This suggests that unburned prairie can support low densities of deer mice, but not high densities. The ratio of density in burned prairie to density in unburned prairie, therefore, increases as overall densities of deer mice increase. The pattern of densities of deer mice in burned and unburned prairie also demonstrates that even strongly fire-positive species can mistakenly appear to be fire-neutral at low densities.

The only other rodent on Konza Prairie that may exhibit a fire-positive response is the thirteen-lined ground squirrel. The pattern observed was marginally significant, with density greater in burned than unburned prairie in 12 of 17 censuses (P < 0.09, Table 5.3). Thirteen-lined ground squirrels were never abundant relative to other species on Konza Prairie; therefore, fire may have relatively little impact on their density in light of other factors impinging on individual ground squirrels.

Responses on Konza Prairie were significantly fire-negative for the western harvest mouse, Elliot's short-tailed shrew, and the southern bog lemming, but only suggestive of a fire-negative response for the prairie vole (Table 5.3). On average, western harvest mice were two to three times more abundant in unburned than burned areas, although consistency in this fire-negative pattern was less than expected (Table 5.3, Fig. 5.1). However, the weak nature of the recorded response was due to three of four exceptions (density in burned prairie > density in unburned prairie) occurring during spring censuses when densities were low. The strong fire-negative response of western harvest mice to conditions during the first growing season after fire was readily apparent in 11 of 12 summer and autumn censuses (P < 0.01). Densities for summer and autumn censuses were 0.9 and 3.0 individuals/trapline in burned and unburned prairie, respectively. This fire-negative response, which was consistent with earlier studies (Table 5.2), was undoubtedly due to the combustion of plant litter and standing dead vegetation used for nesting sites.

The fire-negative response of Elliot's short-tailed shrew was strong, with relative density consistently greater in unburned than burned prairie (15 of 17 censuses; Table 5.3). The two exceptions occurred in autumn 1981 when densities were high (3.2 and 2.8 individuals/trapline in burned and unburned prairie, respectively) and summer 1984 when densities were low (0.5 and 0.4 individuals/trapline in burned and unburned prairie, respectively). This observed fire-negative response for Elliot's short-tailed shrew was consistent with its foraging behavior (searching litter for invertebrate prey) and with the fire-negative pattern reported for its larger, northern congener, the northern short-tailed shrew (Table 5.2). Our observations also point to the need for long-term assessment of fire-response patterns since the strongest fire-positive response by Elliot's short-tailed shrews occurred in the first census.

Results from published studies on microtine rodents (Table 5.2) before we began our long-term censuses led us to expect a negative response of prairie voles to experimental fires on Konza Prairie. In addition, the prairie vole also was expected to be one of the more abundant rodents on Konza Prairie, which has not been the case. Even at the highest density recorded (4.0 and 2.9 individuals/trapline in burned and unburned prairie, respectively), prairie voles were relatively uncommon on Konza Prairie. In our censuses, responses of prairie voles suggested a negative response to fire, since density was lower in burned than unburned prairie in 11 of 16 censuses; however, this pattern was not statistically significant (Table 5.3, $0.15 > P > 0.10$). Examination of response patterns suggested that the potential negative response to fire was stronger in summer than after the end of the growing season. Average density was 0.2 and 0.5 individuals per trapline in burned and unburned sites, respectively, in summer, as compared to 0.6 and 0.6 for burned and unburned sites, respectively, in autumn and spring censuses combined. Additionally, density was greater in unburned than burned prairie in 5 of 6 summer censuses ($P < 0.08$), but only 6 of 10 censuses during autumn and spring ($P >> 0.10$). A negative response to fire was expected due to the combustion of plant litter and standing dead vegetation used for nest building and concealment. Further sampling will be needed to assess the occurrence of a fire-negative response by prairie voles on Konza Prairie.

The significant fire-negative response of the southern bog lemming—relative density greater in unburned than burned prairie in 11 of 12 censuses (Table 5.3)—was expected from the general habitat and food requirements of microtines. However, the significant response was somewhat surprising in light of the low level of abundance observed (0.04 and 0.15 individuals/trapline in burned and unburned prairie, respectively; 0 individuals in 7 of 19 censuses). This negative response was undoubtedly due to folivorous food habits, use of aboveground runways constructed in the litter layer, and frequent construction and use of aboveground nests. Recovery after mid-summer for both microtine rodents (prairie voles and southern bog lemmings) also suggests that availability of high quality foliage is insufficient for recovery until the necessary redevelopment of a protective layer of living and dead plants has occurred.

The white-footed mouse, a woodland form, was the third most abundant rodent caught in prairie habitats—a result unexpected before our censuses. Average densities and the lack of consistent differences in density between burned and unburned prairie suggested that the response of white-footed mice to fire was neutral (Table 5.3). Previous analyses of capture results from Konza Prairie demonstrated that white-footed mice prefer lowland prairie sites near ravines, including those with only an occasional patch of trees or shrubs, over prairie sites farther from ravines (B. K. Clark et al. 1987). It seems likely, therefore, that the presence of white-footed mice in prairie censuses was related to the presence of ravines and trees/shrubs in experimental plots, rather than to fire-induced changes in prairie vegetation. Over an extended time scale, recurring fire on Konza Prairie is expected to reduce the presence of shrubs and trees on frequently burned areas and thereby to have a negative effect on white-footed mice.

RESPONSES OF SMALL MAMMAL ASSEMBLAGES TO FIRE

Differences in species-specific responses to fire should produce differences in assemblage structure and composition between burned and unburned grassland sites. Earlier studies have focused on numerical responses of individual species to fire and have not addressed this issue, except for Schramm and Willcutts (1983). The lack of data on this topic is partly due to the fact that limited trapping efforts do not lend themselves readily to the analysis of patterns of change in assemblages. Schramm and Willcuts (1983) reported a greater increase in diversity on burned sites during the first few weeks after fire than on unburned sites. This difference in diversity undoubtedly was linked to the positive response of prairie voles as well as numerical changes in more typically fire-positive species on burned sites.

On Konza Prairie, assemblages of small mammals were compositionally very different in burned and unburned prairie: postfire assemblages were more dominated by deer mice than assemblages in unburned prairie (Table 5.4). Thirteen-lined ground squirrels also contributed slightly more to assemblages that develop after fire than to assemblages in unburned sites. In contrast, proportional contributions of the other common species to the small mammal assemblages were greater in unburned than burned prairie. Although fire-negative species were proportionately more abundant in unburned than burned prairie, the deer mouse was proportionately the most abundant small mammal in unburned prairie.

Comparison of species richness and diversity of small mammal assemblages in burned and unburned prairie is hampered by the relatively small number of individuals caught per trapline during censuses. Even when numbers of individuals were summed for watersheds (two trap-lines), numbers of small mammals were too few and prevented a direct comparison of

TABLE 5.4 Average percentage abundance of common small mammals (ranked from fire-positive to fire-negative) in burned (B) and unburned (U) prairie, from autumn 1981 to autumn 1987 on the Konza Prairie, with the number of censuses (19 total) in which percentage abundance was greater in burned prairie than unburned prairie (B > U), was greater in unburned prairie than burned prairie (B < U), and was the same in burned and unburned prairie (B = U, values in parentheses are the number of censuses in which B = U = 0)

	Percentage Abundance					
	B	U	B > U	B < U	B = U	P^a
Deer mouse	65.7	40.3	18	1	0 (0)	<0.001
13-lined ground squirrel	5.3	4.3	13	5	1 (1)	<0.09
White-footed mouse	6.4	11.5	7	12	0 (0)	<0.13
Western harvest mouse	6.1	17.1	3	14	2 (2)	<0.05
Prairie vole	4.2	5.9	2	14	3 (3)	<0.05
Southern bog lemming	1.5	2.4	1	12	7 (7)	<0.05
Elliot's short-tailed shrew	7.7	16.6	0	17	2 (2)	<0.001

[a] Probability values (P) are for ranked sign tests in which the ratio of B > U to B < U was tested against a 1:1 ratio.

richness and diversity in burned and unburned prairie. To overcome the effect of small sample size, the pattern between species richness and sample size was examined by plotting average richness values for watershed censuses in both burned and unburned prairie (Fig. 5.2). Average values for species richness were calculated for sample size categories of 1, 2, 3, 4, 5, 6–10, 11–15, . . . 71–75 individuals. Species richness— sample size patterns suggested that numbers of species caught along two traplines set in the same watershed reached a maximal value of 6–7 species for both burned and unburned prairie as numbers of small mammals captured approached 40–50 individuals (Fig. 5.2). Comparison of average values of species richness suggested that species richness was slightly greater in unburned than burned prairie for intermediate sample sizes (6 to 50 individuals/census period; Fig. 5.2). However, species richness appeared similar in burned and unburned prairie as an asymptotic value of 6–7 species was reached when sample size exceeded 50 individuals. Overall, species richness appeared to be little affected by fire (Fig. 5.2), although proportional composition of assemblages shifted considerably between unburned and burned prairie (Table 5.4).

Our average values for the proportional responses of species to fire

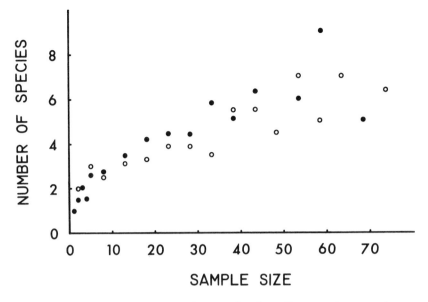

FIG. 5.2 Number of species in the sample of small mammals trapped on a watershed (number of individuals/two traplines) in burned (open circles) and unburned (closed circles) prairie on the Konza Prairie. Values plotted are the average number of individuals in all censuses of 1, 2, 3, 4, 5, 6–10, 11–15, . . . 71–75 individuals (using midpoints of 8, 13, . . . 73).

were somewhat misleading for species that exhibited major fluctuations in density (e.g., western harvest mice) or pronounced seasonal shifts in density (e.g., Elliot's short-tailed shrews). From autumn 1981 to autumn 1982, western harvest mice were abundant on Konza Prairie, and the impact of fire on the proportion of western harvest mice in the small mammal assemblages was especially dramatic (Table 5.5). Low densities from spring 1983 to spring 1986 resulted in similarly low representation of harvest mice in small mammal assemblages in both burned and unburned prairie (2–3 percent of all small mammals). However, with recovery of population densities in 1986 and 1987, the contribution of harvest mice to the small mammal assemblage also increased. At high densities, western harvest mice made up one third to one half of the assemblage in unburned prairie, and the impact of fire resulted in an assemblage with a greatly reduced harvest mouse component in burned prairie. These results emphasize the importance of long-term data sets for examining population responses to natural events such as fire.

TABLE 5.5   Percentage abundance of western harvest mice (HM) and deer mice (DM) in burned and unburned prairie on Konza Prairie during four subperiods within the total study period, with the ratio of western harvest mice to deer mice (HM/DM)

Time Period	Number of Census Periods	Burned			Unburned		
		HM	DM	HM/DM	HM	DM	HM/DM
Autumn 1981– autumn 1982	4	8.9	52.8	0.17	36.2	25.6	1.41
Spring 1983– spring 1986	10	3.0	69.7	0.04	2.0	49.0	0.04
Summer 1986– spring 1987	3	7.9	75.4	0.10	19.1	42.9	0.45
Summer 1987– autumn 1987	2	13.2	56.8	0.23	51.7	22.1	2.34

TABLE 5.6   Percentage abundance of Elliot's short-tailed shrews (SS) and deer mice (DM) in burned and unburned prairie on Konza Prairie during summer, autumn, and spring censuses, with the ratio of Elliot's short-tailed shrews to deer mice (SS/DM)

Time Period	Number of Census Periods	Burned			Unburned		
		SS	DM	SS/DM	SS	DM	SS/DM
Summer 1982–87	6	2.6	79.8	0.03	10.4	43.5	0.24
Autumn 1981–87	7	18.7	52.7	0.35	33.8	27.6	1.23
Spring 1982–87	6	0.0	66.8	0.0	2.8	51.9	0.05

For Elliot's short-tailed shrews, densities were high in autumn and near zero in spring (Table 5.6). Seasonal differences in trappability may confound the differences in estimated relative densities on Konza Prairie. Season appeared to influence the observed importance of shrews in small mammal assemblages of the tallgrass prairie as well as the degree of impact of fire on these small insectivores. In unburned prairie, for example, shrews made up one tenth of the assemblage in summer, increased to one third by autumn, and decreased to only a few percent by spring. The same annual pattern for shrews was found in burned prairie; however, the proportional representation in the small mammal assemblage was much lower.

DIRECT EFFECTS OF FIRE

Casual observations suggest that some small mammals are killed by grassland fires while others are forced to flee ahead of the fire. These direct effects of fire should vary with characteristics of a particular fire, as small mammals can often outrun a slow-moving backfire, but not a fast-moving headfire (for a description of fires, see Hulbert 1978). Fire-caused mortality of small mammals depends partly on whether individuals are (1) active entirely aboveground and have precocial young; (2) active aboveground, nest frequently or entirely aboveground, and have altricial young, (3) active aboveground but nest in belowground burrows; or (4) burrowing forms that seldom come aboveground. Microtine rodents, harvest mice, and woodrats when using aboveground nests should be especially vulnerable to grassland fires. For small mammals that use belowground burrows, the magnitude of direct effects will depend on whether they are active aboveground at the time a fire occurs.

Mortality of meadow and prairie voles caused by a fast-moving headfire (late March) was assessed by Schramm (1970). No deaths due to direct mortality from fire were documented during a search conducted on the day after fire, although several hundred individuals were living on the site before the fire. Additionally, no evidence of mortality due to heat or asphyxiation was found in the few burrows that were excavated after the fire.

Other studies also support the contention that few voles are killed directly by grassland fires. Following a late April 1976 burn of a 22.8 ha tallgrass prairie, Erwin and Stasiak (1979) found 1 young meadow vole dead near 1 of 24 nests examined, and 1 adult prairie vole dead away from nests. After a 0.6 ha burn on this same site in mid-May 1979, none of the 16 meadow voles living partly or entirely on the area was found dead (Vacanti and Geluso 1985).

Geluso et al. (1986) studied the movements and fate of 7 radio-telemetered meadow voles before, during, and after a backfire (mid-May) in tallgrass prairie. One of these voles was found dead on the burned site, whereas 3 voles escaped in belowground burrows and 3 voles escaped while remaining aboveground. The one death that occurred due to fire was questioned as a natural occurrence because it was suspected that an observer prevented the vole from seeking refuge in a burrow located near where the carcass was found. No other dead voles were found, although at least 13 nontelemetered voles were living on the site. Survival of radio-telemetered voles belowground also suggested that deaths due to heat or asphyxiation are unlikely as prairie fires pass over burrow entrances. Of 3 voles monitored aboveground during the fire, 1 was forced to leave the area ahead of the flames. A second vole also was found outside of the burned area, but it was uncertain whether it had been forced to emigrate during the fire or whether it moved from the burned area after the fire. The third vole escaped the fire by staying on the bare mound of a plains pocket gopher as the fire burned around it.

Schramm (1970) also reported forced emigration of voles (five meadow or prairie voles) by watching for their movements ahead of a fast-moving fire. However, these five voles represented only a few percent of voles living on the burned area, and all voles were absent from the grid within a few days.

When tallgrass prairie was burned in Nebraska, Erwin and Stasiak (1979) found a high level of mortality for young western harvest mice. A search of 536 nests yielded 8 nests that contained 27 dead young ranging in age from neonates to pups near weaning. Using estimates of nest density for the area, Erwin and Stasiak calculated that the fire would have killed between 9 and 23 young harvest mice per hectare. In contrast to results for young harvest mice, no adult harvest mice were found dead in nests examined. The effect of the fire on the total population was unknown, because no estimate of the size of the adult population was available.

In concert with Erwin and Stasiak (1979), observations on Konza Prairie suggested that direct mortality is not a primary cause of the decline of trappable-sized western harvest mice following fire. In 1984 and 1987, approximately one half of a 13 ha small mammal grid was burned and one half remained unburned. Censuses before and after the fire were used to assess differential persistence in burned and unburned prairie. For the two years combined, similar proportions of harvest mice present before prairie fires were caught after fire on both burned (53 percent of 30 individuals) and unburned sites (47 percent of 38 individuals; $G = 0.24$, $d.f. = 1$, $P > 0.50$).

For most species examined in detail during fires, direct mortality and forced emigration appear to have only a minimal impact on postfire changes in small mammal populations. This is especially true for trappable-sized small mammals, which can apparently move fast enough to find safe sites—burrows or bare areas on the soil surface—before being killed by burns and heat. However, wildfires driven by very strong winds were undoubtedly more difficult for small mammals to escape than backfires.

When aboveground nests are used by small mammals, dependent young are vulnerable to direct mortality from grassland fires; therefore, the magnitude of impact of fire on aboveground nesting species is related to the timing of fire relative to the time period that young are in nests.

MOVEMENTS AND RECRUITMENT FOLLOWING FIRE

Population densities for both fire-positive and fire-negative species often change dramatically during the first few weeks after a grassland fire. The rapidity of the shift suggests that movements into or out of burned prairie cause population responses immediately following grassland fires. Support for this idea was first provided by Schramm (1970) from movements (25–160 m) of five meadow voles and two prairie voles from burned prairie to adjacent unburned grassy areas within a few days of the fire. The fate of large numbers of other voles that disappeared after the fire was not known; however, the decrease was not due to direct mortality (Schramm 1970). Description of the study site indicated that the unburned grassy edge was small, so it seems likely that other voles made even longer moves to find favorable habitat.

In a small area of burned tallgrass prairie in Nebraska, the fire-negative response of meadow voles occurred within a few days of the fire (Vacanti and Geluso 1985). Five of 10 voles with home ranges exclusively in burned prairie before the fire were trapped in unburned prairie just outside of the burned area after the fire. Within a month after fire, 3 of these 5 individuals had established home ranges exclusively on the unburned study site, as did 3 of 6 voles that had parts of their home ranges on the burned area before the fire. For comparison, 8 of 10 voles with home ranges exclusively in the unburned study site before fire remained there after fire.

Fire-induced movements by small mammals were also examined on a 13 ha study site on Konza Prairie. In 1984, 2 of 10 deer mice in the unburned area before fire shifted to some use of the burned portion in less than five weeks after the fire, and one that used both burned and unburned portions before fire shifted to only the burned portion after fire (D. W. Kaufman, S. K. Gurtz, and G. A. Kaufman, 1988). In contrast, none of the 3 mice in the area to be burned shifted to the unburned area after the fire. For deer mice first trapped less than two weeks after fire and not recorded previously on the grid, shifts from unburned to complete or partial use of the burned area (7 of 11 individuals, with 3 of these to exclusive use of burned prairie) was significantly greater than shifts of deer mice from burned to complete or partial use of unburned areas (1 of 9).

On this same study site in 1987, 1 of 6 resident deer mice caught on the burned area before fire shifted to some use of unburned prairie after fire, whereas 3 of 6 deer mice on unburned prairie shifted to some use of burned prairie after fire (Clark 1989). In contrast, none of 12 western harvest mice living in unburned prairie before the fire was trapped in burned prairie after fire, whereas 13 of 13 residents on the area to be burned shifted to some use of unburned prairie after fire (4 of these used both burned and unburned prairie, but all 4 mice were last trapped in unburned prairie). Prairie voles exhibited a pattern similar to western harvest mice, as neither of 2 voles caught in the unburned area before fire shifted to burned prairie after fire, but 6 of 6 voles caught in the area to be burned shifted to use of only unburned prairie after fire. Finally, 3 of four southern bog lemmings caught in the burned area before fire moved to the adjacent unburned site after fire. The dramatic shift in resident mice in 1987 as compared to 1984 was probably due to two factors. First, densities of small mammals on the study site were much higher in 1987 than 1984. Second, in 1984 the unburned portion of the grid was only one year postfire when the second portion was burned, whereas in 1987 the unburned portion was three years postfire.

Distribution of new individuals of the 5 species on the site during the month following the experimental fire in 1987 was strikingly consistent with expectations (Clark 1989). For new individuals first trapped on the site after fire, 21 of 23 deer mice were captured on burned prairie, whereas 42 of 45 western harvest mice, 24 of 25 Elliot's short-tailed shrews, 3 of 3 prairie voles, and 1 of 1 southern bog lemmings were captured on the unburned portion of the study site. Some of these individuals may have been born on the grid during this time; however, as indicated by their adult body sizes when first trapped, most individuals must have moved from untrapped burned and unburned prairie areas contiguous with the grid.

Generally, the initial decline or increase on burned prairie by fire-negative and fire-positive species, respectively, depends in large part on movements into and out of these sites during the first few weeks after the fire. Predation on fire-negative species during emigration from burned prairie may also result in losses, but the magnitude of this pressure has not been studied. In contrast, reproduction by fire-positive species should contribute to high density in burned grasslands, although this aspect also remains unstudied. As habitat quality for the fire-positive species deteriorates through time, movements should result in net emigration from the burned area. At the same time, these changing habitat conditions should be favorable for fire-negative species, so that immigration plus reproduction should lead to increased densities of fire-negative species.

RECOVERY AND SUCCESSION OF SMALL MAMMALS

Assessing whether species are fire-neutral, fire-positive, or fire-negative is useful, but it is ultimately more important to know the time course of changes in and recovery of populations of small mammals as we try to understand the role of fire in grasslands. In the absence of fire, populations will remain stable (Fig. 5.3,A, all other factors assumed to be constant with no effect on density), as do fire-neutral species following fire (Fig. 5.3,B). In contrast to these patterns, density of fire-negative and fire-positive mammals will shift following fire with recovery to prefire levels taking one to several years. Three general categories of fire responses are (1) shift in density within days to weeks, followed by recovery within one to several years (Fig. 5.3,C and D); (2) delayed shifts in density, with maximum impact in the second or later years after fire and recovery after that (Fig. 5.3,E and F); and (3) shifts in density, followed by an opposite response before recovery to prefire levels (Fig. 5.3,G and H).

Nonneutral fire responses can create temporal variation in total biomass, species richness, and species diversity of assemblages. For example, assemblage characteristics may increase or decrease soon after fire due to changes in the presence/absence and/or proportional composition of species. In other cases, assemblage characteristics may not change immediately or over time although the presence/absence and/or proportional composition of species shifts. This is especially true for species richness, which can change only with the net addition or loss of species.

Based on observed changes in habitat features following fire, recovery of populations and, therefore, assemblages of small mammals to prefire status undoubtedly extends past the first growing season. Assessment of recovery, like other aspects discussed above, requires not only the study of burned prairie, but also of unburned prairie to provide a statistical control. Additionally, populations should be assessed at frequent intervals during the first several years after fire to gain the most insight into patterns of recovery.

Cook (1959) traced small mammal populations through three growing seasons following a wildfire in annual grasslands in California. After an immediate fire-negative response by western harvest mice, immigration to the burned site began at the time of maximum grass seed production about six months after the autumn fire. Densities of harvest mice were similar in burned and unburned grassland until the second growing season after fire, when densities in the burned area increased dramatically above densities on unburned areas. Densities remained low on both sites in the third year of study. In contrast to this pattern, California voles reached an annual high density in unburned grassland while remaining

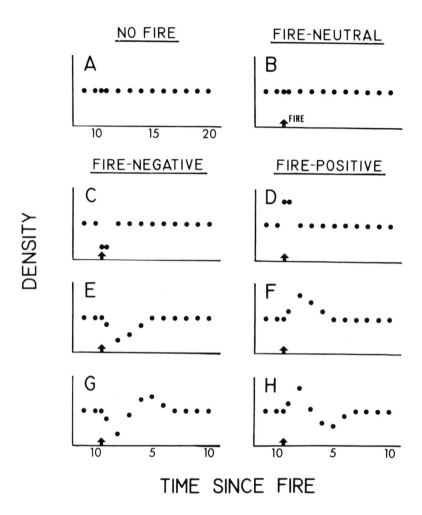

FIG. 5.3 Hypothetical patterns of change in the population density of animals, including small mammals, with time since fire, when all other influences on density are constant. Values plotted are for density during the growing season as well as immediately after a spring grassland fire (B–H) and the equivalent time in A. Predicted densities are for species in the absence of fire (A), fire-neutral species (B), species exhibiting immediate response and then a fast recovery to prefire density (C, D), species exhibiting a slow response and a slow recovery (E, F), and species exhibiting a slow response, maximum density a few years after fire, and a slow recovery to unburned density (G, H).

near zero in burned grassland during the first summer after fire. By the second summer, density was high in both burned and unburned areas, although density in the burned area was only 60 percent of that in the unburned area. Whether this recovery in the burned area would have continued or whether this difference between burned and unburned areas was due to spatial variation is unknown as trapping ended before the third summer.

Schramm and Willcutts (1983) examined changes in small mammals from May through August 1981 following a mid-April fire in tallgrass prairie. Data for prairie voles, meadow voles, deer mice, and white-footed mice demonstrated considerable shifts in density during the 18 weeks of the study. Much of the variation is difficult to ascribe to fire and the recovery from the fire. However, it is certain that recovery of small mammals to prefire status had not occurred by late summer.

For meadow voles in tallgrass prairie in Nebraska, use of adjacent burned and unburned sites was similar before fire (10 individuals on each site); however, use of the burned area declined drastically within a few days after a May fire (1 and 15 individuals on burned and unburned sites, respectively; Vacanti and Geluso 1985). Differential use was still evident the following spring (1 and 17 on burned and unburned sites, respectively). However, meadow voles had recovered on burned prairie by the end of the second summer, with similar use of burned and unburned prairie (15 and 13 residents, respectively).

To assess recovery of small mammals in tallgrass prairie habitats on Konza Prairie, relative densities at different times after fire were calculated for deer mice, western harvest mice, and Elliot's short-tailed shrews (Table 5.7). Numbers of individuals of each species captured on traplines set in watersheds in a topographically similar portion of Konza Prairie were used to compute relative densities by season. Numbers of individuals included in year 1 are from watersheds that were burned in spring and trapped in the subsequent summer, autumn, and spring censuses. Data were also collected for years 2, 3, 4, 5–7, and 9–15 after fire. The mean value for years 5–7 was based on repeated sampling of one watershed, whereas the mean for years 9–15 was based on one unburned watershed trapped from 1981–87. Because of the composite nature of the data (all censuses in all years) and use of the same watershed multiple times, no detailed statistical analysis is possible. Therefore, only general patterns are summarized in Table 5.7 and described here.

For each of the three species, the number of individuals captured per trapline varied considerably within most categories of season and time since fire (Table 5.7). The general pattern for deer mice was that density

TABLE 5.7   Changes in relative density of the 3 common small mammals with time since fire during summer, autumn, and spring censuses on Konza Prairie; values given are the mean ($\bar{x}$) and standard deviation (sd) of numbers of individuals per trapline for all traplines falling into each category of season and year after fire during the study

		Years after Fire [a]					
		1	2	3	4	5–7	9–15
Deer mouse							
Summer	$\bar{x}$	11.15	4.86	3.43	3.71	3.33	2.08
	sd	5.56	3.91	1.48	2.45	2.75	0.80
Autumn	$\bar{x}$	8.46	4.12	4.81	3.19	2.50	1.36
	sd	4.53	2.10	1.73	2.58	1.50	0.85
Spring	$\bar{x}$	5.50	1.95	1.71	1.43	4.25	0.83
	sd	4.58	1.52	2.20	1.81	1.77	0.87
Western harvest mouse							
Summer	$\bar{x}$	1.08	6.57	7.83	7.00	2.75	5.83
	sd	0.86	5.19	6.51	0.50	1.06	4.75
Autumn	$\bar{x}$	4.20	6.50	4.17	6.33	8.50	8.33
	sd	4.06	3.11	0.76	1.26	—	3.62
Spring	$\bar{x}$	2.00	1.20	0.83	1.67	0.75	0.67
	sd	1.00	1.15	0.76	1.44	1.06	0.76
Elliot's short-tailed shrew							
Summer	$\bar{x}$	0.35	0.09	0.29	0.57	2.33	1.58
	sd	0.24	0.20	0.57	0.73	2.25	1.24
Autumn	$\bar{x}$	3.38	4.27	5.31	4.83	5.83	5.00
	sd	1.87	2.15	3.39	1.68	1.15	2.77
Spring	$\bar{x}$	0.0	0.05	0.14	0.0	0.25	0.17
	sd	—	0.16	0.38	—	0.35	0.26

[a] Year 1 after fire is the time period from fire to the first year after fire, year 2 after fire is the time period from the start to the end of the second year after fire, etc.

was two to three times greater in year 1 than in year 2 for all three seasons. In the second summer after fire, numbers of deer mice remained in transition from the high density of burned prairie to the low density of unburned prairie, as the summer value is 30 percent higher than the highest subsequent density estimate from year 3 to years 9–15. The impact of fire on deer mice, therefore, appears to have ended by the completion of the second growing season after fire (autumn).

In contrast to the pattern for deer mice, the impact of fire on western harvest mice appeared to last only through the first growing season (Table 5.7). Density of western harvest mice in the first summer was about one sixth that of the second summer, whereas the density in the first autumn may be lower or higher than autumn densities in unburned prairie. In spring, 11 months after fire, no effect of fire-induced changes was apparent.

For Elliot's short-tailed shrews, only density in autumn was sufficiently high to suggest any temporal pattern of recovery (Table 5.7). The negative impact of fire on shrews was evident in the first autumn, with densities recovering to unburned levels by the third autumn. Density in the second autumn was intermediate between densities in years 1 and 3. But with the high variability in density among traplines and years, it is difficult to know whether populations were still in transition or had recovered by the second autumn.

Available data on recovery of populations of small mammals suggest that both fire-negative and fire-positive mammals are most heavily influenced during the first growing season after fire (more closely resembling Fig. 5.3,C and D than E and F). Recovery for fire-negative species may occur in the second growing season, but has surely occurred by the start of the third growing season after fire. Variation in density among years and sites (Table 5.7) suggests that length of time needed for small mammals to recover likely varies with primary productivity, available food, and structural features of the habitat.

FREQUENCY OF FIRE

Fires with a constant frequency of recurrence are expected to induce cyclic changes in densities of fire-positive and fire-negative species that reflect the cycle of fire (Fig. 5.4). When the cycle of fire is longer than the time to recovery, a regular cycle with return to unburned densities before the end of the cycle is expected to develop for both fire-negative (Fig. 5.4,A) and fire-positive mammals (Fig. 5.4,B). However, when the cycle of fire is shorter than the time to recovery, a cycle in density will develop where the average density during the cycle decreases for fire-negative species (Fig. 5.4,C) and increases for fire-positive species (Fig. 5.4,D) until a stable cycle is reestablished.

As suggested by the postfire temporal change in density of deer mice, western harvest mice, and Elliot's short-tailed shrew on Konza Prairie (Table 5.7), a recurring fire with a 2-year to 10-year frequency should create a cycle of population density of small mammals in tallgrass prairie. Analyses of deer mice, western harvest mice, and Elliot's short-tailed shrews on Konza Prairie strongly suggest that 2-year and 4-year cycles of

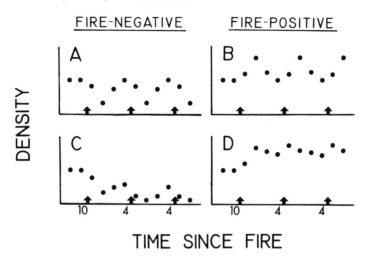

FIG. 5.4   Hypothetical patterns of change in the population density of animals, including small mammals, in grasslands experiencing recurring fire (every 4 years after the initial fire in the figure occurred in year 10). Values plotted are for the density in the growing season in each year. Predicted patterns are for species that recover to unburned densities before the next fire (A, B) and species that fail to recover to unburned density before the next fire (C, D).

density develop in watersheds burned at 2-year (two watersheds burned in different years) and 4-year intervals (four watersheds burned in different years), respectively (D. W. Kaufman et al. unpublished).

Because patterns of temporal change in density of small mammals suggest that recovery does not always occur by the second year after fire (Table 5.7), it seems that a directional change in average density of small mammals would more likely occur over time in areas burned every two years than in areas burned every four years. Variability in density that is unrelated to fire has been quite high, and we cannot test for such a shift.

Data from annually and quadrennially burned sites demonstrated an effect of fire frequency on postfire density and average density during the cycle of fire. In the first case, relative density in the first year after a four-year fire was greater than density in an annually burned site for deer mice during 18 of 19 censuses (ranked sign test, $P < 0.001$), western harvest mice during 8 of 10 censuses ($P = 0.10$), and Elliot's short-tailed shrew during 7 of 9 censuses ($P = 0.15$). Average relative density in years 1, 2, 3, and 4 of the four-year cycle (average of four different sites trapped during each census) was greater than density in annually burned prairie for deer mice during 12 of 19 censuses ($P < 0.05$), western harvest mice during 14 of 17 censuses ($P < 0.01$), and Elliot's short-tailed shrew during 9 of 12 censuses ($P < 0.02$).

SIZE AND SHAPE OF BURN

Spatial extent and shape of a grassland burn undoubtedly affect the response of small mammals to a fire. For very small burns, emigration and immigration should be minimal for fire-negative and fire-positive species, respectively, since individuals using the area of the burn will be mostly influenced by their use of the contiguous unburned area. In contrast to small burns, fire-created conditions will have the primary impact on small mammal use for larger, two-dimensional burns. Although no studies of the size and shape of burns have yet been conducted, time to recovery of fire-negative species should be shorter when individuals can readily move to the middle of the burned area than when the distance to the middle is large.

On a 2 ha area with a mosaic of small burned and unburned areas (< 0.05 ha) on Konza Prairie, deer mice used burned plots more than the unburned plots, whereas the opposite pattern was found for western harvest mice (Peterson et al. 1985). Although home ranges of both species would have included both burned and unburned prairie, use patterns by individuals reflected the pattern of population responses seen on much larger burned and unburned areas on Konza Prairie.

INTENSITY OF FIRE

With abundant dry fuel and strong winds, a grassland fire burns nearly all litter and standing dead vegetation. In contrast, patches of grassland are left unburned when fuel is limited or damp. No specific predictions are possible for small mammal responses when fires burn incompletely across a landscape. In general, however, the assemblage of small mammals on an incompletely burned area should have a greater proportion of individuals of fire-negative species than the proportion of individuals of fire-negative species in a grassland experiencing an intense, complete burn.

No studies of fire and small mammals have examined the effect of a mosaic of burned and unburned patches created by an incomplete burn that occurs naturally. However, the mosaic of small patches created by controlled burns (Peterson et al. 1985) and the mosaic of large patches created by experimental fires on watersheds on Konza Prairie simulate a range of patch sizes that could be created by a fire that burns patchily. Results of censuses in small patches (Peterson et al. 1985) as well as those given in Table 5.3 support the prediction that an area burned by a patchy fire, creating patches up to tens of hectares in size, would have more of a mixture of individuals of both fire-positive and fire-negative small mammals than either burned or unburned prairie.

SEASONALITY OF FIRE

In North American grasslands, wildfires could have occurred during any season of the year, although the occurrence of fire would have been more likely in some months than others due to annual weather patterns. In the Great Plains, for example, most fires caused by lightning would have occurred from late spring to early autumn (Hulbert 1973, Bragg 1982). Grassland small mammals are undoubtedly influenced by seasonality of fire, due to their adaptation to particular habitat features and conditions. An area burned at the end of a growing season would be without vegetative cover for several months longer than if it were burned the following spring. For fire-negative mammals requiring the protective cover of litter, standing dead vegetation, and/or growing plants, an early fall to winter fire should have a greater impact on small mammals over the next year than would a spring fire. In contrast, fall and spring fires should cause early summer densities of fire-positive species to be more similar than the early summer densities of fire-negative mammals. In tallgrass prairie in eastern Kansas, plant species composition, primary productivity, and large mammal (cattle) weight gain differ among areas burned at different times of the year (e.g., K. L. Anderson 1964, Hulbert 1986, Smith and Owensby 1973, Towne and Owensby 1984). Although plant composition and productivity are altered by the seasonality of fire, the effects on small mammals of differences in composition and productivity between autumn and spring burns would probably be less important than the impact of the lack of litter and plant cover for several months (result of November or December fire) as compared to a much shorter time period (April or May fire).

Although effects of fire on small mammals—e.g., mortality of young and rate of recovery—surely vary with the season in which fire occurred, no studies have focused on this issue. Since most of the effects of season on population responses will undoubtedly be more subtle than general fire-negative and fire-positive responses, studies of differences in effects of season of grassland fires on small mammal populations will require intensive, replicated studies. In fact, Tester and Marshall (1961), C. E. Bock and J. H. Bock (1978, 1983), and J. H. Bock et al. (1976) examined the response of small mammals in spring and autumn or spring and winter burn plots; however, due to a lack of replicates (only one or two plots of each type in each study), no effects of season were evident, and their analyses focused on only the general effects of fire on small mammals.

INTERACTION OF FIRE WITH CLIMATIC CONDITIONS

Since primary productivity is greatly reduced by drought, the amount and architecture of living vegetation should be more alike on burned and unburned grasslands previously stressed by a multiyear drought than on those whose climate was favorable for plant growth during the few years before fire. Assemblages of small mammals on burned and unburned areas affected by a multiyear drought should, therefore, be more alike than assemblages on burned and unburned areas experiencing climatic conditions favoring plant growth. This difference in pattern would occur because mammalian assemblages in grasslands affected by drought would be dominated by small mammals requiring open habitat (likely fire-positive species, especially deer mice on Konza Prairie) rather than those requiring heavy litter and vegetation (likely fire-negative species). Changes in plant species composition and quality and quantity of seed production due to drought should also alter use by small mammals relative to use when not affected by drought.

No studies have examined the interactive effects of fire and climate on small mammals; however, long-term research on Konza Prairie is directed toward this issue for small mammals as well as other consumers, plant composition and productivity, and ecosystem processes. It is impossible to discern how climatic conditions may alter fire effects for small mammals with our first 6 years of data; however, effects of climate on fire effects for small mammals in tallgrass prairie should become evident as 20–30 years of data on small mammal populations, climatic variables, and primary productivity are accumulated.

INTERACTION OF FIRE WITH TOPO-EDAPHIC CONDITIONS

Plant species composition, primary productivity, and litter/standing dead vegetation vary with soil type and topography in grasslands (Knapp and Seastedt 1986, Abrams and Hulbert 1987, Gibson and Hulbert 1987, Abrams et al. 1986). As a result, fire-induced changes in vegetation should vary with topo-edaphic factors, such as moisture, nutrient availability, exposure, and slope. Due to the typically higher production and moister soils of lowland over upland grassland (Abrams et al. 1986), fire should also have a differential influence on assemblages of small mammals in upland and lowland sites, although precise predictions are not possible.

Use of upland sites, limestone break sites, and lowland sites by deer mice and western harvest mice was assessed for capture data from autumn

1981 and spring and summer 1982 (G. A. Kaufman et al. 1988). Distribution of the use of topo-edaphic sites for deer mice indicated that use of lowland was less than use of upland and breaks when prairie was left unburned. Following a spring burn, however, deer mice used lowland sites in a similar fashion to upland and break sites. In contrast, the effect of fire on western harvest mice was apparently not dependent on topo-edaphic conditions.

INTERACTION OF FIRE WITH GRAZING

Since grazing prevents or retards the accumulation of litter and standing dead vegetation, the proportional abundance of fire-positive small mammals should be high in moderately to heavily grazed grasslands. In contrast, if grazing pressure is light and, therefore, patchily distributed, individuals of fire-positive small mammals should be proportionately less abundant than in heavily grazed prairie, because ungrazed patches would be more suitable for fire-negative than fire-positive species. Therefore, the effect of fire in altering the population densities of different small mammals should decrease as grazing pressure increases from light to heavy.

From our review, it appears that none of the studies of fire and small mammals in North American grasslands were conducted in research sites where grazing by large mammals was an interactive influence on fire. Because studies of fire effects have been conducted where grazing by large mammals has little or no influence, the results of such studies show dramatic changes in populations of small mammals during the first year after a nonannual fire. Yet studies of small mammals in cattle-grazed and ungrazed sites in mixed-grass prairie of north-central Kansas (similar grasses and small mammals) indicate that deer mice are abundant and western harvest mice and prairie voles are uncommon in moderately to heavily grazed sites that have not been burned for more than 20 years (G. A. Kaufman and D. W. Kaufman unpublished). The proportional abundance of these species presumably would not change much if these moderately to heavily grazed sites were burned.

CONCLUSIONS

Fires in ungrazed grasslands have negative impacts on small mammal species that are folivorous (microtine rodents and cotton rats), frequently or usually use surface nests of plant debris (microtine rodents, harvest mice, and woodrats), and forage in the litter layer for invertebrates (short-tailed shrews). Such fires have positive impacts on small species that forage for seeds and/or insects in habitats with little litter cover (heteromyid rodents, peromyscine rodents, grasshopper mice, ground squirrels, and zapodid rodents). These responses are apparently related to changes in the litter and standing dead vegetation layers that occur with fire.

Fire could potentially cause the death of small mammals, especially species that nest aboveground; however, most of the decreases in numbers of individuals of fire-negative species after a fire are undoubtedly due to the emigration of individuals shortly after fire as a result of the loss of litter and live and dead vegetation. The initial increase in numbers of individuals of fire-positive species is also due to movements of individuals, but in this case the burned area offers more suitable habitat conditions than nearby unburned sites.

Immediate changes following a fire and the subsequent recovery by deer mice, western harvest mice, and Elliot's short-tailed shrews, with differing kinds of habitat requirements, suggest that recovery or return to "unburned" densities would occur by the end of the second or third year after fire for most, if not all, species in burned, ungrazed grassland. As a result, recurring fires with frequencies of two or more years should create cycles in population density of both fire-negative and fire-positive species; however, it is uncertain how much average density for different species will vary through time due to the frequency of recurring fire.

Other factors, such as intensity of fire, seasonality of fire, general climate, weather conditions, and topo-edaphic conditions, undoubtedly affect the impact of fire. However, so little work has been done on these issues that the general and specific effects are unknown or unconfirmed.

Finally, continued study of the effects of fire on small mammals requires long-term replicated studies to assess the temporal variation in response patterns as well as patterns of recovery and succession of the grassland in general and the small mammals in particular. Continued study of fire and small mammals will require the analysis of the interaction of fire and grazing, as grazing was a component of native grasslands. This does not diminish the work already done on fire and small mammals, but rather is meant to encourage work on a range of grazing intensities. Since patches of presettlement prairie undoubtedly remained ungrazed for periods of time, a better understanding of the role of small mammals in grasslands requires knowledge of how small mammals used and moved between the mosaics of habitat conditions created by grazers, weather patterns, and fire.

ACKNOWLEDGMENTS

We thank D. M. Kaufman for preparing the figures. Research on Konza Prairie was supported by NSF grants DEB-8012166, BSR-8307571, and

BSR-8514327. Data and supporting documentation are stored in the Konza Prairie Research Natural Area data bank (Data Set Codes = CSM01, CSM04). Konza Prairie Research Natural Area, a preserve of The Nature Conservancy, is operated by the Division of Biology, Kansas State University. This is contribution No. 89-75-B, Division of Biology, Kansas Agricultural Experiment Station, Kansas State University, Manhattan.

6
Effects of Fire on Community Structure in Tallgrass and Mixed-Grass Prairie

By Scott L. Collins
and David J. Gibson

Fire is a commonly recognized component of the disturbance regime in grassland ecosystems, but the importance and beneficial aspects of fire have only recently been acknowledged (Wright 1974). Weaver and Albertson (1936) and Hopkins et al. (1948), for example, commented on the destructive aspects of dormant season fires on grassland vegetation. These authors were also mainly concerned with effects of the great drought (Weaver and Albertson 1936, Tobey 1981), a period when burning may have had detrimental impacts on plant growth and soil erosion. With the realization that burning at certain times of the year tended to increase growth, nutrient content, and palatability of forage species (Aldous 1934), prescribed burning has now become a frequently used management tool for improving quality of rangelands (Wright 1974, Wright and Bailey 1980) and prairie restoration (Cottam and Wilson 1966, R. C. Anderson 1972a). Because of the predominant range management perspective (McMurphy and Anderson 1965, K. L. Anderson et al. 1970), much modern fire research in grasslands has focused on the mechanisms associated with nutrient cycling (Risser and Parton 1982; chapter 8), as well as increased productivity of individual species (Knapp 1985; chapter 3) or whole communities (Hulbert 1988).

General reviews of fire effects in grasslands have been provided by Daubenmire (1968), Vogl (1974), Kucera (1981), and Wright and Bailey (1982). Other than Vogl (1974), these reviews focus primarily on changes in community productivity following burning. Increasing evidence suggests, however, that fire also has dramatic short- and long-term effects on plant community structure in grasslands (Abrams and Hulbert 1987,

Collins 1987, Gibson and Hulbert 1987, Gibson 1988, Collins and Glenn 1988). In particular, fire may alter species richness, diversity, competitive interactions, micro-succession, and patch structure. Because productivity effects have often been described (see chapters 3 and 7), the purpose of this chapter is to review and discuss fire effects on plant community structure in tallgrass and mixed-grass prairie vegetation. Specifically, we will discuss fire effects on species *richness* (the number of species per unit area), *evenness* (the distribution of dominance among species), *diversity* (the relationship between richness and evenness), and *patch structure* (the association of species at various spatial scales). In addition, we will discuss how the interaction of fire and other disturbances, such as grazing, alters community structure. Our data are derived from several studies in (1) mixed-grass prairie in the Wichita Mountains Wildlife Refuge, southwestern Oklahoma, (2) tallgrass prairie at the U.S. Department of Agriculture Forage and Livestock Research Station in central Oklahoma, and (3) tallgrass prairie at Konza Prairie Research Natural Area in northeastern Kansas.

DISTURBANCE REGIME IN GRASSLANDS

The composition, species richness, and diversity of grasslands are a function of edaphic conditions (Barnes et al. 1983, White and Glenn-Lewin 1984), climate (Borchert 1950, Sauer 1950), and a complex disturbance regime, which includes grazing, especially by large ungulates (Stebbins 1981, Archer and Tieszen 1986), and fire (R. C. Anderson 1982, Axelrod 1985). In general, climate, fire, and grazing affect grassland communities over large spatial scales (see chapter 9; Table 6.1). In the absence of dis-

TABLE 6.1   General characteristics of the disturbance regime in North American grasslands (modified from Collins and Barber 1985)

Disturbance Type	Scale	Intensity	Frequency
Drought	large	light-severe	periodic
Grazing	large	light-moderate	1–3 months
Fire	large	light-moderate	1–5 years
Soil disturbances			
Buffalo wallows	small	severe	1–3 months
Mound building/excavation	small	moderate-severe	continuous

Source: Collins and Barber 1985.

turbances such as fire, mesic grasslands may become dominated by woody vegetation (Bragg and Hulbert 1976, Collins and Adams 1983). It is interesting to note that Clements developed the rudiments of his theory that vegetation is controlled by climate (Clements 1936) while he was studying grasslands in Nebraska. Clements considered fire to be a rare and destructive element in grasslands. Many climate-based life zone diagrams (e.g., Holdridge 1967), however, do not predict the occurrence of mesic grasslands but instead predict dominance by woody species in regions now occupied by tallgrass prairie. Thus, the persistence of tallgrass and mixed-grass vegetation, in particular, is a function of the interaction of several large-scale disturbances. Superimposed on these factors are numerous small-scale soil disturbances created by a diverse native fauna which was at one time very abundant across North America (England and DeVos 1969). Together the biotic and abiotic disturbances interact to form a complex disturbance regime, which helps to maintain grassland ecosystems (Towne and Owensby 1984, Axelrod 1985, Collins and Barber 1985, Collins and Glenn 1988).

At a small scale, grassland vegetation is dominated by a few common matrix-forming species (Fig. 6.1), such as big bluestem (*Andropogon gerardii*), Indian grass (*Sorghastrum nutans*), prairie dropseed (*Sporobolus asper*), little bluestem (*A. scoparius*), goldenrod (*Solidago* spp.), and ironweed (*Vernonia baldwinii*). These species occupy the majority of space in the community (see Weaver and Fitzpatrick 1934, Mentzer 1951). Numerous interstitial species (e.g., *Ambrosia psilostachya*, *Oxalis stricta*, *Conyza canadensis*, *Senecio plattensis*, *Artemisia ludoviciana*) occur in the spaces between the larger dominants. Different disturbances have a differential effect on the matrix species, which in turn affects richness of interstitial species. For example, native ungulates like bison (*Bison bison*) generally graze graminoids in preference to forbs (Krueger 1986). Grazing will reduce the dominance of matrix species, thereby increasing space available for interstitial species (Fig. 6.1,A). This generally enhances diversity (Peet et al. 1983, Looman 1983, Collins 1987). Fire, on the other hand, may increase the dominance and competitive ability of some matrix species and kill many nonmatrix species (Abrams and Hulbert 1987), which in turn reduces richness and diversity (Fig. 6.1,B). Small-scale animal disturbances, such as gopher mounds or buffalo wallows, may destroy matrix species and expose soil which is then colonized by ruderals (Fig. 6.1,C). Thus, grassland vegetation may be differentially affected by fire and grazing, and these large-scale disturbances interact with numerous soil disturbances to enhance patch structure and community diversity.

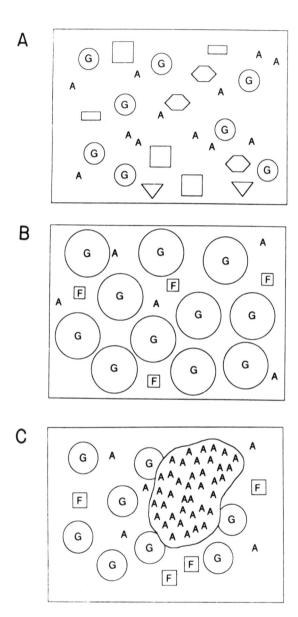

FIG. 6.1 A schematic diagram showing the matrix structure of grasslands and the impact of (A) grazing, (B) fire, and (C) small-scale soil disturbance on community structure. G = matrix grass, F = forb, A = annual. Different-shaped symbols in A indicate different species of forbs. Grazing reduces cover of matrix species, whereas fire increases matrix cover. Soil disturbances may kill matrix species and expose a site for colonization by annual forbs.

FIRE EFFECTS ON SPECIES RICHNESS

In Oklahoma, the number of species in 0.5 ha plots of mixed-grass prairie subject to different disturbances ranged from 33 to 64 (Collins and Barber 1985). However, the average number of species per 0.5 m^2 quadrat (alpha-diversity of Whittaker [1977]) in these areas ranges from only 6.7 on a prairie dog town to 12.6 in an area that was burned and grazed, and contained buffalo wallows. Using larger quadrats, Peet et al. (1983) reported an average of 18 species per m^2 in mesic grassland. In contrast, frequently burned pine-wiregrass communities in North Carolina (Walker and Peet 1983) average about 40 species per m^2. So point diversity in grasslands is relatively low. However, a larger area contains many species because of numerous disturbances in various stages of micro-succession which increase community heterogeneity and promote high species richness (gamma-diversity of Whittaker [1977]).

Fire has a strong effect on species richness. At Konza Prairie, a series of different watersheds has been burned at intervals of 1, 2, 4, 10, and 20 years beginning in 1972 (Hulbert 1985). Vegetation on these watersheds has been sampled since 1981 three times each growing season in 20 permanent quadrats of 10 m^2 per watershed, using a modified Daubenmire (1959) scale (see Abrams and Hulbert 1987). Species richness on these watersheds fluctuates between years in response to climatic variation, and the year-to-year variation in richness on unburned and annually burned watersheds is highly correlated (Fig. 6.2,A). Annually burned grasslands have fewer species than unburned grasslands. The decrease in richness on annually burned watersheds results from a diminished soil seed pool (Abrams 1988). Many annual species which initiate growth early in the growing season or late in the preceding season are killed by fire and are therefore unable to set seed and complete their life cycle (Gibson 1988).

In more northern regions, H. G. Anderson and Bailey (1980) found that species richness increased with annual spring burning in the aspen parkland region of Alberta. These grasslands are primarily dominated by cool season C$_3$ grasses which are often damaged by spring fire. In addition, fire removed the litter layer, providing a favorable seed bed for forb species (H. G. Anderson and Bailey 1980). The dominance of C$_3$ and C$_4$ species may also be correlated with available soil moisture. Steuter (1987) reported that burning in spring, mid-summer, and fall increased C$_3$ production on a xeric northern mixed prairie. On a nearby mesic site, production of C$_4$ species was enhanced by spring burning.

A more interesting pattern is apparent in the plots of richness on the two-year and four-year burn cycles (Fig. 6.2,B,C). In all cases, species richness increased the year following a fire. This does not reflect a correla-

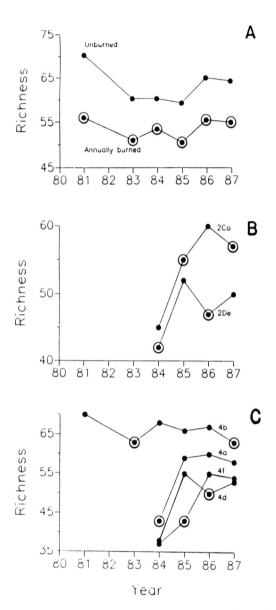

FIG. 6.2 Species richness on several different watersheds subjected to different fire frequencies at Konza Prairie Research Natural Area, Kansas. Circles surrounding a dot indicate a year during which a watershed was burned. Fires occur in early–mid-April. A, annually burned (average of 2 watersheds) and unburned (average of 3 watersheds); B, 2-year burns; C, 4-year burns.

tion between richness and precipitation because in watersheds 2De and 4A (Fig. 6.2,B,C) species richness increased following a fire in years when richness decreased on the annually burned and unburned watersheds. Although Daubenmire (1968) noted that fire may enhance richness, he provided no supporting evidence. Relative to other aspects of grassland ecology, there are few studies reporting fire effects on species richness in grasslands. There appears to be no clear relationship between fire and species richness during the year in which the fire occurred. For example, Dix (1960) showed that richness increased on one grassland and decreased on two others following burning in northern mixed-grass prairie. Adams et al. (1982) found that richness decreased immediately after fire in tallgrass prairie in southern Oklahoma. G. R. Hill and Platt (1975) and Abrams and Hulbert (1987) found no difference in richness between burned and unburned tallgrass prairies. In contrast Collins (1987), Humphrey (1984), Curtis and Partch (1948). Netherland (1979), H. G. Anderson and Bailey (1980), and Blankespoor (1987) all reported an increase in species richness following burning. The disparity between studies is a function of many factors, including season during which burning occurred, time since the previous burn, grazing history, precipitation, and fire temperature. Results from Konza Prairie are preliminary but represent the best long-term experimental design to address community response to different fire frequencies. Nevertheless, no one study has attempted to address the causal mechanisms associated with increased or decreased richness in response to fire.

In mesic grasslands, differences in richness are often a function of changes in the number of forb rather than grass species (e.g., Blankespoor 1987). This pattern may be reversed in arid areas. In Arizona, for example, Bock et al. (1976) reported that the number of forbs increased but grasses actually decreased following burning in February or April. Many common grassland forbs require only a moist cold treatment to germinate (Sorensen and Holden 1974). It is also conceivable that fire or leachate from ash after a fire may stimulate seed germination of some grassland species, as has been found in the chaparral (Keeley 1987). Glenn-Lewin et al. (see chapter 4) report that the effects of fire on seed germination may extend into the second growing season. Although fire may affect seed set in grassland species (Hulbert and Wilson 1980, Knapp 1984a, Knapp and Hulbert 1986, Davis et al. 1987), we could find no studies determining whether or not fire actually stimulates seed germination of prairie plants. Circumstantial evidence exists, however. Martin and Cushwa (1966) and Martin et al. (1975) reported that moist heat, such as would affect seeds in the soil during a fire, increased germination of some legume species.

Heitlinger (1975) suggested that the heat of a prairie fire may break down the hard outer shell of *Melilotus alba*, a nonnative species, thus promoting germination after spring or summer burning. In contrast, R. C. Anderson and van Valkenberg (1977) observed a decrease in abundance of several legume species after fire in Illinois.

Grasslands may burn at almost any time (Bragg 1982), and the season during which burning occurs may have a dramatic effect on composition and structure of grasslands. Towne and Owensby (1984) reported that annual winter burning decreased productivity. In contrast, Penfound and Kelting (1950), Kelting (1957), and James (1985) recorded increased productivity following infrequent winter burns. In general, fires that occur when most species are dormant have little effect on richness, although some winter annuals may be eliminated. These species are usually uncommon in grasslands (Collins and Uno 1983). Burning in the spring after many cool season species initiate growth may decrease evenness because cover of C_3 species is often reduced and dominance by C_4 grasses enhanced by fires.

Studies reporting effects of fires during different seasons have been conducted in grasslands from Oklahoma to Alberta. However, results from several studies in mesic tallgrass prairie in Oklahoma, Kansas, and Iowa show no clear patterns. If moisture levels are at or above normal, both productivity and richness may increase after burning. Following April fires, Collins (1987) Netherland (1979), and H. G. Anderson and Bailey (1980) reported increased richness in Oklahoma and Alberta grasslands, respectively. Abrams and Hulbert (1987) and G. R. Hill and Platt (1975) reported no change in richness in Kansas and Iowa. Burning earlier or later in the growing season generally decreased richness (Dix 1960, Adams et al. 1982, Antos et al. 1983) in the same year as the fire. Perhaps the timing of fire has less to do with the system response than do the ratio of cool season to warm season species, fire frequency and intensity, and climatic conditions following fire (Engle and Bultsma 1984). Ewing and Engle (1988) conducted a detailed study of production and microclimate changes following September fires. With high fuel loads, intense fires reduced production by bunchgrass species the year after the burn.

Fire effects on species diversity are somewhat less variable than the effects on species richness. Although Adams et al. (1982) and Humphrey (1984) noted that burning increased diversity, most studies report that species diversity decreased after fire (Netherland 1979, Collins and Barber 1985, Collins 1987, Gibson and Hulbert 1987). The decrease in diversity is attributed to the increased cover of matrix species, which results from enhanced productivity. This increase in productivity of a few species de-

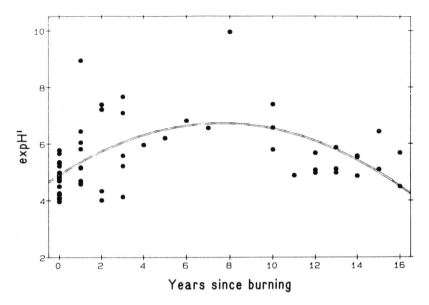

FIG. 6.3   Changes in species diversity (expH') during postfire succession at Konza Prairie Research Natural Area, Kansas (modified from Gibson and Hulbert 1987). $r^2 = 0.26$, $P = 0.001$.

creases species evenness, which in turn decreases community diversity (Collins 1987).

Within a watershed, species diversity (based on the Shannon-Weiner index) increased for six to seven years following burning, at which point diversity declined (Gibson and Hulbert 1987; see Fig. 6.3). Humphrey (1984) found that diversity decreased within only two to three years after a fire in sagebrush grassland. The decline in diversity in tallgrass prairie is attributed to the development of a thick layer of litter and standing dead material, which may inhibit germination and growth of many species (Knapp and Seastedt 1986). Maximum species richness and diversity in grasslands, therefore, will occur in areas with periodic but not annual burning (Kucera and Koelling 1964, Gibson 1988). For example, T. F. H. Allen and Wyleto (1983) found that richness on the Curtis Prairie in Wisconsin was positively correlated with the number of fires (up to three) that occurred over a five-year period.

The number of forb, grass, annual, and woody species increases during postfire succession in grasslands (Gibson and Hulbert 1987). The number of C_4 species peaks a few years after burning and then declines. Cover of grasses peaks the year of the burn and then decreases for a number of years before reaching equilibrium. Cover of annuals also decreases with time since burning, even though their richness is increasing during post-fire succession. However, cover of forbs and woody vegetation increases over time. Bragg and Hulbert (1976) reported a 40 percent increase in woody plant cover over a 30-year period on unburned prairie in Kansas. Within only 15 years without fire, woody species dominated mesic grassland vegetation on coarse textured soils in Oklahoma (Collins and Adams 1983). Thus, in the absence of fire, species interactions and the accumulation of litter lead to a rapid replacement of grasses by shrubs. Once established, these shrubs may facilitate the establishment of tree seedlings (Petranka and McPherson 1979) and further enhance the rate of succession.

At larger spatial scales, burning may alter patch structure within and between communities (see chapter 9). To determine the effect of fire on within-community heterogeneity, we established transects in annually burned and adjacent long-term unburned watersheds at Konza Prairie. Each transect consisted of 50 contiguous 0.5×0.5 m^2 quadrats. Cover values were estimated for each species occurring in each quadrat. The transects were sampled in May, July, and September 1987. Community pattern was analyzed using the methods described in Gibson and Greig-Smith (1986). For each sample period, quadrat data were first analyzed with detrended correspondence analysis (DCA; M. O. Hill and Gauch 1980). Ordination scores for quadrats along the first DCA axis were then subjected to two-term local variance analysis (M. O. Hill 1973), which produces a trace that reflects changes in community heterogeneity at different spatial scales.

On both burned and unburned areas in May and July, heterogeneity increased as the area sampled increased (Fig. 6.4,A,B), which indicates a patch structure greater than or equal to 12 m. At scales above 10 m in May and 5 m in July, the trace of community heterogeneity was lower on the annually burned versus the unburned grasslands (Fig. 6.4,A,B). This implies that at any spatial scale community composition is less variable on annually burned grasslands during the growing season. In other words, fire *decreases* community heterogeneity. This occurs because frequent burning reduces cover or eliminates many interstitial species and increases cover of matrix species. Differences in community pattern are evident during September when productivity is declining (Fig. 6.4,C). At this time, patchiness occurs at a greater spatial scale on the burned grassland, whereas patch size on the unburned watershed peaks at about 5 m. Here we see a more heterogeneous decay of patch structure in the unburned area, leading to a peak at a smaller spatial scale than that which occurs within the more homogeneous burned area.

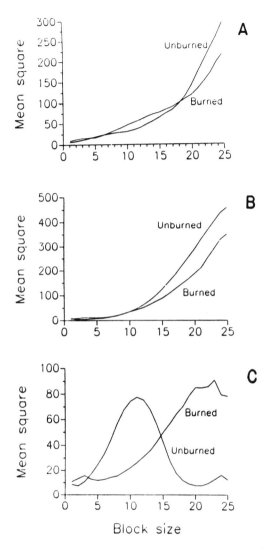

FIG. 6.4 The effects of fire on patch size on burned and unburned watersheds in
May, July, and September 1987, at Konza Prairie Research Natural Area, Kansas.
During May and July, mean square values are lowest on the burned grassland,
indicating that fire reduces community heterogeneity. In September, heterogeneity is much higher on the unburned grassland until block size 10 (5 m), where
patches in the unburned grassland begin to fuse and decrease heterogeneity.

INTERACTION OF FIRE WITH GRAZING

Most of the studies described thus far have not explicitly considered the effects of fire in the context of other disturbances. The need for such studies has been noted by R. C. Anderson (1982), Looman (1983) and Loucks et al. (1985). Grazing, in particular, is a natural disturbance in grasslands, which also alters diversity and community heterogeneity at different spatial scales (Senft et al. 1987). Ungulates are attracted to recently burned areas and preferentially graze them. Indeed, indigenous Indian tribes used fires to increase palatability of grasses to attract animals for hunting purposes (Pyne 1986). Thus, it is not unexpected that fire and grazing will interact to affect community structure (Looman 1983).

The design and execution of complex field experiments to study the individual and interactive effects of disturbances are often prohibitive. Such studies require large areas, which can only be weakly considered as replicates. As a result, only a limited number of studies have attempted to address the interaction of disturbances, such as fire and grazing, in tallgrass prairie communities. In the Wichita Mountains Wildlife Refuge, Collins and Uno (1983) found that fire had an effect on species assemblages within buffalo wallows, small hard-panned bottom soil depressions created by the wallowing activity of bison. The primary vegetation gradient in this study represented compositional differences from outside to inside the wallows (Fig. 6.5). However, the vegetation inside burned wallows was distinct from that of unburned wallows. In addition, the zonation from edge to interior of wallows was more distinct on the burned grassland. This may be caused by increased grazing and wallowing activity by ungulates on the burned grassland. Thus, burning increased beta-diversity (sensu Whittaker 1977) within wallows and altered species composition compared to unburned wallows.

In a second study in the same refuge, vegetation was sampled on grasslands subjected to different combinations of natural disturbances (Collins and Barber 1985). Two groups of sites were examined. The first group contained sites that were (i) undisturbed, (ii) grazed only, and (iii) grazed areas with buffalo wallows. The second group contained grasslands that were (i) burned, (ii) burned and grazed, and (iii) burned, grazed, and wallowed. Richness was lowest on the burned grassland (Table 6.2). For each group of sites, grazing increased species richness. The addition of wallows further increased richness and diversity. From these empirical results it was concluded that natural disturbances increase heterogeneity (beta-diversity) in grasslands and that a combination of disturbances will interact to further increase diversity.

This hypothesis was tested with a complete block design field experi-

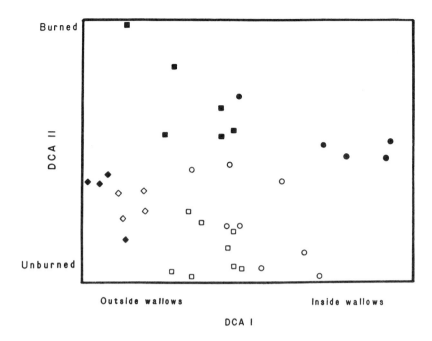

FIG. 6.5   Detrended correspondence analysis (DCA) of vegetation samples from exterior (diamonds), edge (squares), and interior (circles) portions of buffalo wallows on burned (filled symbols) and unburned (open symbols) grasslands in the Wichita Mountains Wildlife Refuge, Oklahoma (from Collins and Uno 1983). The primary gradient (DCA I) separates samples from outside to inside the wallows. This gradient is more distinct for the burned wallows. DCA II separates samples from burned and unburned areas.

TABLE 6.2   Average values (N = 3) of diversity (expH′), evenness, and richness for plant species in 4 disturbance treatments in tallgrass prairie in central Oklahoma (+G = grazed, −G = ungrazed, +B = burned, −B = unburned)

		Treatment			
Variable	Year	−G, −B	+G, −B	−G, +B	+G, +B
Diversity	1985	7.7	8.6	4.7	9.1
	1986	8.3	8.3	5.1	9.0
Evenness	1985	0.57	0.56	0.43	0.44
	1986	0.61	0.61	0.46	0.51
Richness	1985	26.7	30.7	31.1	32.7
	1986	24.3	24.7	27.7	29.0

Source: Collins 1987.

ment with replicated sample areas of (i) unburned, ungrazed; (ii) unburned, grazed; (iii) burned, ungrazed; and (iv) burned, grazed treatments. The treatments and vegetation sampling were conducted in 1985
and repeated in 1986. Species richness increased along the disturbance
gradient from undisturbed to burned, grazed treatments (Table 6.2). Species diversity was lowest on the burned, ungrazed treatment and highest
on the burned, grazed treatment. Two-way analysis of variance indicated
that fire and grazing significantly enhanced species richness in this tallgrass prairie. Thus, this study provided experimental evidence that disturbances like fire and grazing do interact to affect community structure.

INTERACTION OF FIRE WITH SMALL-SCALE DISTURBANCES

Although the interaction of fire with grazing may seem intuitive, fire
effects on small-scale patch dynamics are poorly understood. In many systems, small-scale patch dynamics provide the heterogeneity necessary to
maintain high species diversity within a community (Sousa 1984, Pickett
and White 1985). In tallgrass prairie, K. L. Anderson (1965) maintained
that competition from perennial grasses limited the distribution of annuals to disturbed habitats, such as trails, eroded banks, rodent diggings,
and other disturbances. Small-scale patch disturbances are created by the
burrowing activity of ants and numerous small mammals, such as prairie
dogs (*Cynomys ludovicianus*), badgers (*Taxidea taxus*), and gophers (Geo-
myidae). These disturbances are qualitatively and quantitatively different
from buffalo wallows (Collins and Glenn 1988) because soil disturbances
are formed by piling excavated soil on top of existing vegetation. The potential impacts of this may or may not include mortality of preexisting individuals. Also, the exposed soil may provide suitable germination sites
for seeds in the seed bank as well as those dispersed onto the disturbed
area (Platt 1975, Rabinowitz and Rapp 1985, Belsky 1986).

To determine the effects of fire on small-scale patch dynamics, we established two field experiments in which we created artificial soil disturbances in ungrazed tallgrass prairie in Oklahoma and Kansas. In each experiment, we created replicated soil disturbances on plots of about 0.10 to
0.25 m^2. In Oklahoma, 50 disturbances were created in the fall of 1985, 25
of which were on a grassland that was burned in April 1986, the other
25 on unburned grassland (see Collins 1989). In spring of 1987, both
grasslands were burned. At Konza Prairie, 20 disturbances were created
on an unburned watershed and 20 on an annually burned watershed in
April 1987, immediately after prescribed burning. At both sites, the disturbances were created by clipping aboveground vegetation, removing
roots and crowns, and fluffing the soil by hand. Cover of all species was

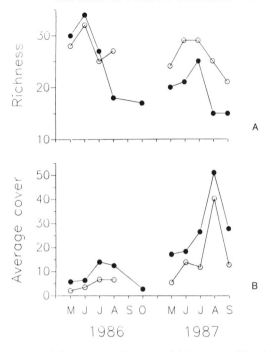

FIG. 6.6   Changes in (A) species richness and (B) cover of big bluestem (*An-dropogon gerardii*) over two growing seasons (May [M] to October [O] 1986 and May [M] to September [S] 1987) on artificial soil disturbances in tallgrass prairie burned annually (filled circles) and one time (open circles, spring 1987) at El Reno, Oklahoma. Fire may increase the rate of succession by increasing the spread of big bluestem onto disturbances.

sampled on disturbed treatments and adjacent control areas four or five times during the growing season.

In Oklahoma, the total number of species was slightly higher on the annually burned compared to the unburned disturbances during the first three sample periods (Fig. 6.6,A). From August 1986 until September 1987, richness was higher on the grassland that was burned only one time. In most cases, however, the differences were rather small; thus, it does not appear that burning has a significant impact on the number of species that occur on soil disturbances.

One measure of succession is the rate at which plant cover accumulates over time (Tilman 1985). Big bluestem is the most common matrix species on this site (Collins 1987). The rate of increase by big bluestem is there-fore an indication of the rate of micro-succession, that is, the rate at which space is occupied by a superior competitor. It appears that fire may increase the rate of succession on these disturbances (Fig. 6.6,B). In 1986, cover of big bluestem increased at a greater rate on the burned versus the unburned plots. In 1987, after both grassland areas had been burned, cover of big bluestem increased dramatically on the disturbances. By the end of the second year, big bluestem cover on the annually burned grassland was still much greater than on the grassland burned only one time. Because burning has been shown to increase the tillering rate of big bluestem (Hulbert 1969, Peet et al. 1975), fire may actually increase the rate of succession by enhancing the ability of big bluestem to invade and dominate areas of exposed soil (Collins 1989).

As on the Oklahoma plots, there were few differences in species richness between burned and unburned soil disturbances at Konza Prairie (Fig. 6.7,A). The only difference between the two plots was in October, when a flush of germination by winter annual species increased richness on the unburned soil disturbances. In addition, fire affected the number of seedlings that colonized these areas. Although the number of seedlings

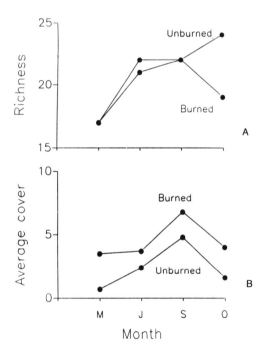

FIG. 6.7 Changes in (A) species richness and (B) cover of big bluestem (*Andropogon gerardii*) on annually burned and unburned tallgrass prairie at Konza Prairie Research Natural Area, Kansas. As in Oklahoma, cover of big bluestem was greater on the burned vs. the unburned disturbances.

TABLE 6.3 Total number of all seedlings and grass seedlings found throughout the growing season on control plots and artificial soil disturbances in annually burned and unburned grasslands at Konza Prairie, in northeastern Kansas (B = annually burned, U = unburned).

Seedlings	Control		Soil disturbance	
	B	U	B	U
Grass	0	45	23	90
Total	3	57	45	175

Source: Collins and Gibson, unpublished.

occupying disturbances was greater than on control plots, the total number of seedlings and the number of grass seedlings was dramatically lower on the annually burned versus unburned treatments (Table 6.3). Again, this may reflect the smaller seed pool that Abrams (1988) reported for annually burned versus unburned grasslands at Konza. In addition, the number of propagules from local seed sources may be lower on burned watersheds. In annually burned grasslands at Konza, fewer annuals colonized soil around badger dens than similar areas in unburned grasslands (Gibson 1989). Cover of big bluestem was again greater on the burned versus the unburned soil disturbances throughout the growing season (Fig. 6.7,B), lending further support to the notion that burning may increase the rate of succession on small patches in grasslands.

SUMMARY

Grasslands provide an excellent vegetation type for the analysis of community theory both because they can be experimentally manipulated and because, unlike forest systems, the response time in grasslands is relatively short. It is clear from this review that experimental studies leading to generalities concerning fire effects on grassland community structure are frustratingly few. To some extent, this reflects a previous research focus on grassland productivity rather than community structure per se. Additional problems occur due to variation in conditions before and after burning, and differences among methods. Nevertheless, changes in the productivity of matrix-forming species following fire are clearly reflected by changes in community structure. In mesic grasslands, spring fires usually enhance production by C_4 grasses, which increases dominance and reduces diversity. This may occur despite an increase in species richness following burning. Fire also tends to reduce community heterogeneity.

However, burning increases the palatability of grasses, which may ultimately lead to increased heterogeneity imposed by large grazers. There is a clear interaction between fire and other components of the disturbance regime in grasslands. This occurs because most other disturbances reduce cover of matrix species. Furthermore, fire appears to enhance the rate of micro-succession on small-scale soil disturbances.

ACKNOWLEDGMENTS

Financial support to DJG was provided by NSF grant BSR-8514327 for Long-Term Ecological Research to Kansas State University. Support for SLC was provided by two Junior Faculty Summer Research Fellowships through the Graduate College (1985) and College of Arts and Sciences (1987), University of Oklahoma. Susan Glenn provided many helpful comments on the manuscript.

7

The Influence of Fire on Belowground Processes of Tallgrass Prairie

By T. R. Seastedt
and R. A. Ramundo

Fire occurred frequently in pristine tallgrass prairie (Pyne 1982, 1986), and it was used as a management tool by European settlers during the 1800s (Weaver and Fitzpatrick 1934). Nonetheless, early investigators of the tallgrass prairie held a poor opinion of burning. "Fire was damaging and destructive" was Weaver's (1954, p. 271) terse summary of fire effects. Weaver, perhaps influenced by Aldous (1934), reported that "*despite* annual burning in spring, the large well managed ranges (in the Flint Hills of Kansas) . . . are still in good to excellent condition" (Weaver 1954, p. 213, emphasis added). With the exception of Aldous's (1934) efforts, fire was simply not studied as an ecological factor until the construction of the Curtis Prairie in Wisconsin (see R. C. Anderson 1972a). The combination of heavy grazing by cattle and the drought of the 1930s apparently directed investigators towards other areas of research. Moreover, much of the tallgrass prairie had already disappeared under the plow. The remaining tracts on the western fringes were more sensitive to water limitations and, historically at least, were much farther from seed sources for woody plant species than the eastern portions. Accordingly, fire would be much less important as a management tool than in the more easterly areas.

Even before Weaver's curt dismissal of fire, burning of the tallgrass prairie was recognized as a necessary management practice for maintaining the dominant grass species and stimulating plant production (Curtis and Partch 1950). By the 1960s, the beneficial aspects of fire were reported by both basic and applied ecologists (Kucera and Ehrenreich 1962, Kucera et al. 1967, Kucera 1981, Owensby and Anderson 1967, Owensby et al. 1970, Daubenmire 1968, Hulbert 1969, 1973, Old 1969; Fig. 7.1).

FIG. 7.1   Konza Prairie (left side of highway) in April 1974, before the purchase of the land to the left of the fencerow on upper left. Note the difference in the grazed (left) and ungrazed (right) prairie. Burned watersheds visible in this photo include 2 annually burned and 1 4-year burned plot.

This reversal in opinion about fire effects resulted in part from efforts to save and rebuild prairies in agricultural or forested areas east of the Missouri River as well as to protect western remnants from woody species invasion (Bragg and Hulbert 1976; Fig. 7.2). At the same time, Owensby and his colleagues were demonstrating the value of fire as a means of maximizing the productivity of warm season (C_4) grasses (Owensby and Anderson 1967, Owensby et al. 1970, Smith and Owensby 1972). Until the early 1980s, however, knowledge of the mechanisms for the responses of prairie to fire remained speculative. While Weaver and his students pioneered root studies of the prairie, their disinterest in fire as an ecological factor delayed the accumulation of information on the responses of plant roots and other soil biota to fire.

Studies of belowground processes in grasslands remain few. The problems of dealing with the soil medium have discouraged many investigators. However, work by Hadley and Kieckhefer (1963) and Old (1969) in Illinois; efforts by Kucera and his students in Missouri (e.g., Dahlman and Kucera 1965); a combination of modeling and empirical studies in

FIG. 7.2 Grazed prairie with and without fire treatments. Area on left was frequently burned, while right side has not been burned for many years. (Photo by Tom Bragg, reproduced with permission from Bragg and Hulbert 1976.)

Kansas by Schimel, Parton, and Ojima (e.g. Ojima 1987, Ojima et al. 1988, Parton et al. 1987); and our work as part of the Konza Prairie Long-Term Ecological Research (LTER) program allow us to make statements that, we hope, will remain valid longer than Weaver's 1954 summary.

AN OVERVIEW OF THE BELOWGROUND PRAIRIE SYSTEM

We have used nutrient cycling models to conceptualize important components and processes in the tallgrass prairie (Fig. 7.3). The example shown here lacks representations of gaseous fluxes, such as nitrogen (N) fixation, denitrification, etc., but does emphasize the importance of the belowground system in nutrient cycling processes. The belowground system contains primary producers (roots and rhizomes), herbivores (many arthropods and nematodes), detritivores (earthworms, many arthropods, nematodes, and microfauna) and decomposers (bacteria, fungi). The belowground system controls nutrient inputs aboveground, while the canopy controls the amount of fixed energy inputs belowground (Seastedt et al. 1988b). We see no benefit in separating aboveground from belowground

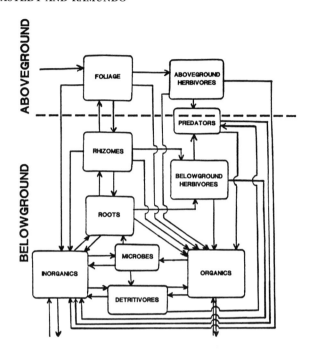

FIG. 7.3 Conceptual model of the tallgrass prairie, emphasizing the biotic components (rhizomes, roots, herbivores, detritivores, predators, and microbes) and the abiotic components (organic and inorganic storage reservoirs). Fire seldom directly affects the belowground system, but it has a profound effect on energy, water, and nutrient inputs to the soil.

components, except to point out the futility of trying to understand the prairie by concentrating one's efforts in either medium. Here, we treat canopy phenomena as factors influencing the inputs of energy, nutrients, and water to the soil system.

The belowground system is both larger (in terms of biomass or densities) and more active (in terms of respiration or nutrient cycling indices) than are the portions of producers, consumers, and decomposers found aboveground. Nutrient budgets constructed for the tallgrass prairie (Sheedy et al. 1973, Risser et al. 1981, Risser and Parton 1982, Callahan and Kucera 1981, Ojima 1987, Ojima et al. 1988, Seastedt 1988; chapter 8) emphasize the importance of the nutrient reservoir contained in the soil organic matter component. Roots, microbes, and invertebrates are tiny fractions of the total nutrient pool, but their sensitivity to fire produces the immediate changes that are both causes and results of the visible, aboveground responses to fire.

FIRE EFFECTS ON ENERGY, NUTRIENT,
AND WATER INPUTS TO SOIL

Our research on Konza Prairie Research Natural Area, a site owned by
The Nature Conservancy in the Flint Hills of Kansas, has focused on how
standing dead and litter function as an energy, nutrient, and water filter
(Knapp and Seastedt 1986). Knapp (1984b, 1985) summarized changes in
the surface energy budget with respect to the emerging vegetation. A reduction in the input of solar energy to the soil surface translates to relatively cooler soils in unburned areas, particularly during the first few
weeks after the fire (Ehrenreich 1959, Hulbert 1969, Old 1969). The ash-
covered soil surface of burned prairie absorbs most of the solar input instead of having this energy reflected or absorbed above the soil surface by
the standing dead and litter in the canopy of unburned watersheds (see
Fig. 7.1). The soil, and especially the moisture in the soil, acts as a ther-
mal sink and an overall warming trend continues until the regrowth of the
canopy shades the soil, much like the standing dead of the unburned
sites. Research being conducted as part of the NASA-supported study of
surface climatology currently under way at Konza Prairie will undoubtedly
produce an extensive data set that precisely quantifies these differences.

Fires in the tallgrass prairie are possible at any time of the year (Bragg
1982). Fire in different seasons produces many different effects on the energy, nutrient, and water inputs to the soil. Hence, the time of year at
which a fire occurs is critical in determining the type and magnitude
of the vegetation response (e.g., K. L. Anderson 1965, McMurphy and
Anderson 1965, Owensby and Anderson 1967, Towne and Owensby 1984,
James 1985). The time of year of a fire determines whether or not the
vegetation is active, vulnerable, and/or capable of reacting to energy
changes. A very different vegetation response is observed if fire occurs in
autumn or winter, when the plants are dormant, or in mid-summer when
the dominant C_4 plants are vulnerable. Indeed, a visit to a prairie following a summer fire immediately allows one to concur with Weaver (1954):
such fires are extremely "damaging and destructive." In the remainder of
this chapter we restrict ourselves to discussing the effects of late spring
(specifically, late April) burns. Fire at this time of year produces the maximum growth response in the dominant C_4 grasses, while reducing the
abundance of C_3 grasses and forbs (Owensby and Anderson 1967, Hulbert
1988). Burning the prairie at this time is the common management proce-
dure used in the Flint Hills, the last large remnant of tallgrass prairie in
North America.

Increased temperatures on burned prairie were hypothesized to stimulate belowground nutrient cycling and to be a potential major factor in

enhancing plant productivity (Rice and Parenti 1978, Ojima 1987, Ojima et al. 1988). Plant roots and organisms exhibiting standard Q_{10} responses to temperature will substantially increase their respiration rates due to this warm-up. But increases in respiration by roots and microbes do not necessarily translate into increased cycling rates of elements other than carbon (C). Moreover, enhanced root respiration could potentially decrease overall net primary production (NPP). Studies that have measured soil microbial responses to fire have produced mixed results (e.g., compare Rice and Parenti 1978 with Lussenhop 1981). Mineralization studies by Ojima (1987) and data presented in this chapter document the effects of temperature on other ecosystem processes that interact to produce the observed production response.

Changes in the amounts and composition of nutrient inputs to the soil do occur because of fire. For some elements, burning may only affect the seasonality and form of the input. Phosphorus (P), for example, appears to be deposited in equal amounts on burned and unburned watersheds (Seastedt 1988), but burning converts the P to an inorganic form that is readily usable by plants (Eisele 1985, A. P. Schwab, personal communication). Other elements, such as N, are lost due to volatilization during the fire. The input of these elements is about equal to the amounts found in litterfall. Since litter tends to remain in the canopy of the prairie for an extended period, this deposition may be small in frequently burned areas. For example, we estimated an average of 1.9 g/m^2 of particulate N deposited on the soil surface in litter of unburned watersheds versus 0.5 g/m^2 on burned watersheds (Seastedt 1988). Ojima (1987) presents detailed information on N deposition in ash and losses due to volatilization.

Supplements of ash to unburned prairie have no stimulatory effect on plant productivity (Old 1969, Petersen 1983, Hulbert 1988). The input of ash therefore is not of concern in understanding the mechanisms responsible for the short-term growth differences observed on burned and unburned prairie. Since this ash is high in available inorganic P, the absence of a plant response to ash inputs demonstrates that burned prairie is not P-limited, a fact that has been substantiated with an LTER fertilization experiment. Over the long term, however, this input of inorganic P may stimulate N fixation, which does contribute to the sustained productivity of the system (Eisele 1985). Experiments conducted by Hulbert (1988) indicated that the heat of the fire does not induce tillering. Perhaps the last major unknown about the immediate effects of fire on the soil interface concerns the potential for rapid ammonia volatilization from the soil shortly after fire (Raison 1979, Woodmansee and Wallach 1981). This question awaits measurement with the new procedures capable of large scale, in situ methods, such as the Fourier-transform infrared radiometry (FTIR) technology (Gosz et al. 1988).

A particular focus of our research on Konza Prairie has been the effect of standing dead and litter on the amounts and composition of N in rainfall and throughfall (Seastedt 1985, Gilliam 1987). Nitrogen inputs exceed 1 g/m²/yr, and, given the sensitivity of the prairie to N availability (Old 1969, Owensby et al. 1970), this input is significant to the annual N budget of the tallgrass prairie. Competition between the autotrophs and heterotrophs for available N is a major factor influencing the pattern of N cycling on tallgrass prairie. Our measurements of throughfall have consistently shown that microbes on standing dead and litter intercept much of the inorganic N in rainfall and are a source of organic N in throughfall (Table 7.1). The accumulation of litter on and above the soil surface may reach amounts several times the mass represented by living foliage (Weaver and Rowland 1952). Prairie litter can act as a substantial N sink (Seastedt 1988). Thus, inputs of inorganic N are reduced on unburned prairie. This reduction may, however, be biologically insignificant, given the presence of microbes capable of immobilizing all of the inorganic N in rainfall and throughfall in the top few centimeters of the soil. Still, plant roots are abundant in this zone, and on unburned prairie these roots grow

TABLE 7.1   Nitrogen concentrations of bulk precipitation, soil water, and streams of annually burned and unburned tallgrass prairie[a]

| Source | Concentration (μg/l) | | | | | |
| | Ammonium-N | | Nitrate-N | | Organic-N | |
	Burned Sites	Un-burned Sites	Burned Sites	Un-burned Sites	Burned Sites	Un-burned Sites
Bulk precipitation	456	456	530	530	420	420
Throughfall	344	196	345	258	1,669	2,155
Soil Water						
20 cm deep	< 2	< 2	11	32	358	389
80 cm deep	< 2	< 2	13	12	213	182
Stream water	nd	nd	3	14	186	259

[a] Bulk precipitation and throughfall data from Seastedt (1985); soil water results from unpublished LTER data, and stream results from McArthur et al. (1985).

into the litter layer as well, suggesting considerable competition for nutrients in this zone.

The surface area and geometry of live foliage, standing dead, and litter have a large effect on the amount of rainwater reaching the soil surface (O. R. Clark 1940, Seastedt 1985, Gilliam et al. 1987). Virtually 100 percent of small (e.g., 5 mm or less) rainfall events can be intercepted and evaporated in the canopy. The decaying mulch on the soil surface intercepts another fraction of this input. The ability of flowering stems and tillers to funnel water to the roots of grasses (much like stemflow of forests) has not been measured and is probably significant (Seastedt 1985). The fraction of rainfall that is intercepted and the differences in inputs between burned and unburned sites are a function of the amount and duration of rainfall events as well as the amount of aboveground surface area. Water inputs to the soil of unburned prairie are, on average, about 10–15 percent less than inputs on burned prairie. However, litter can influence the outputs of water from the soil as well as the inputs. The reduction in inputs on unburned sites appears to be more than negated in some years by a concurrent reduction of evaporation at the soil surface (K. L. Anderson 1965). Increased rates of evaporative losses on burned areas explain why burning is detrimental in years of low late-spring and summer rainfall (Towne and Owensby 1984). Higher rates of plant productivity that occur in most years on burned sites also dictate more rapid drying of soils below the evaporative zone.

FIRE EFFECTS ON BELOWGROUND PRIMARY PRODUCTIVITY

Previous studies of fire effects on tallgrass prairie roots and rhizomes have consistent, albeit not always statistically significant, results regarding root response to burning (Table 7.2). Old's (1969) Illinois study compared the response to burning in the current year to plots burned three years earlier. No differences were observed. Hadley and Kieckhefer's (1963) study compared recently burned with long-term unburned plots and found about a 20 percent increase in biomass with burning. Kucera and Dahlman (1968) compared annually burned plots with plots not burned for five or six years and found a marked difference. Ojima (1987) reported the largest difference by comparing plots burned either 1 or 2 years in a row with plots not burned for about 10 years. Obviously, fire frequency, or time since the last fire, is important in determining the magnitude of the difference between treatments.

Interpretation of the differences in root and rhizome responses to fire is complicated by the fact that root biomass measurements are influenced both by root productivity and root senescence and decomposition rates.

TABLE 7.2   Comparison of root and rhizome mass of burned and unburned tall-grass prairie (average of all data reported)

Depth of Sample	Study Site	Burned Prairie (g/m²)	Unburned Prairie (g/m²)	Reference
35 cm	Illinois	1,064	839	Hadley and Kieckhefer 1963
5 cm	Missouri	956	669	Kucera and Dahlman 1968
100 cm	Illinois	2,107	1,908	Old 1969
30 cm	Kansas	1,002	790	Ojima 1987[a, b]
30 cm	Kansas	1,086	859	Seastedt (unpubl.)[b]

[a]Based on C data; mass assumed to be 2.5 times the amount of C.
[b]Rhizomes not included.

Fire can affect production of new roots as well as their rates of decay. If the cooler soils of unburned prairie slow the decay of roots, and if a portion of these roots appears in the biomass estimates, then differences in root production are underestimated.

In 1986 we measured root lengths from plots with and without litter, using root windows described by Hayes and Seastedt (1987). The average root length to a depth of 30 cm on plots containing litter was 70 percent of that on plots without litter—a ratio similar to biomass values observed by Kucera and Dahlman (1968) and Ojima (1987) (Fig. 7.4). Note that these results are based on lengths of roots calculated for a rectangle 1 m long by 30 cm deep. Disappearance estimates using the root window indicated no significant differences between treatments, and thus the difference in average lengths of roots was attributed to significantly greater production on burned areas. Thus, these results suggest that the higher amounts of root mass observed on burned sites are largely due to a production response. Biomass differences of roots and rhizomes are therefore not strongly influenced by differences in decomposition rates on burned versus unburned prairie.

Results from root windows suggest about a 400 percent turnover rate in root lengths per year—a value much higher than the 30–40 percent turnover rate estimated for biomass (Dahlman and Kucera 1965, Hayes and Seastedt 1987). A portion of the estimate of root length turnover is caused by methodological problems associated with repeated tracings. By tracing the same window on two consecutive days and assuming that all new roots

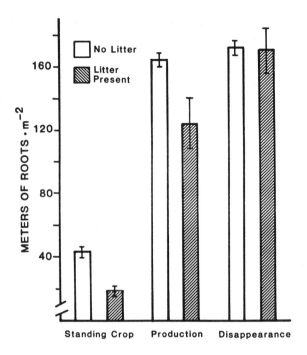

FIG. 7.4   Root lengths and estimates of production and disappearance of roots from root window tracings. Values are means and standard errors of 4 windows per treatment. Estimates are expressed as the length of roots found in a profile 1 m² long by 30 cm deep.

(production) or roots that had disappeared (decomposition) were the result of investigator error, we found that root window measurements will overestimate production and decay rates by 25–40 percent. Even with this bias, however, we believe that the results from root windows do correctly document the high rate of turnover by the smaller, lateral roots that branch from the longer-lived main roots.

An interesting and unresolved question regarding plant productivity and fire concerns the role of mycorrhizal fungi. Strong relationships between spore densities of vesicular-arbuscular mycorrhizae and fire frequency, or species composition and fire frequency, have not been observed at our site (Gibson and Hetrick, 1988). Elsewhere, Dhillion et al. (1988) have shown a negative relationship between fire and mycorrhizal colonization of little bluestem roots. However, fire clearly increases the positive energy balance of the dominant grasses, which, theoretically at least, should make them more nutrient-limited. Moreover, mycorrhizae may affect root-shoot ratios and assist in resistance to drought stress or grazing (Miller 1987, Wallace 1987, Wallace and Svejcar 1987). Thus, the benefits of mycorrhizal infection should be more substantial on burned prairie, and we would therefore predict either higher incidences of infections or simply higher mycorrhizae biomass and activity on recently burned areas.

BELOWGROUND HERBIVORE AND DETRITIVORE RESPONSES TO FIRE

Very few soil organisms appear to be directly harmed by prairie fires. Burning does not increase soil temperatures to lethal values, except at the soil surface (Wright and Bailey 1982). An inspection of the surface of burned prairie in late spring occasionally reveals substantial numbers of dead millipedes and adult June beetles, yet densities of these organisms are generally higher on annually burned watersheds (Seastedt 1984a). The responses of individual species are highly variable (Warren et al. 1987); however, of the major invertebrate groups, only the microarthropod fauna that live and feed on surface litter exhibit declines in densities (Seastedt 1984b). This response probably results more from the loss of habitat than from direct mortality. True soil-dwelling microarthropods have been reported to increase in densities in response to frequent fires (Lussenhop 1976, 1981). Fire results in increases in earthworm populations (James 1982, 1988), and in macroarthropod herbivores, such as the white grubs and root xylem-sucking cicada nymphs (Seastedt 1984a, Seastedt et al. 1986). Millipede densities are also higher on burned watersheds, even though the amount of foliar litter is significantly reduced. We lack data on nematode responses to fire, but we do know that this group responds to C supplements (Seastedt et al. 1988a). Thus, we would expect a positive response of nematodes to burning in most years. The soil fauna appears to respond to aspects of both resource quality and quantity (Seastedt et al. 1988b). Burning increases the quantity, but may have at most a neutral effect on quality. For reasons discussed later in this chapter, the soil consumer group may be particularly sensitive to fire frequency, which may increase resource quality as well as quantity.

In contrast to other ecosystems, the soil invertebrates of the tallgrass prairie appear to have a neutral net effect on plant productivity. While the root herbivores have a significant negative impact on plant productivity (e.g., Ingham and Detling 1986, Andersen 1987), the beneficial effects of the detritivores apparently negate the damage of the herbivores. A four-year experiment using insecticides in the soil did not affect either foliage or root production (Seastedt et al. 1987, 1988a). However, exclusion of earthworms and larger arthropods from decaying roots slows decomposition and mineralization (Seastedt et al. 1988a), and insecticide treatment of soil can reduce nitrate concentrations of soil water (Seastedt and Hayes 1988). The increased productivity of the root system, in conjunction with higher densities of herbivore and detritivore soil fauna, should stimulate the amount of belowground nutrient cycling. Detecting these increased rates, however, is difficult and governed by concurrent changes in microbial activity (Seastedt et al. 1988a, Seastedt and Hayes 1988).

THE EFFECTS OF FIRE ON BELOWGROUND NUTRIENT PROCESSES

The direct influence of prairie fires on soil chemistry parameters is slight at best. To date we have seen no fire-related changes in soil chemistry as a result of annual burning over a 10-year interval (Table 7.3). So far, only site effects (as opposed to fire effects) have been observed. The decline in organic matter inputs (via litterfall) appears to be more than compensated for by increased root production. Nitrogen content of soil organic matter is hypothesized to decline in response to long-term annual burning, and such a response has occurred in the Aldous plots, sites that have been burned annually for more than 50 years (Ojima 1987, Ojima et al. 1988). We may, however, have yet to appreciate the potential interaction between a fire and subsequent heavy rain. Massive erosion losses of nutrients on watersheds lacking standing dead and litter may occur if heavy rains follow burning. While we have not recorded such an event at Konza Prairie, a once-in-100-years episode might be sufficient to alter long-term average soil conditions.

TABLE 7.3   Soil characteristics of annually burned and unburned tallgrass prairie[a]

Treatment	pH	Bulk Density	% Organic Matter	Total N[b]
Unburned	6.0 A	0.93 B	6.50 A	0.25 A
Unburned	6.2 BC	1.05 A	6.25 A	0.24 A
Unburned	6.3 BC	1.04 B	6.05 A	0.25 A
Annually burned	6.0 AB	0.91 B	6.95 A	0.26 A
Annually burned	6.1 AB	1.04 A	6.40 A	0.24 A

[a] Values are means of four 25 cm deep soil cores. Each core represents a composite obtained along a transect. Values followed by different letters are significantly different (Duncan's Multiple Range Test, $p < .05$).
[b] Expressed as percentage of dry mass.

As previously mentioned, the vast majority of nutrients in the tallgrass prairie system are belowground, with most elements bound as insoluble organic or inorganic forms, which are essentially immune to all but the most extreme disturbances, such as conventional agricultural tillage practices. Not only are most of the nutrients belowground, but the rates of decomposition and mineralization of belowground organic matter are also more rapid than those occurring on or above the soil surface. A two-year study of foliage in litterbags on the surface and roots contained in litterbags buried just below the soil surface emphasized these facts. Decay of foliage, which initially contained 0.6 percent N, averaged about 28 percent mass loss per year, versus about 35 percent mass loss per year for roots, which initially contained 0.5 percent N (Fig. 7.5). Nitrogen and P were immobilized in foliage but not in roots during this two-year interval (Fig. 7.6). We have conducted several studies of foliage and stem decay where no N was released during the first few years of the study (Seastedt 1988), and similar results have been reported by Pastor et al. (1987). In contrast, these elements in roots exhibited apparent mineralization rates averaging about 25 percent per year (Fig. 7.6). Given the C to N to P ratios of the substrates, neither N nor P should have exhibited net miner-

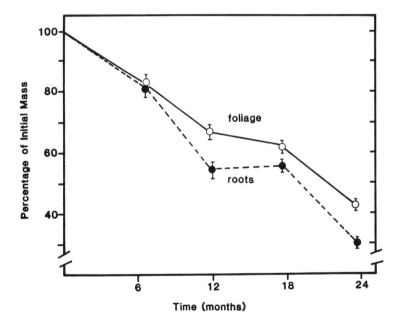

FIG. 7.5   Foliage and root decay rates estimated with litterbag methods. Values are means and standard errors of a minimum of 12 samples per substrate per date.

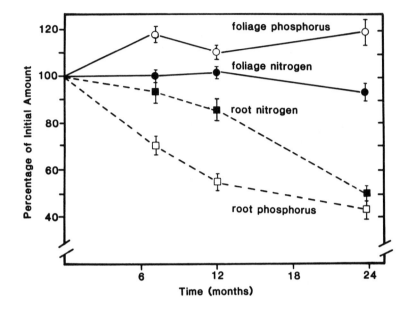

FIG. 7.6   Amounts of N and P contained in foliage and roots in litterbags (from Fig. 7.5).

alization (c.f., Alexander 1977). However, microbial immobilization of N may occur in the soil away from the roots, while this process must occur on and within the foliage aboveground. A viable alternative hypothesis is that grazing of the decaying roots by microbivores and detritivores may circumvent restrictions imposed upon microbes (J. M. Anderson et al. 1983, Seastedt et al. 1988a).

The increase in belowground biomass of roots low in N content reduces net mineralization rates of soils on burned prairie (Ojima 1987). Available N is in scarce supply to both plants and microbes, as demonstrated by experimental manipulations. We have evaluated the importance of N as a limiting factor to tallgrass prairie using fertilization experiments. Preliminary results from annually burned sites suggest a 60 percent increase in NPP on plots fertilized with 10 g/m^2 of inorganic N. Owensby et al. (1970) reported similar responses for a nearby pasture.

The ability of soil microbes to immobilize available inorganic N and prevent it from reaching plant roots was demonstrated in a short-term experiment that added C (as sucrose, table sugar), ammonium nitrate, both materials, or neither chemical to 16 plots. Plant biomass and soil water inorganic N content were measured for four weeks following treatment, and plant biomass was harvested at the end of the growing season (Table

TABLE 7.4   Plant biomass and soil water inorganic N response to fixed C (sucrose) and N (ammonium nitrate) additions[a]

Variable	Treatment			
	C	N	C + N	Untreated
Soil water				
NO$_3^-$N (μ/l)	650 B	86,900 A	80 B	60 B
Soil water				
NH$_4^+$N				
(μg/l)	30 A	50 A	20 A	280 A
Plants (g/m^2)				
Foliage mass	1,025 AB	1,360 A	820 B	950 B
Foliage N	6.8 AB	7.9 A	4.3 C	4.8 BC
Root mass				
Live	810 A	630 A	680 A	520 A
Dead	480 A	590 A	410 A	310 A
Rhizomes				
Live	380 A	480 A	360 A	380 A
Dead	200 A	160 A	170 A	170 A
Total Plant				
Mass	2,920 A	3,220 A	2,460 A	2,360 A
Nitrogen	16.9 AB	18.4 A	11.9 B	11.8 B
Detritus N^b	5.9 A	7.0 A	4.6 A	4.2 A

[a] From Seastedt et al. (1988a) and Seastedt and Hayes (1988). All plots were burned before the growing season. Means followed by different letters are significantly different (Duncan's Multiple Range Test, $p < .05$).
[b] Dead roots and rhizomes.

7.4). Both production and soil water chemistry values were unusual for Konza Prairie, perhaps because the experiment was conducted on a particularly productive site. Nonetheless, the results demonstrate that inorganic N can be prevented from reaching plant roots over an entire growing season by adding a source of fixed C. These findings indicate that the plants were able to obtain about 60 percent of the added N, but were inhibited from doing so if sugar was added to the soil. The addition of sugar alone appeared to subsequently increase the N content of the plants, but this effect was not statistically significant and was not observed when sugar and N were added together. The presence of a readily usable C source along with an inorganic N source may have stimulated denitrification on the watered plots (e.g., Alexander 1977).

Porous cup lysimeters have been used since 1982 to measure organic and inorganic N content of soil water on Konza Prairie (Seastedt and Hayes 1988). Averages for the 1982 through 1986 growing seasons are shown in Table 7.4. Also shown are estimates of bulk precipitation inputs and stream water measurements (McArthur et al. 1985, see also Tate 1985). Ammonia values for soil and stream water are not routinely measured because concentrations are low, with values for most samples below our detection limits of 2 $\mu g/1$. These results suggest that nitrate concentrations at the 20 cm depth in soil are significantly lower in annually burned soil. However, organic N, whose concentrations are unaffected by burning, is the dominant dissolved form of N in soil and stream water. Quantitative estimates of export of N in surface and ground waters have yet to be calculated. Koelliker et al. (1986) estimate that the average export of water at Konza Prairie is about 15 percent of inputs. Multiplying values shown for soil water or streams in Table 7.2 by 0.15 and comparing those numbers in rainwater inputs suggests that N losses in surface and ground waters are, on average, small compared to inputs. Preliminary investigations by Schimel et al. (unpublished) and Groffman (unpublished) suggest that gaseous losses of N are also small. Thus, the tallgrass prairie probably is accruing N in the soil system except during those years with unusual storm events (Woodmansee 1978).

Increased soil temperatures, accompanied by increased fixed C inputs from plants and increased secondary productivity by soil invertebrates on burned sites, should result in increased microbial activity and enhanced rates of nutrient cycling. While we suspect that this is indeed the case, supporting data are few (cf. Rice and Parenti 1978, Ojima 1987), and the overriding effect of N limitation via microbial immobilization may negate positive effects. Plant N amounts do increase on burned areas; however, external cycling (via mineralization) remains low (Ojima 1987). Instead, the perennial grasses appear to internally recycle this enhanced amount of N (Adams and Wallace 1985, Hayes 1985, 1986; Fig. 7.7). Plants are simply more efficient (i.e., produce more biomass per gram of N) on burned sites. We estimate that the annual N needs of plants from the soil are only about 4–5 g/m^2 of N, about the same amount translocated to the foliage each year. This estimate assumes an annual loss in foliage of 2 g/m^2 and an annual loss from roots of about twice that amount. Since rainfall inputs can provide about 1 $g/m^2/yr$, mineralization requirements are not large. Nonetheless, the fertilization studies show how inorganic N availability in soil controls productivity. Nitrogen should be most limiting to productivity following years of especially good flowering by the grasses. When flowering is extensive, plants apparently allocate their N to flowering stems and seeds rather than retranslocating it belowground. Since

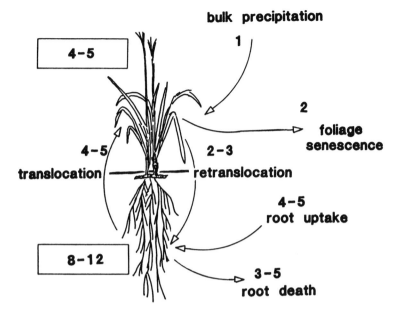

bulk precipitation

FIG. 7.7 Nitrogen budget for tallgrass prairie. Values are reported in g/m² for amounts in boxes, or in g/m²/yr for estimates of fluxes. Amounts and fluxes for dead plant materials are not shown, but can be estimated from Table 7.4.

flowering is usually more extensive on burned sites, we predict greater year-to-year variability in the productivity of burned prairie, a prediction that will be tested with the LTER data.

An important variable we have avoided addressing until now is fire frequency. Our discussion so far has compared annually burned versus long-term unburned prairie. The data are consistent in showing that, during years of adequate rainfall at least, annually burned prairie is strongly N-limited while long-term unburned prairie is strongly energy-limited. Obviously, when a long-term unburned site is finally burned, the site is no longer energy-limited; since this area lacks the high root biomass responsible for the immobilization of N, the site is not nearly as N-limited as the annually burned prairie. The net result is that the productivity of such areas greatly exceeds that of either annually burned or unburned sites (Hulbert 1986). The consequences of these shifts in energy and nutrient limitations at less-than-annually burned sites on secondary productivity and soil nutrient dynamics is the subject of a 1988 experiment at Konza Prairie. We predict that both primary and secondary productivity will exhibit maximum growth responses under these conditions. Of particular interest is whether or not these conditions might be responsible for out-breaks of white grubs and other root-feeding herbivores (e.g., Ueckert 1979).

FIRE, GRAZING, AND SPATIAL HETEROGENEITY

A recent emphasis in ecology has been understanding the influence of spatial patterns on population and ecosystem processes (e.g., Risser et al. 1984, Forman and Godron 1986). Collins and Gibson (chapter 6) have dis-cussed these phenomena for the prairie in general, and only a few specific remarks are added here. Fire and grazing by large ungulates can be re-garded as "patchy phenomena," contributing to the diversity of the land-scape. Grazing negates or at least diminishes fire effects by removal of fuel, but grazing functions similarly to fire by removing (or at least tram-pling) the standing dead and litter layer. Indians used fire to attract grazers (Pyne 1986); hence, an inequitable distribution of grazing on burned and unburned sites is expected. Since the prairie evolved under the influence of both fire and grazing, these factors need to be addressed concurrently to gain an understanding of the nominal operating condi-tions of pristine prairie. Accordingly, the next phase of our LTER re-search effort will include both variables.

Spatial pattern is important to belowground phenomena *if*, for ex-ample, we can demonstrate that soil phenomena occurring adjacent to a point of reference affect the behavior of that point. The existence of "edge effects" or ecotones attests to the importance of spatial patterns. Hillslope variation (e.g., Schimel et al. 1985) is an obvious example. Since soil phe-nomena are so strongly influenced by energy, water, and nutrient inter-actions, we should quickly recognize that the specific combination of patches of burned and unburned, and grazed and ungrazed, areas on un-even terrain such as the Flint Hills will affect average productivity of the area. For example, an unburned area above a burned area could provide soil water and soil water N downslope such that the overall productivity of the area is enhanced. We look forward to testing these questions with the new technologies developed as part of the NASA-FIFE study of the Konza Prairie.

SUMMARY

The major effect of late spring fire on the belowground components of the tallgrass prairie results from increases in usable solar energy inputs, a consequence of the removal of the standing dead and litter (Knapp and Seastedt 1986). The absence of detritus results in increased efficiency of C fixation by primary producers (Knapp 1985, Hulbert 1988). A portion of this fixed C is translocated belowground, which stimulates soil herbivore and detritivore densities. Larger amounts of root detritus, which is low in N content, enhance the immobilization potential of the soil and result in reduced amounts of inorganic N in soil and soil water. This occurs in spite of higher inorganic N inputs to the soil from rainfall and throughfall. Frequent burning therefore creates conditions for severe N limitation to plant productivity. These conditions are maintained until detritus accumulation caused by an absence of fire reduces C inputs. The reduction in C inputs to the soil reduces the C to N ratio and allows for accumulation or export of inorganic N.

ACKNOWLEDGMENTS

We appreciate the efforts of current and former colleagues in developing the below-ground data sets. The works of A. K. Knapp (photosynthesis), D. C. Hayes (roots, retranslocation), S. W. James and T. C. Todd (soil invertebrates), and several others were essential to our efforts. These studies were initiated under the careful guidance of the late L. C. Hulbert, Director of Konza Prairie Research Natural Area. We have benefited greatly from the advice and findings of D. S. Schimel, W. J. Parton, and D. S. Ojima from Colorado State University. Research was supported by NSF grants DEB-A012166, BSR-8305435, BSR-8514327, and BSR-8505861, and NASA grant NAG-5-897 to Kansas State University. Data and supporting documentation are stored in the Konza Prairie Research Natural Area Data Bank, Division of Biology, Kansas State University.

8
Simulated Impacts of Annual Burning on Prairie Ecosystems

By Dennis S. Ojima,
W. J. Parton,
D. S. Schimel,
and C. E. Owensby

Aboveground plant production in mesic, ungrazed grasslands generally increases following a fire. Increased production has been attributed to release of readily available nitrogen (N) and phosphorus (P), increased N mineralization rates, enhanced N fixation, and altered microclimatic conditions (Rice and Parenti 1978, Biederbeck et al. 1980, Old 1969, Hulbert 1969, Sharrow and Wright 1977, Daubenmire 1968, Raison 1979, Ewing and Engle 1988). Most of these fire effects occur immediately after the fire and are associated with short-term microclimatic fire effects, which include increased soil temperature and light, and decreased soil moisture (Old 1969). Frequent fires have long-term effects, such as decreasing soil organic matter and changing species composition (Vogl 1974, Kucera 1981, Old 1969, Risser et al. 1981; chapter 6) and often result in maintenance of greater productivity in spite of apparent loss of labile soil organic matter and large volatile losses of N (Daubenmire 1968, Biederbeck et al. 1980).

Short-term abiotic effects of burning have been well studied (Hulbert 1969; Old 1969; Sharrow and Wright 1977). Removal of litter and standing dead by fire increases the amount of solar radiation reaching the soil surface and results in an increase in soil temperature (Old 1969, Hulbert 1988). Higher soil temperatures increase plant residue decomposition rates and the mineralization rates of organic matter (Risser and Parton 1982, Woodmansee and Wallach 1981, Sharrow and Wright 1977). Soil moisture is reduced after fires as a result of increased bare soil evaporation rates and enhanced transpiration rates due to earlier green-up (K. L. Anderson 1965, Kucera and Ehrenreich 1962; chapter 3). Another positive effect of fire is that it eliminates the high air temperature within the litter layer (10 to 15 cm above the soil surface), which has been shown to reduce photosynthesis rates of big bluestem growing through the extensive litter layer associated with an unburned prairie (Knapp 1985, Knapp and Seastedt 1986; chapter 7).

The mechanisms by which short-term effects of fire are translated into long-term behavior of the tallgrass ecosystem are not well understood. This chapter shows how the cumulative effect of short-term responses to burning results in long-term changes in ecosystem properties of the Konza tallgrass prairie site in Kansas. We will demonstrate this conclusion with recent field results from a variety of nutrient cycling and plant production studies at the Konza and Aldous sites and from a modeling study (Ojima et al. 1988, Ojima 1987) in which we used the CENTURY soil organic matter model (Parton et al. 1987, 1988) to simulate short-term (1–5 y) and long-term (5–20 y) impacts of fire on plant production and nutrient cycling (N and P). The field data and modeling study will demonstrate how annual burning of the tallgrass prairie results in the maintenance of greater productivity despite a reduction in soil organic matter and large losses of N ($1-2$ g/m^2/y^1) associated with each fire.

In this chapter, we will synthesize the data from a variety of recent papers, where the field data are presented in much greater detail. The long-term (20–80 y) impact of fire on aboveground production is presented by Towne and Owensby (1984), while short- and long-term impacts of fire on aboveground and belowground production, mineralization rates of soil organic matter, and N immobilization are presented by Ojima (1987). N$_2$ fixation rates have been evaluated by Eisele et al. (1989), and leaching NO$_3$ losses have been presented by Hayes and Seastedt (1989). The short-term impact of fire is evaluated with data from the Konza prairie site, while the long-term impact of fire is determined using data from the Aldous plots (both sites are near Manhattan, Kansas).

KONZA AND ALDOUS SITES

The field sites are located in the Flint Hills near Manhattan, Kansas, along the western border of the tallgrass prairies. The vegetation is dominated by *Andropogon gerardii* Vittm., *Sorghastrum nutans* Nash, and *A. scoparius* Michx. The Aldous and Konza sites used in this study are both established on ungrazed areas. The Aldous site was initiated in 1926 to evaluate the impact of burning at four different times of the year (Aldous 1934, Towne and Owensby 1984). Soil at the Aldous site is a loess-derived Smolan silt loam, classified as a Pachic arguistoll. Annual mowing of the unburned sites was done from 1927 to 1967. After 1967 the mowing was stopped for the unburned site, which thus reflects the impact of not burning or mowing during the past 20 years.

The Konza site is located on Konza Prairie Research Natural Area (KPRNA) Long Term Ecological Research (LTER) site near Manhattan, Kansas. At our Konza site burning was excluded for 20 years until we started burning in 1983. Our site is on a relatively flat north-facing bench, soil depth is approximately 70 cm, and the soil is a Clime clay loam (classified as Udic haplustolls). This area was extensively grazed until the early 1970s and then left ungrazed and unburned until 1983.

ECOSYSTEM FIRE EFFECTS

In this section we will present a synthesis of recent data from Konza and Aldous tallgrass prairie sites and will attempt to show how short-term fire effects translate into the observed long-term effect of annual burning. Table 8.1 shows the observed short- and long-term effects of annual burning on a tallgrass prairie. The table summarizes recent data from the Konza and Aldous sites (Ojima 1987) and shows the effect of annual burning (percentage change from unburned control) after 1, 2, and 18 years on nine ecosystem characteristics.

Plant Production

Aboveground and belowground plant biomass C and N were collected in late August 1984 (time of peak root and shoot biomass) at the Konza and Aldous sites for both burned and unburned treatments. The results (Table 8.1) show that short-term annual (two years) burning increased aboveground and belowground live biomass by 102 percent and 79 percent, respectively. The total N content of live shoots and roots was little influenced by burning, thus resulting in a decrease in the N concentration of shoots (−21 percent) and roots (−46 percent). Burning had relatively little impact on C and N content of dead shoots and roots (data not shown). These results suggest that the nitrogen use efficiency (NUE) of plants was increased, since burning resulted in more plant biomass with similar uptake of N from the soil (see chapter 7). Short- and long-term effects of annual burning were similar for live root C (79 percent and 68 percent increases), while the positive effect of annual burning on aboveground plant production appeared to be reduced for long-term annual burning (102 percent vs. 30 percent respectively, for short- and long-term burning).

Plant Combustion Losses

Volatile losses of aboveground C, N, and P were monitored at the Aldous plots during the spring of 1983 (Ojima 1987). Biomass losses ranged from

TABLE 8.1   Short- and long-term observed effect of fire (% change from un-burned control) on microbial C and N, belowground net N mineralization, labile P, inorganic N, live root and shoot biomass, and live root and shoot N concentration (values are calculated for data presented by Ojima [1987]).

Variable	Short-Term		Long-Term
	1 y	2 y	18 y
Microbial C[a]	+9	+6	−13
Microbial N[a]	+9	+2	−16
Belowground net N mineralization[a]	+25	+5	−190
$NO_3 + NH_4$[a]	+14	−8	−32
Labile P[a]	+19	—	+8
Aboveground live shoots[b]	—	+102	+30[c]
Belowground live roots[b]	—	+79	+68
Live shoot N concentration[b]	—	−21	—
Live root N concentration[b]	—	−46	−38

[a] Average changes for April to September growing season.
[b] Based on live shoot and root biomass data observed in August 1984.
[c] Difference after 15–20 y of annual burning at the Aldous plots (Towne and Owensby 1984).

3,090 to 4,350 kg/ha, while the percentage loss of aboveground material ranged from 63 to 89 percent. Combustion losses of N ranged from 12.5 to 30.0 kg N/ha, and losses on a percentage basis were similar for both biomass and N. Phosphorus losses were negligible for two of the three burns and were 50 percent for a burn where wind redistributed ash material. Some of the other direct effects of fire were a slight increase in soil pH (0.16 to 0.24) following the fire; increases in mean soil temperature, which ranged from 1 to 3°C (5 cm depth); and decreased soil moisture for one to two months after the fire (Ojima 1987).

Soil Nutrients

The effect of fire on soil nutrient levels and mineralization rates was determined by measuring soil microbial C and N, soil NO_3 and NH_4, labile P, total soil C and N, and belowground net N mineralization rates for Aldous plots and the Konza prairie sites during the 1983 and 1984 growing seasons (Ojima 1987). The one- and two-year burning effects were determined from the Konza site, while the Aldous plots show the long-term (18 y) effects of annual burning (Table 8.1). Table 8.1 shows the average April to September changes (percentage change compared to unburned control) for the nutrient variables as a function of time since the initiation of annual burning. Microbial C and N levels increased during the first year after burning and then decreased until they were 13 and 16 percent lower than controls after prolonged annual burning. The initial increase was a result of increased decomposition rates (higher soil temperatures) following a fire, while the long-term decrease may be a result of a decrease in C and N inputs from aboveground litter. The results also suggest that fire causes the C:N ratio of microbial biomass to increase.

Belowground N mineralization was increased 25 percent 1 year after a fire and then decreased with repeated fires (190 percent decrease after 18 years). The short-term increase in N mineralization was caused by increased soil temperature, which increases decomposition rates. This interpretation was based on data from the buried-bag transfer experiments, where the transfer of burn treatment soils into unburned plots significantly decreased net mineralization, while the transfer of unburned soils into burned plots increased the N mineralization rates (Ojima 1987). The long-term decrease in N mineralization was a result of the increased root production and decreased N content of the burned plots (higher N immobilization). The observed changes in the N mineralization rates are consistent with the changes in the total soil mineral N levels (NO_3 + NH_4), which increased by 14 percent in the first year and decreased by 32 percent after prolonged annual burning. Labile P levels followed a different pattern, with increased labile P levels for both short- and long-term burning treatments, which probably resulted from deposition of P in the ash with each fire. The overall effect of annual burning was to decrease the ratio of mineral N to labile P. Total soil C was increased by 4 percent, while soil N was decreased by 10 percent on the long-term burned site. Our best explanation for these results was that the increased soil C comes from an increase in root production, while the decreased soil N results from combustion N losses.

A summary of these results shows that the turnover rate of soil organic matter (SOM) increased with fire because of the increased soil temperatures. Fire causes decreased belowground net N mineralization rates because of an increase in N immobilization by dead roots. We have not monitored aboveground N immobilization rates in this study; however, preliminary estimates of N immobilization rates suggest that fire would reduce N immobilization by 10 to 30 kg N/ha. The net effect of fire on the total system net N mineralization rate was not measured, but the modeling results suggest that annual burning reduced total system net N mineralization rate by 10 kg N/ha after 20 years of annual burning.

Nitrogen Losses and Inputs

Nitrogen inputs from N fixation by blue-green algae (cyanobacteria-Nostoc) are potentially very significant in the tallgrass prairie (Eisele et al. 1989). We found (Eisele et al. 1989) that blue-green N_2 fixation decreases linearly as a function of the natural log of the ratio of available N to available P. In the previous section we showed that fire caused the ratio of available N : available P to decrease because fire increased available P and decreased available N ($NO_3 + NH_4$). Thus N_2 fixation increases and partially compensates for the fire-induced combustion N losses.

Knapp and Seastedt (1986) have compared NO_3 leaching losses for burned and unburned sites and found that burning decreases NO_3 leaching. The significance of the difference is minor, since NO_3 losses are low for burned or unburned prairies ($0.02-0.03$ g m^{-2}y^{-2}). Recent denitrification data from the Konza site (Mosier et al. unpublished data) shows that N_2O fluxes are an order of magnitude lower for the burned site; however, the magnitude of the N losses is low for both sites (< 0.1 g N m^{-2}y^{-1}). The reduction in NO_3 leaching and N_2O fluxes with fire is probably a result of the fire-induced decrease in soil NO_3 and NH_4 levels.

In summary, our conceptual model (Fig. 8.1) identifies the biological processes affected by fire (changes relative to unburned control). Aboveground and belowground biomass are enhanced by burning due to the removal of the aboveground plant residue and an increase in growing season length (two to four weeks). Belowground biomass is increased more than aboveground biomass, and amount of plant production per gram of N uptake is increased substantially (NUE). An immediate effect of burning is the combustion of aboveground plant material with the volatile loss of C and N and the deposition of P in the ash. The deposition of P may induce higher N-fixation rates of blue-green algae in the soil surface. This input of N would help to counterbalance the combustion losses of N. Aboveground inputs to soil organic matter are reduced as a result of combustion of aboveground plant material. This loss is partially compensated by an increase in root production. Net N mineralization from soil organic matter is influenced by burning. The higher soil temperatures resulting from the removal of aboveground plant material increase SOM mineralization rates. Aboveground plant removal causes a decrease in aboveground N immobilization, while belowground N immobilization is increased as a result of increased root production and lower N contents for burned roots

ECOSYSTEM FIRE EFFECTS

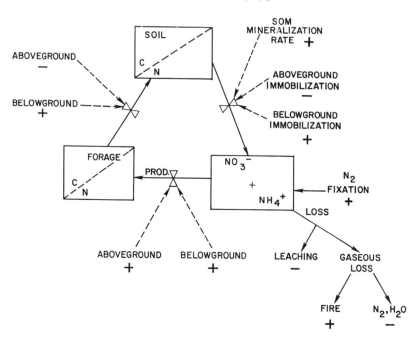

FIG. 8.1   Conceptual flow diagram of the effect of annual burning on a tallgrass prairie. The fire effects are expressed as changes relative to an unburned control.

(Table 8.1). Fire influences N losses from the system by reducing NO_3 leaching loss and gaseous N losses associated with nitrification (N_2O) and denitrification (N_2O and N_2). These reductions in gaseous N losses only partially compensate ($<$ 5 percent) for the larger combustion N losses (1 to 2 g N m^{-2} per fire). The net result of the direct fire effects is sustained long-term increases in plant production, which are maintained in spite of large C and N plant combustion losses because of the increase in NUE of the plants, decrease in leaching of soil NO_3, decrease in N_2 and N_2O gaseous losses, and increase in N inputs due to N fixation.

MODELING ECOSYSTEM FIRE EFFECTS

We will describe our recent ecosystem modeling work incorporating the observed direct impacts of fire into the CENTURY model. The objective of this effort was to test whether adding the direct effects of burning into the model allows us to simulate the observed short- and long-term effects of annual burning on ecosystem properties. We will briefly describe the structure of the CENTURY SOM model and the changes to the model added to represent the impact of fire, and compare the observed and simulated effect of annual fire for a 20-year simulation.

The CENTURY SOM model simulates the biogeochemistry of C, N, and P in the plant-soil system of natural grasslands and agro-ecosystems using a monthly time step. The plant production submodel simulates the dynamics of C, N, and P in the live and dead aboveground plant material and live and dead roots, using a simple model where maximum plant production is controlled by precipitation and is reduced as a function of available soil nutrients. In the SOM submodel, plant residues are decomposed by microbes, and the resulting microbial products become the substrates for SOM formation. We divide SOM into three fractions:

1. An active soil fraction consisting of live microbes and microbial products (1 to 4 y turnover time).
2. A protected fraction that is more resistant to decomposition as a result of physical or chemical protection (20 to 40 y turnover time).
3. A fraction that is physically protected or chemically resistant and has a long turnover time (800 to 1,200 y).

The flow diagrams for C, N, and P submodels of CENTURY (Fig. 8.2) show that the organic C, N, and P flows have a similar structure, with the N and P following the C flows. The N and P submodels also include the flows of mineral N and P compounds. The C:P ratio of the SOM fractions floats as a function of the labile P level (lower values with higher labile P levels). The driving variables for the model include soil texture, monthly precipitation, average monthly maximum and minimum air temperature, and the plant lignin content. A detailed description of the CENTURY model is presented by Parton et al. (1987, 1988).

The CENTURY model has been modified to include the direct effects of burning on the ecosystem (Ojima 1987). The changes are primarily based on an analysis of the observed fire effects at Konza prairie and the Aldous plots and include:

1. Calculating biological N_2 fixation rates as a function of the ratio of mineral N to labile P (high N_2 fixation with low ratios).
2. Developing a plant production model where maximum plant production is a function of monthly precipitation and soil temperature and the standing dead biomass.
3. Allowing the C:N ratio of the active SOM to float from 6 to 14 as a function of the mineral N level (low values for high mineral N levels).
4. Increasing the NUE for burned plants (higher C:N ratios for burned plant material).
5. Incorporating the combustion losses of aboveground C, N, and P into the model.

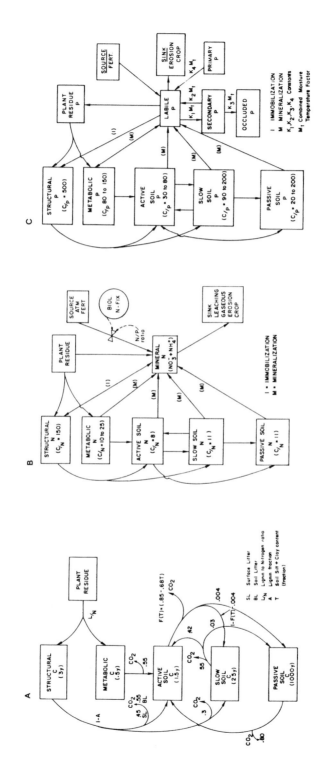

FIG. 8.2 Flow diagrams for C (A), N (B), and P (C) submodels in the CENTURY model (modified from Parton et al. 1988).

MODEL RESULTS

The effects of annual burning are shown by comparing an unburned simulation with an annual burning simulation (same initial conditions for both runs). The results for aboveground and belowground production (Fig. 8.3) show that burned aboveground production is 80 percent higher than unburned production immediately after the first fire and then decreases with time, so that burned aboveground production is 35 percent above unburned production after 18 years. Belowground production follows a similar pattern to aboveground production. The observed effect of burning on aboveground production is similar to the simulated results, with an

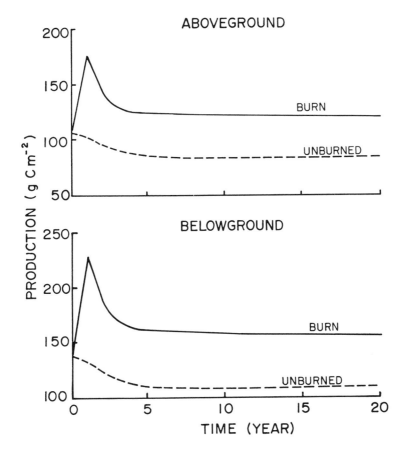

FIG. 8.3 Simulated impact of an unburned and annually burned treatment on aboveground and belowground plant production for a 20-year simulation.

increase of more than 100 percent immediately after the fire and 17–25 percent after 15 years of annual burning (Towne and Owensby 1984). Higher belowground production with burning is also supported by the observed data, since burned live root biomass is 79 percent higher after 2 years of annual burns and 67 percent higher after prolonged (18 y) annual spring burning.

Simulated annual burning caused total soil C to increase for the first 2 years after annual burning (Fig. 8.4) and then decrease to values similar to initial values after 20 years of annual burning. The unburned soil C increases throughout the 20-year run. Simulated soil N levels are stable ini-

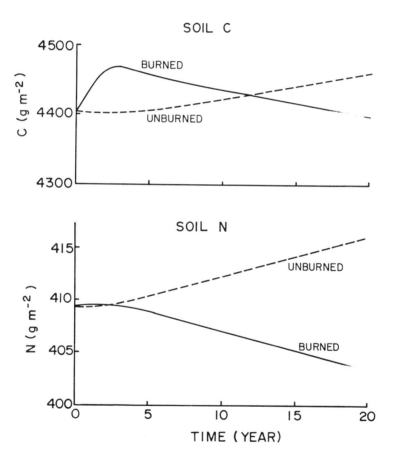

FIG. 8.4   Simulated effect of annual burning on soil C and N levels for a 20-year simulation.

tially (1–3 y) and then decrease with annual burning, while soil N levels increase continually for the unburned simulation. The observed data show that prolonged annual burning causes soil C levels to be increased by 4 percent while soil N levels are decreased by 10 percent. The model correctly predicted that burning would decrease soil N and that soil C would change less with burning than soil N. Our interpretations of both the observed data and model results are that the increased soil C with burning is a result of the increase in root production (Table 8.1), while the decrease in soil N with burning results from the loss of N in combustion.

The simulated total system net N mineralization and belowground net mineralization (excluding N immobilization into aboveground plant residue) are shown in Fig. 8.5. The results show that belowground net N mineralization increases slightly with time in the unburned run, while N mineralization decreases rapidly during the first three years for the annually burned simulation. Total system net N mineralization decreases for both the unburned and burned simulations, but after three years of annual burning the unburned N mineralization rates are approximately 1.0 g N m^{-2}y^{-1} higher than the burned values. The observed decrease in belowground N mineralization of 190 percent after prolonged annual burning is similar to the model simulation results, where burned belowground N mineralization rates are 91 percent lower than the unburned run. The simulated decrease in the total system net N mineralization rates cannot be verified by observed data because aboveground immobilization was not measured at our site. The decrease in belowground net N mineralization rates with burning is caused by the increase in root production and decreased N concentration of the burned plant residues (higher N immobilization rates).

The microbial C and N for the annual burned and unburned runs (Fig. 8.6) show that microbial C increases during the first five years for the unburned run and then stabilizes. Microbial C for the annual burning run increases initially and then decreases. Microbial N increases slightly for the unburned run, while microbial N decreases rapidly after the first year for the burned run. The simulated C:N ratios of the microbial biomass are higher in the burned run (10.5) than the unburned run (9.5). The long-term decrease in microbial N and C for the burned run compared to the unburned run is in agreement with the observed data (Table 8.1), which show lower microbial N (16 percent) and C (14 percent) for the annually burned treatment relative to unburned treatments. Similarly, the observed data show that the C:N ratio of the annually burned treatments is higher compared to the unburned treatment.

The effect of burning on N$_2$ fixation in the soil is simulated by the model (data not presented) and shows that the average annual N-fixation rate for

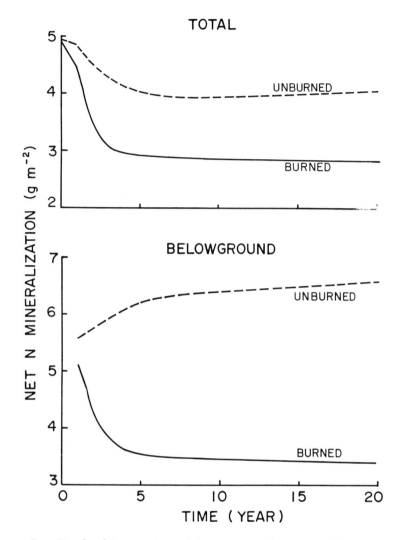

FIG. 8.5   Simulated impact of annual burning on total system and belowground net N mineralization for a 20-year simulation.

the annual burning run is 0.52 g N m^{-2}y^{-1} and 0.42 g N m^{-2}y^{-1} for the unburned run. The increased N fixation with burning is caused by the simulated decrease in the ratio of available N to available P, which is a result of an increase in available P (P returned in the ash) and a decrease in the available N levels ($>$ N immobilized by burned dead roots).

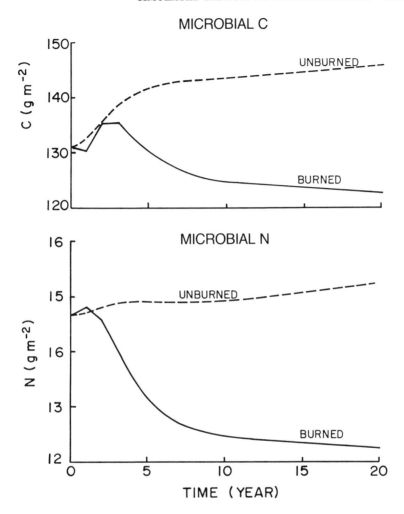

FIG. 8.6   Twenty-year simulation of the effect of annual burning on microbial C and N in the soil.

SUMMARY

We have incorporated the observed direct effects of fire on a tallgrass prairie into the CENTURY SOM model and tested whether the resulting model could predict the observed short- and long-term impact of annual burning on ecosystem properties. The direct fire effects we incorporated into the model include: (1) calculating biological N_2 fixation rates; (2) developing a plant production model that included the impact of standing dead plant material; (3) allowing C:N ratios of the microbes to float; (4) changing the NUE of burned plants; and (5) including the fire-produced combustion losses of aboveground plant material and their impact on soil temperatures and soil moisture. The results show that the model correctly predicts the short- and long-term effects of annual burning on ecosystem properties. The ecosystem properties we represented included aboveground and belowground plant production, microbial C and N, soil C and N, and belowground N mineralization rates. These ecosystem properties have different short- and long-term responses to annual burning, with a general pattern of increased values following the initiation of annual burning (one to three years) followed by a long-term decrease after prolonged annual burning. Our modeling results suggest that the most influential direct effect of fire is the increase in NUE produced by burning, which allows the observed sustained increases in plant production in spite of large N losses associated with long-term annual burning.

9
Landscape Processes and the Vegetation of the North American Grassland

By Paul G. Risser

The grasslands of North America have provided an ecological system from which several fundamental ecological principles have been derived and tested. Succession and its role in range management, the importance of roots and other belowground processes in ecosystem function, changes in plant composition along topographic and moisture gradients, and the ways that grassland plants affect soil processes are among these important ideas and their applications. In addition, much has been learned about the physiology and demography of individual plant species, especially in response to drought, grazing, and burning (Fowler 1984, Risser 1985). In general, these studies have focused on the spatial scale of individual plants or small, relatively homogeneous grassland areas. Furthermore, most earlier simulation models of grassland ecosystems have acknowledged, but not explicitly included, spatial heterogeneity at the scale of the landscape (Urban et al. 1987). Curiously, many of these studies have neither accommodated spatial variation nor included an assessment of how the results can be extrapolated to broader geographic areas.

More recent investigations have begun to examine ecological processes that operate over broader spatial scales than those of individual plants and in particular have been directed toward landscape-level processes. These studies have continued the linkage between plant growth and soil characteristics—an emphasis that has been a hallmark of North American grassland ecology since early in this century. The concept of landscape ecology has encouraged an expansion of research on these plant-soil relationships and also widened the scope of investigations to other phenomena, such as regional hydrological processes and changes in atmospheric conditions. This approach focuses on the transfer of energy, information, and materials across heterogeneous landscapes. That is, burning of rangelands has proximate effects on plant productivity, soil temperature, and other variables. In addition, however, burning may affect nutrient conditions in both the immediate drainage streams and farther downstream, may affect the migration and grazing patterns of wide-ranging ungulates, and may influence precipitation patterns by providing nuclei in the atmosphere. Thus, landscape ecology deals with spatial pattern, has particular concern with processes that cross boundaries of relatively homogeneous ecological systems, and explicitly recognizes the ecological consequences of heterogeneous resources and their use.

This chapter summarizes some of the important understandings about North American grasslands, bringing together ideas that have arisen at various spatial scales, showing connections between these ideas, and, finally, describing some future directions in grassland ecology.

THE SETTING

The species composition of the grasslands of North America has been described (Risser et al. 1981, Weaver 1954, 1968, Weaver and Albertson 1956, Weaver and Fitzpatrick 1934, Diamond and Smeins 1988). Near the eastern border with the deciduous forest, the tallgrass prairie is dominated by grasses such as big bluestem (*Andropogon gerardii*), little bluestem (*A. scoparius*), Indian grass (*Sorghastrum nutans*), and switchgrass (*Panicum virgatum*). The shortgrass steppe on the western Great Plains is dominated by blue grama (*Bouteloua gracilis*), buffalo grass (*Buchloe dactyloides*), and western wheatgrass (*Agropyron smithii*); the intervening mixed-grass prairie contains these grass species and many others, especially species of *Stipa*, *Bouteloua*, and *Agropyron*. Forbs occur throughout these grasslands, and the particular species composition of the grassland in any one locality at a specific time depends upon combinations of soil, topography, climate and the history of use.

When viewed from the perspective of the regional climate, North American grasslands have a greater risk of rainfall deficiency in the summer than have the bordering forest regions, and the shortgrass steppe has a markedly lower summer rainfall even compared with the remainder of these grasslands. The grassland regions have fewer days with rain, more drought, and lower relative humidity during July and August than adjacent forest regions, and hot winds are frequent during dry summers (Borchert 1950, Sims 1988).

A pronounced climatic gradient exists from the tallgrass prairie westward to the shortgrass steppe. Annual rainfall decreases from more than 75 cm in the eastern area of the tallgrass prairie to about 25 cm on the shortgrass steppe (Parton et al. 1981; Risser et al. 1981). In the east, two peak periods of rainfall occur, one in early summer and a smaller one in

September; west of the tallgrass prairie, the September peak disappears. Relative humidity decreases westward, especially during the growing season; mixing ratios also decrease, as does cloud cover; in addition, wind speed, solar radiation, and potential evapotranspiration increase westward. Further, variability in total rainfall, rain-days, and average rainfall amounts increase to the west (Risser et al. 1981). Thus, most climatic data suggest that the environment is inherently more variable and more stressful to plants in the westward portions of the North American central grasslands.

The most notable herbivore on the Great Plains was the bison (*Bison bison*), which probably invaded North America via the Bering land bridge in the early Pleistocene. Historic herds may have descended from a second migration in the late Pleistocene (Meagher 1973). Rigorous population counts of these herds were not made, but most estimates range from 50 to 125 million. Grazing habits of the bison are not completely known (Peden et al. 1974), but each herd probably grazed over wide geographical areas. As forage became limiting because of grazing, drought, or plant phenological stage, the bison—like the pronghorn (*Antilocapra americana*) today—moved to locations with more forage (Ellis and Travis 1975; England and De Vos 1969). Currently these grasslands are grazed by domestic herbivores with more restricted ranges and somewhat different grazing patterns (Senft et al. 1987).

Rangelands have been subjected to fires set by lightning or humans for thousands of years. As discussed elsewhere in this volume, burning under dry conditions, especially in the mixed-grass and shortgrass steppe (Wright and Bailey 1982) can be quite deleterious. In the more humid regions, elevated temperatures are usually brief, and the perennial grasses themselves experience minimum damage (R. C. Anderson 1982; Danbenmire 1968), though there are other landscape-level effects. In the tallgrass prairie, burning has been routinely recommended as a management approach, particularly to reduce invasion by woody species and to control cool season grasses (R. C. Anderson 1982; Launchbaugh and Owensby, 1978).

Definitions of drought frequently are based on rainfall amounts, but the duration of low soil water content, the presence of high soil and air temperatures, drying winds, and abrasive wind-blown material are also important (Coupland 1950). The responses of central North American grasslands to drought, especially in the 1930s and 1950s, have been described in considerable detail (Weaver and Albertson 1936, 1956), and these drought conditions interact with the frequency and severity of effect from burning.

Grasses probably emerged during the late Cretaceous, and by the early Miocene they had achieved a significant place in the earth's vegetation (de Wet 1981). Coexistence of grasslands and ungulates since the early Tertiary has led to a number of presumed protective or compensatory adaptations by plants (Dahl and Hyder 1977, Detling and Painter 1983, Dyer et al. 1982, McNaughton 1979). Thus, from prehistoric times, grasslands have been exposed to drought, grazing, and fire (R. C. Anderson 1982, Axelrod 1985, Singh et al. 1983). As a result, evaluations of grasslands today depend upon this historical perspective—namely, that ecological processes have evolved over long periods of time, but that current changes in global climate may be occurring at a faster rate than ever before. If so, it is an open question just how the grasslands will respond at any spatial and temporal scale to global changes occurring at apparently unprecedented rates. In the following discussion, it is argued that local processes are necessary for understanding landscape-level processes, but that landscape-level processes are important in predicting the future of grasslands under burning and conditions of changing environment.

FIRE AS A FACTOR IN LANDSCAPE HETEROGENEITY

Like grazing, fires can have significant influence on pattern, diversity, and dynamics within and among landscapes. Historically, fires burned extensively throughout the North American prairies; however, natural firebreaks, such as gallery forests along streams (Abrams 1986), served as boundaries which eventually contained fires and affected their distribution. A single fire would influence landscape pattern and process in at least two ways. First, the variable distribution of factors such as fuel, soil moisture, and wind patterns would produce a patchy fire, which would result in heterogeneity within the burned area. This patchiness would then affect other components within the grassland, including plant community heterogeneity (see chapter 6) and distribution of small mammal habitat (see chapter 5). Physical features within the landscape, such as buffalo wallows, may interact with fires by remaining as unburned patches and serving as refugia for some taxa. If fires do burn through wallows, vegetational heterogeneity increases within and among wallows (Collins and Uno 1983). Additionally, burning may increase the transfer of materials across landscape boundaries (Wiens et al. 1985). For example, leaching of nutrients by heavy rains immediately after a burn may enhance productivity in the streams draining a burned watershed while reducing nutrients necessary for regrowth of terrestrial plants (see chapter 7).

Second, at larger spatial scales, the patchy distribution of burned and unburned areas would dramatically impact landscape processes. In particular, ungulates preferentially graze vegetation in burned areas because of the greater productivity and nutritive quality of forage following fire. Also, the removal of standing dead material and deep litter would facilitate grazing. Therefore, the movement and impact of grazing animals within a landscape (Senft et al. 1987) may be strongly tied to the spatial distribution of burned patches. The overall effect of grazing would be concentrated in the most recently burned units of the landscape. These grazing patterns would impose a feedback system, in which the heterogeneous distribution of fuel as a result of grazing would lead to variable fire effects within a burned area following the next fire.

Fire frequency will also impact regional-level phenomena. Assuming that fires occurred at different times of the year and at different frequencies over a given period of time, then grasslands would have reflected a heterogeneous pattern of vegetation among areas subjected to different burning regimes. Gibson and Hulbert (1987) showed that plant species composition changed rapidly following fire and, furthermore, that grasslands burned annually contained plant communities quantitatively different from areas that remained unburned for varying lengths of time. These regional patterns due to variable fire frequency would also impact animal populations, energy flows, and nutrient cycles. Clearly, fire at the landscape and regional levels has direct and important effects which interact with other large- and small-scale phenomena (grazing, topography, and edaphic conditions) to enhance spatial and temporal heterogeneity in grassland ecosystems.

SPACE AND TIME SCALES AND SPECIES COMPOSITION

Time and space provide useful frameworks for analyzing the processes that determine the persistence and change of species composition. Equilibrium theories attempt to explain the coexistence and persistence of species on the basis of niche separation among habitat conditions—i.e., habitat separation within a landscape—and niche differentiation, involving coevolution or preadaptation to reduce competition among plants sharing the same location (Bazzaz and Parrish 1982). Nonequilibrium explanations pay less attention to competition and niche differentiation and give more importance to the unpredictability of disturbance and therefore of species interactions at many time and space scales (Pickett and White 1985). Disturbance, microhabitat heterogeneity, climatic fluctuation, and the regenerative attributes of plant species may be so overwhelming that compositional equilibrium with the physical environment rarely arises.

Time scales of concern range from the immediate successional responses to processes such as burning, to relictual dynamics, where a perennial species may persist but not reproduce under changed environmental conditions, all the way to the time scales of evolution. Space scales again range from the adaptive reproductive tactics employed by a plant in a specified locality to broad regional changes in species composition in response to burning, changes in climate, or other controlling factors. Thus, a wide variety of spatial and temporal scales are applicable to grassland ecology. The focus of this chapter, however, is at the landscape and decadal scales—that is, processes that occur over time scales of a few years to a few decades, and over spatial scales of tens of meters to a few kilometers. Understanding these patterns depends upon processes that operate at faster and smaller scales; the implications of these processes may be manifest at broader and slower scales (Allen and Starr 1982, Urban et al. 1987).

Translation between spatial scales can be illustrated with a specific example from the shortgrass steppe. Both blue grama (*Bouteloua gracilis*) and buffalo grass (*Buchloe dactyloides*) tolerate heavy grazing and drought conditions (Gould 1977). Blue grama may be the more drought-tolerant (Albertson and Tomanek 1965), but buffalo grass may increase relative to blue grama under conditions of continuous heavy grazing (Savage and Jacobson 1935) and may have higher photosynthetic rates at lower temperatures (Monson et al. 1983). Both are C_4 species that grow well under warm conditions and have approximately the same phenology (Dickinson and Dodd 1976).

Under conditions of light to moderate grazing intensity, one would expect buffalo grass to expand under climate conditions with increased drought. Future climate scenarios predicting increasing aridity would presumably anticipate a regional expansion of the importance of buffalo grass. If, however, such nonequilibrium climatic changes were associated with increasing grazing pressures, blue grama would have a competitive advantage and become more important across the landscape. Broad geographic changes in the relative importance of the dominant species may be caused by changes in burning, drought, and grazing regimes, and these changes will become a part of any scheme predicting the responses of grassland landscapes to changes in the global environment.

Similar analyses can be extended to other comparisons. For example, blue grama and western wheatgrass (*Agropyron smithii*) occur together in the shortgrass steppe landscape. Different photosynthetic pathways in these two species allow a partitioning of resources and account for the relationships observed in the field. Western wheatgrass is a C_3 species, whereas blue grama is a C_4 species which grows under warmer (Kemp and Williams 1980) and more variable soil moisture conditions (Sala et al. 1982). Under warmer climatic conditions, blue grama would be expected to expand, but under a cooler climate western wheatgrass would benefit.

The soil water status varies over the landscape and is influenced not only by the prevailing climate but also by grazing pressure, burning regime, topography, soil, and vegetation (Sala et al. 1981). Several studies have been designed to relate these soil water conditions to the productivity and survival of C_3 and C_4 species (Brown and Trlica 1977, Kemp and Williams 1980, Power 1980, Smoliak and Dormaar 1985). In the 1930s, large areas of the Great Plains were seeded with crested wheatgrass (*A. cristatum*), and these areas have persisted without being invaded by native grassland species, such as blue grama, buffalo grass, and western wheatgrass. In general, the introduced crested wheatgrass has a high aboveground rate of primary production, allocating a lesser proportion of carbon (C) to the belowground parts of the system. In theory, this practice would make the crested wheatgrass more vulnerable to periodic droughts, so one would expect broad landscape-level changes in response to severe or prolonged droughts. That crested wheatgrass has persisted under periodic dry periods to date may be due to earlier growth of the C_3 species when more moisture is likely to be available (Kemp and Williams 1980), or to the fact that the native grassland is more likely to deplete the water in shallow soil horizons than is crested wheatgrass. With more pervasive and extended changes in drought conditions, the native species may eventually invade landscapes now composed of crested wheatgrass, or the introduced species may prove to be more adaptable.

These examples of species are based on the shortgrass steppe, but similar ones could be raised for the tallgrass prairie. Species characteristic of the shortgrass steppe, which occur in shallow soils in the tallgrass region, would be expected to expand their importance under drier conditions. Indeed, broad geographical changes in relative importance of these species have been observed under drought conditions (Albertson and Tomanek 1965, Weaver and Bruner 1954). The significant point is that processes at spatial scales of individual plants and their competitors translate into processes at the landscape level under changing climatic regimes. The potential rates of individual adaptation versus the rates of climate change are unknown. It is also interesting that to predict the landscape-level consequences of changes in global climate as discussed in the late 1980s, the most appropriate data sets are those collected 30 and 50 years earlier during the droughts on the Great Plains.

SPACE AND TIME SCALES OF PLANT AND SOIL PROCESSES

There are a number of straightforward and well-documented relationships between plant productivity and species composition, and soil moisture regimes (Risser et al. 1981). This discussion will acknowledge that literature and then focus on more recent ideas involving nutrients.

Swanson et al. (1988) considered the ways in which land forms affected patterns and processes from several different types of ecosystems. For example, in semi-arid grasslands, cattle preferentially graze the lowlands, which usually produce more and higher quality forage than the uplands (Schimel et al. 1986, Senft et al. 1985). Organic C, nitrogen (N), phosphorus (P), and soil depth increase down the slope (Schimel et al. 1985). Typically higher plant biomass production is caused in part by higher moisture availability and in part by accumulations of fine soil particles and organic matter as a result of surface and subsurface water flow from upslope.

This expected pattern of marked differences between uplands and lowlands, however, is altered in several ways. For example, grazing patterns of cattle may redistribute nutrients (Schwartz and Ellis 1981; Senft et al. 1985) and snow (Woodmansee and Adamsen 1983). Also, wind reworks the soil surface, depositing fine soil material across the landscape. On the shortgrass steppe in eastern Colorado, these processes tend to result in a relatively uniform soil horizon with similar water retention capabilities. As a consequence, the vegetation is spatially more uniform than might otherwise be expected (Swanson et al. 1988). Thus, at the landscape level, hydrological processes tend to exacerbate distinctions between topographic positions while aeolian, and to some degree biological, processes tend to minimize these differences. Thus, changes in global climate, particularly hydrological and aeolian, will alter these landscape-level ecological processes.

This discussion can be extended to another level of complexity by considering how the wind patterns affect soil moisture patterns in the sagebrush steppe by influencing the distribution of snow drifts. In addition to the direct effects on soil moisture and length of growing season, wind also affects the distribution of mycorrhizal spores. Vesicular-arbuscular mycorrhizae may influence the growth of plants in several ways (Allen and Allen 1984, 1986): improvement of competitive advantage of later successional species, reduction of leaf senescence, improved water relations, and increase of N uptake and leaf survival. In southwestern Wyoming, the interaction of wind, soil moisture, and mycorrhizal spores produced a complicated interaction affecting the species composition of the sagebrush steppe (Allen and Allen 1988, Warner et al. 1987). The presence of mycorrhizae provided a competitive advantage to the grasses, but the consequent reduction of forbs lowered the snow capture, leading to reduced soil moisture, which in turn was disadvantageous to both the grasses and forbs. On the lower slopes, however, more snow was deposited, which caused an increase in a pathogenic fungi (snow mold), parasitic on the mycorrhizal fungi. Topography, wind, snow, soil moisture, and mycorrhizal and parasitic fungi all interacted in the control of species composition across the heterogeneous landscape. Any monotonic changes in snowfall patterns would impact this system, with consequent changes of the ecological system.

Mycorrhizal relationships in the grasslands appear to be quite complex in both time and space scales (Hays et al. 1982, Miller et al. 1987). Hetrick and Bloom (1983) described colonization of prairie soils as erratic, with fluctuations from month to month and between sample areas, ranging from 12 to 50 percent. In a sand prairie in Illinois, Dhillion et al. (1988) found that fire significantly reduced colonization levels of vesicular-arbuscular mycorrhizae in little bluestem during the first growing season after burning, but not in subsequent years. Hays et al. (1982) demonstrated a reduction in tillering in mycorrhizal blue grama, but mycorrhizal western wheatgrass produced more tillers. Ebbers et al. (1987), studying prairie dropseed (*Sporobolus heterolepis*) and vesicular-arbuscular mycorrhizal spore abundance across a soil moisture–nutrient gradient, found that an ordination of 49 stands resulted in a Gaussian distribution of prairie dropseed, but spore abundance was dissimilar to dropseed distribution, decreasing from upper to lower slopes. Dickman et al. (1984) found the reverse for little bluestem and spore abundance—i.e., spore abundance increased from upper to lower slopes. It seems clear that mycorrhizal patterns of abundance and colonization are operating at many spatial and temporal scales, but meaningful patterns have not yet arisen, nor have these relationships been linked to burning or other landscape-level environmental conditions.

SPATIAL AND TEMPORAL SCALES BROADER THAN THE LANDSCAPE

Kebart and Anderson (1987) correctly note that much more attention has been devoted to the east-west gradient across the North American prairie than to the north-south gradient (but see Diamond and Smeins 1988). An exception was McMillan (1959), who examined phenotypical differentiation from the northern plains with a short growing season to the south with shorter photoperiods and a longer growing season. R. C. Anderson and Adams (1981) compared the number of species in flower in the southern portion of the tallgrass prairie (Oklahoma) with a more northern site in Wisconsin. In the south, there was a significant correlation between long-term monthly rainfall and the bimodal distribution of the number of species in flower. The authors concluded that this was a long-term adaptation for maximizing flowering during seasons with more plentiful rainfall. At the northern end of the gradient (Wisconsin), the number of plants in flower gradually increased during the months of the growing season. In a comparison of Oklahoma, Illinois, and Wisconsin sites, Kebart and Anderson (1987) found that in most species that occurred in all three sites, flowering occurred first in the most northern site and last in the southern location. Kebart and Anderson (1987), Dickinson and Dodd (1976), and Leopold and Jones (1947) all reported that precipitation following drought encouraged additional periods of flowering in some species. In the North American grasslands, there are east-west gradients dominated by rainfall, and north-south gradients influenced by temperature and photoperiod. But as indicated here, changes in global climate (e.g., drought) will alter the vegetation along these gradients and, in so doing, alter the landscape-level patterns.

Herbivores affect vegetation, but most previous investigations have been directed toward localized grazing strategies (Coppock et al. 1983, Dwyer 1961). In an attempt to broaden these considerations and apply optimal foraging theory to large herbivores, Senft et al. (1987) developed a spatial hierarchy of the following: (a) small patch or feeding station, (b) large patch or plant community/soil plant association, (c) landscape system, and (d) regional system. Foraging behavior involves different processes at each level—for example, diet selection at the level of plant communities, general feeding area selection for the landscape level, and processes such as migration and home range at the level of the regional system. Clearly, fire, a large-scale phenomenon, may alter landscape structure and, thus, the hierarchy of foraging behavior of large mammals.

These processes also have a time dimension. Plants that are not burned or grazed periodically during the growing season usually develop a coarse structure, which makes them less palatable and limits net primary production (McNaughton 1979). In the tallgrass and mixed-grass prairies, animals tend to graze and regraze the same areas (Ring et al. 1985), although this process may not be so important in the shortgrass steppe. The high intensity, short-rotation management strategy is based on this concept—namely, ensuring that all of the rangeland will be heavily grazed by high stocking rates means that there will be a relatively uniform and palatable plant canopy for future grazing. In this case, grazing strategy reduces landscape heterogeneity.

Various combinations of grazing intensity and climatic conditions result in changes in species composition. For example, under wet climate conditions and light grazing pressure, species typical of the tallgrass prairie become relatively more important in a mixed-grass and shortgrass steppe (Fig. 9.1,A). Also, invading species are more likely to penetrate the dry portions of the North American grassland continuum because there is a relaxation in the severity of the environment. Under light grazing pressure, mesic climatic conditions, and occasional burning (approximating

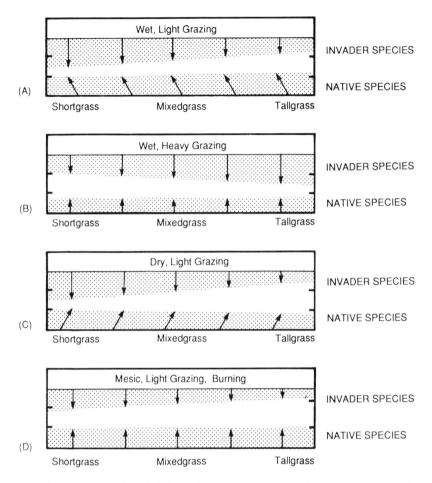

FIG. 9.1 Conceptual model of grassland responses to weather and grazing conditions. Arrows indicate geographic expansion of plant species; stippled area indicates change in the importance of native and invading plant species.

historic conditions), the species composition across the North American grasslands remains relatively unchanged (Fig. 9.1, D).

As described previously, climatic conditions of the shortgrass steppe are drier and more variable than those in the tallgrass prairie. Because of the greater biomass, and therefore fuel, tallgrass prairies are more likely to burn. However, because of the moister conditions, fires are less likely to adversely impact the plants. Today, grazing is equally likely to occur in all the grasslands of North America, but except under heavy grazing pres-

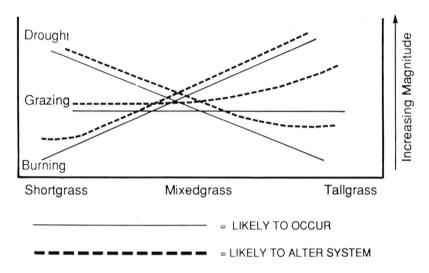

FIG. 9.2   Diagram of grassland responses to drought, grazing, and burning. Solid lines represent the likelihood of occurrences at these driving variables. Dashed lines indicate the relative rates of change in species composition associated with each of the 3 driving variables.

sure which results in major shifts in species composition, the tallgrass prairie is compositionally more sensitive to grazing than the shortgrass (Fig. 9.2). These relationships are useful for predicting how the grassland landscape will change under future combinations of climate, burning, and use.

As a final example of ecological processes operating at scales broader than the landscape, but with effects at the landscape level, it is useful to consider atmospheric constituents. Vegetation composition of grasslands may be influenced by atmospheric constituents, though the extent of this process is not well quantified. Toxicity, especially that caused by acidification via SO_2 pollution, has altered species composition and other characteristics of grassland vegetation (Heil et al. 1988, Lauenroth and Preston 1984). Susceptibility to acidification may be particularly acute on nutrient-poor sites. Thus, from a landscape perspective the spatial distribution of soil types may have a role in addition to the more conventionally defined edaphic characteristics. Nutrient-poor soil conditions not only may select for the species tolerant to low nutrients, but also may offer sites most likely to be affected by air pollutants.

Though changes in species composition due to differential susceptibility to acidification are more widely recognized, the opposite effect of eutrophication may also be important. In a study conducted not in the

TABLE 9.1 Ammonium captured (kg ha^{-1}) by undisturbed and mown grasslands in the Netherlands

Month	Undisturbed Grassland	Mown Grassland
June	0.02	0.04
July	0.15	0.21
August	0.47	0.36
September	0.32	0.20
Total	0.96	0.81

Source: Heil et al. 1988.

North American grasslands, but in the Netherlands, Heil et al. (1988) showed that NH_4 deposition in undisturbed grassland canopies during the summer was equal to that of forest canopies (Table 9.1). In those measurements, 4.7 kg per ha was captured and assimilated by the plants, and this amount is sufficient to change the competitive relations between plants grown under experimental conditions. Specifically, under nutrient-poor conditions, the competitive position of fast-growing species was improved over species with a slower growth rate. The importance of this phenomenon is that atmospheric pollutants can change the grassland species composition in two ways: by selective toxicity, and by providing an advantage to faster growing species. Early successional species which grow rapidly may experience a competitive advantage, thus prolonging early successional stages over the landscape.

FUTURE RESEARCH

Grassland research during the next decade will focus on spatial and temporal scales, identifying processes at all dimensions. There will be a greater recognition of small-scale variability and how this heterogeneity affects broader ecological processes. For example, Gibson (1986) used ion-exchange resins to measure nutrient availability along a 3.2 m transect during summer and autumn in a British dune grassland. There were significant differences among the nutrients between the seasons. The coefficient of variation along the transect averaged 45.7 percent to 66.9 percent with PO_4 (154.5 percent), NO_3 (145.5 percent), and Mn (100.0 percent) showing the greatest variability. Significant relationships were found among comparisons of nutrient availability, grazed and ungrazed treatments, microtopography, and density of tillers of dominant species. Thus, the wider patterns discussed above will be influenced by variation at these much smaller scales.

Understanding landscape-level ecological processes will involve studies at small scales. Major questions revolve around the rates of adaptation to changing climatic conditions, and whether these adaptations will occur as rapidly as the climate changes. Also, experimental approaches will be used to determine competitive interactions among grassland plants under burning and changing environments, especially changes in atmospheric constituents and in altered periodicities of drier and warmer conditions. At landscape scales, investigations will be enhanced by new technologies. The evolution of trace gases and other gases will be measured across the landscape and related to vegetation and soil conditions (Gosz et al. 1988). Similarly, geographic information systems, perhaps connected with remotely sensed data bases, will permit measurement of various parameters of grassland uplands, which will predict the biotic and abiotic components of riparian zones and drainage streams. These two approaches—process studies at small scales and observations at the landscape scale—will lead to an understanding of grassland landscapes that is necessary for predicting the status of North American grasslands in the next century.

10
Epilogue: A Search
for Paradigms

By Linda L. Wallace

As I write this, it is October 1988, and I have spent the past five months in Yellowstone National Park, Wyoming. This was the summer when Yellowstone burned. Fire behaviors were witnessed this year that had never been seen by fire modelers, fire managers, or fire fighters. Among the many scientists and other experts who viewed this once-in-centuries phenomenon, one thought emerged clearly: We do not understand fire very well at all. By compiling this book, we hoped to bring together process-level studies focusing on another fire-dependent ecosystem, the North American tallgrass prairie. Although tremendous inroads have been made in fire research, I wish to emphasize the lesson we learned in Yellowstone: we have much to learn.

With the passage of time, we have seen attitudes change concerning the role of fire in grasslands. Although fires can be devastating to personal property, they are no longer considered detrimental to many ecological systems. Fire is now used as an important management tool and is considered to be a natural and frequent component of the disturbance regime of prairie ecosystems (see chapter 2).

Given this important change in viewpoint, research has begun on the effects of fire on various ecological processes in grasslands. Perhaps the most basic areas, the physiological responses of the producers themselves, is the most poorly studied (see chapter 3). For example, the physiological responses of *Andropogon gerardii* (big bluestem) are fairly well understood. However, little is known about the physiological or morphological responses of other tallgrass prairie dominants. Indeed, little is known about the physiological responses of any other prairie plant to fire. This is a startling gap in our knowledge. This lack of information generates gaps of understanding at other ecological levels as well. Successional processes following fires do not follow classical Clementsian succession (see Chapter 6). Why is that? Knapp (1985) tells us that the physiological responses of both *A. gerardii* and *Panicum virgatum* lead us to believe that the processes that Odum (1969) ascribes to succession are present without species shifts. Is this entirely true? Important shifts in species growth and dominance may be the result of the subtle and indirect effects that fire has on plant physiology and growth.

The importance of the indirect effects of fire on prairie plants may be one of the paradigms that we draw from grassland fires. We see that litter accumulation in unburned grasslands acts to shade and cool plants and soils. Thus both plants and soil organisms are constrained in their activities. The removal of this litter accumulation results in qualitative and quantitative changes in the energy regime at the soil level. In addition to affecting plant growth, litter loss will influence the activities of soil organisms, small mammals, ground-nesting birds, and invertebrate assemblages (see chapters 5 and 7). The importance of the removal of the litter layer is not a new concept (Knapp and Seastedt 1986) but is sufficiently critical to deserve repeating here.

Logically, one would expect that if plant physiology and growth form are affected by fires, then there should also be an effect on plant population dynamics. Population growth will be influenced in two ways, through sexual and asexual reproduction. Asexual reproduction will be enhanced by increased tillering after a fire. This will occur in concert with other morphological changes, including changes in leaf production, leaf display, tiller density, and so forth. It is here that we see some differences of opinion (see chapters 3 and 4). These differences may occur primarily because of small data bases. This issue deserves much closer scrutiny, since tillering may be crucially important in the response of matrix-forming species following fire (see chapter 6).

Fire influences on plant sexual reproduction are as varied as the plant species studied. However, most impacts appear to occur through changes in the number of inflorescences and timing of flower production, rather than through seed set per inflorescence (see chapter 4). How long following a fire will these influences last? Does fire represent an important opportunity for new genotypic establishment in the grassland? What are the effects of fire on pollination vectors or on agents of diaspore dispersal?

Part of the answer to this latter question comes from the extensive work that has been done on small mammal assemblages (see chapter 5). However, the studies that have been conducted are difficult to compare due to methodological inconsistencies. In addition, differences in spatial scales of various studies can yield conflicting results. This yields what may be another important paradigm of fire research: Scaling, an important consideration in all ecological studies, is particularly important when considering fire. At some scales, fire may appear to be stochastic, even chaotic. At other scales, fire may be considered to be a coarse-grained environmental signal, overriding many other fine-grained signals, such as grazing (see chapter 6).

As with the effects of fire on plants, the effects of fire on small mammal assemblages occur primarily through indirect actions. The assemblages of fire-positive, fire-negative, and fire-neutral species are responding primarily to the presence or absence of litter cover. Species dependent on deep litter cover for foraging, nesting, and so forth are fire-negative, with fire-positive species requiring more open habitat. All species are more subject to predation, particularly by raptors, following litter removal.

Ecosystem-level processes integrate these lower levels of hierarchical organization. Nutrient flows will be influenced by the removal of litter and other interceptive surfaces (see chapter 7). The loss of these shading structures will also increase soil temperatures and will result in a temporary increase in the availability of soil water (see chapter 3). This will increase mineralization. However, this effect is temporary, due to the rapid regrowth of aboveground structures and the concomitant increase in evapotranspiration. Therefore, on a long-term basis, what will be the net effect of repeated fires? Soil organic matter can become depleted, and soil nitrogen (N) levels could become reduced as well. Studies by Bragg (1982) tell us that the prairie could burn at any time of the year and could burn in two successive years. Would annual burning be a common phenomenon? It is at this level that fire may take on a more stochastic appearance. The occurrence of lightning strikes, the actions of aboriginal peoples, and subsequent activities of European settlers could have had important consequences for fire behavior. In addition, grazing ungulates are attracted to areas that have been recently burned. Grazers are currently used as part of the range manager's arsenal against grassland fires, since they reduce the production of fine fuels. One of the areas of greatest importance for future research, therefore, is the interaction between fire and grazing and how it influences all levels of ecological response. It is possible that, by their actions in reducing leaf area index, grazers could prolong the period of time when soil temperatures are increased and therefore increase mineralization. This, coupled with direct grazer impacts on nutrient cycling via urine and dung deposition, may be one of the more important ecosystem-level expressions of the ungulate/fire interaction in grassland ecosystems.

The scales of different components of the disturbance regime in grasslands (see chapter 6) will yield different degrees of landscape patchiness (see chapter 9). This is one of the newer areas of ecological study and is thus subject to the highest degree of speculative thought. Fires that move quickly across the landscape tend to burn more patchily. Areas will remain unburned as winds push flames past otherwise flammable vegetation. What role do these unburned patches play? First, they could operate as important refugia for species that would be otherwise negatively affected by fire (see chapter 5). In addition, they may reduce nutrient loss from the system, acting to trap fluvial flows and blowing ash. Will both of these phenomena increase with increased patchiness? For small organisms, this may be the case. However, larger organisms will find very small refugia unusable. Nutrient "trapping" may be increased, however, by increased patchiness of fire. Thus, not only will fast fires have direct effects on nutrient levels in the ecosystem since they burn less thoroughly, but also they may result in a decreased fluvial loss of nutrients to the system.

Large-scale patches also have influences on ungulate behavior. It is at this level—due to the putative effects of ungulates on prolonging periods of increased soil mineralization and due to the known effects of ungulate waste production on rates of nutrient cycling—that we see a different effect of scale. Small-scale patches would be unattractive to large ungulates, which need larger foraging sites to maintain bulk flow of forages. Although forage quality is typically improved by fires, forage quantity is reduced for a short time. Therefore, ungulates are more likely to be attracted by large-scale fires. These large-scale burns result from slower moving fire fronts and would also be expected to experience greater nutrient losses by fluvial processes. Do ungulates act to counter this potential nutrient loss? For too long now, the ecosystem- and landscape-level influences of grazing ungulates have been ignored in grasslands. These ecosystems evolved in the presence of a rich, diverse herbivore fauna. Their removal by Europeans and subsequent replacement by domestic herbivores have dramatically influenced ecosystem behavior. We must include their influences in future studies on grassland fire if we are to understand how this system operates at all hierarchical levels.

Many exciting questions are being addressed by ecologists studying fire, but several problems remain. The first of these is partly methodological and partly conceptual. The extreme heterogeneity of fires in terms of patch size, severity, time of year, and so forth make "fire" impossible to replicate. Consequently, the statistical problems described by Glenn-Lewin et al. in chapter 4 are difficult to surmount.

In addition, some standardization of data collection must occur so that results between studies can be more readily compared. Timing of fire must be reported precisely (e.g., 11 July 1988) rather than merely stating that the fire was a summer burn. In addition, weather conditions before and after the fire need to be noted and reported. Fire frequency must be known as well and reported as precisely as possible. Fire intensity will vary with time since the last fire due to differences in fuel load. Fuel loadings themselves will be influenced by abiotic factors, such as snow compression of litter, and by biotic factors, such as ungulate grazing. Intensity will also depend on weather conditions, including wind direction, speed, and so forth. Some attempt at determining fire temperature across the burned area would yield a quantifiable measure of intensity. As new technologies become available (see chapters 7 and 9), our abilities to understand fire at several scales will increase.

In summary, what are the emerging paradigms concerning fire in grasslands? In a system that has evolved in the presence of grazing, drought, and fire (see chapter 2), it should not be surprising that fire effects are primarily *indirect*, as opposed to the direct effects that we are familiar with in forest fires. However, as in all ecological studies, these effects are highly scale-dependent. It is on this front that some of the most exciting research in fire ecology is yet to come.

Literature Cited

Abrams, M. D. 1986. Historical development of gallery forests in northeast Kansas. *Vegetatio* 65: 29–37.

———. 1988. Effects of burning regime on viable seed pools and canopy coverage in a northeast Kansas tallgrass prairie. *Southw. Nat.* 33: 65–70.

Abrams, M. D., and L. C. Hulbert. 1987. Effect of topographic position and fire on species composition in tallgrass prairie in northeast Kansas. *Amer. Midl. Nat.* 117: 442–45.

Abrams, M. D., A. K. Knapp, and L. C. Hulbert. 1986. A ten-year record of aboveground biomass in a Kansas tallgrass prairie: Effects of fire and topographic position. *Amer. J. Bot.* 73: 1509–15.

Adams, D. E., and R. C. Anderson. 1980. Species response to a moisture gradient in central Illinois. *Amer. J. Bot.* 67: 381–92.

Adams, D. E., R. C. Anderson, and S. L. Collins. 1982. Differential response of woody and herbaceous species to summer and winter burning in an Oklahoma grassland. *Southw. Nat.* 27: 55–61.

Adams, D. E., and L. L. Wallace. 1985. Nutrient and biomass allocation in five grass species in an Oklahoma tallgrass prairie. *Amer. Midl. Nat.* 113: 170–81.

Aikman, J. M. 1985. Burning in the management of prairies in Iowa. *Proc. Iowa Acad. Sci.* 62: 53–62.

Albertson, F. W., and G. W. Tomanek. 1965. Vegetation changes during a 30-year period in grassland communities near Hays, Kansas. *Ecology* 46: 714–20.

Aldous, A. E. 1934. *Effects of burning on Kansas bluestem pasture.* Kansas State Agric. Exp. Sta. Tech. Bull. 38. Manhattan, Ks.

Alexander, M. 1977. *Introduction to soil microbiology.* New York: John Wiley and Sons.

Allen, E. B., and M. F. Allen. 1984. Competition between plants of different successional stages: Mycorrhizae as regulators. *Can. J. Bot.* 2625–29.

———. 1986. Water relations of xeric grasses in the field: Interactions of mycorrhizae and competition. *New Phytol.* 104: 559–71.

———. 1988. Facilitation of succession by the nonmycotrophic colonizer *Salsola kali* (Chenopodiaceae) on a harsh site: Effects of mycorrhizal fungi. *Amer. J. Bot.* 75: 257–66.

Allen, T. F. H., and T. B. Starr. 1982. *Hierarchy: Perspectives for ecological complexity.* Chicago: University of Chicago Press.

Allen, T. F. H., and E. P. Wyleto. 1983. A hierarchical model for the complexity of plant communities. *J. Theoret. Biol.* 101: 529–40.

Andersen, D. C. 1987. Below-ground herbivory in natural communities: A review emphasizing fossorial animals. *Quart. Rev. Biol.* 62: 261–86.

Anderson, H. G., and A. W. Bailey. 1980. Effects of annual burning on grassland in the aspen parkland of east-central Alberta. *Can. J. Bot.* 58: 985–96.

Anderson, J. M., P. Ineson, and S. A. Huish. 1983. Nitrogen and cation release by macrofauna feeding on leaf litter and soil organic matter from deciduous woodlands. *Soil Biol. Biochem.* 15: 463–67.

Anderson, K. L. 1964. Burning Flint Hills bluestem ranges. *Proc. Tall Timbers Fire Ecol. Conf.* 3: 89–103.

———. 1965. Time of burning as it affects soil moisture in an ordinary upland bluestem prairie in the Flint Hills. *J. Range Manage.* 18: 311–16.

Anderson, K. L., E. F. Smith, and C. E. Owensby. 1970. Burning bluestem range. *J. Range Manage.* 23: 81–92.

Anderson, R. C. 1972a. The use of fire as a management tool on the Curtis Prairie. *Proc. Tall Timbers Fire Ecol. Conf.* 12: 23–35.

———. 1972b. Prairie history, management and restoration in southern Illinois. Pp. 15–22 *in:* J. Zimmerman, ed. Proc. Second Midwest Prairie Conference, Madison, Wi.

———. 1982. An evolutionary model summarizing the roles of fire, climate and grazing animals in the origin and maintenance of grasslands: An end paper. In *Grasses and grasslands: systematics and ecology,* ed. J. R. Estes, R. J. Tyrl, and J. N. Brunken, 297–308. Norman, Okla.: University of Oklahoma Press.

———. 1983. The eastern prairie–forest transition—An overview. In *Proc. Eighth North American Prairie Conference,* ed. R. Brewer, 86–92. Kalamazoo, Mich.: Western Michigan University.

Anderson, R. C., and D. E. Adams. 1978. Species replacement patterns in central Illinois white oak forests. In *Proc. Central Hardwood Forest Conference II,* P. Pope, ed., 284–301. West Lafayette, Ind.: Purdue University.

———. 1981. Flowering patterns and production on a central Oklahoma grassland. In *Proc. Fifth North American Prairie Conference,* ed. R. Stuckey and K. Rees, 232–35. Ohio Biological Survey Publ. 15. Columbus, Oh.

Anderson, R. C., and M. Anderson. 1975. The presettlement vegetation of Williamson County, Illinois. *Castanea* 40: 345–63.

Anderson, R. C., and L. E. Brown. 1983. Comparative effects of fire on trees in midwestern savannah and adjacent forest. *Bull. Torrey Bot. Club* 110: 87–90.

———. 1986. Stability and instability in plant communities following fire. *Amer. J. Bot.* 73: 364–68.

Anderson, R. C., and C. V. Van Valkenberg. 1977. Response of a southern Illinois grassland community to burning. *Trans. Illinois Acad. Sci.* 69: 399–414.

Antos, J. A., B. McCune, and C. Bara. 1983. The effect of fire on an ungrazed western Montana grassland. *Amer. Midl. Nat.* 110: 354–64.

Archer, S. R., C. Scifres, C. R. Bassham, and R. Maggio. 1988. Autogenic succession in a subtropical savanna: Conversion of grassland to thorn woodland. *Ecol. Monogr.* 58: 111–27.

Archer, S. R., and L. L. Tieszen. 1986. Plant response to defoliation: Hierarchical considerations. Pp. 45–59. In *Grazing research at northern latitudes,* ed. O. Gudmundsson, 45–59. New York: Plenum.

Axelrod, D. I. 1985. Rise of the grassland biome, central North America. *Bot. Rev.* 51: 163–202.

Barnes, P. W., L. L. Tieszen, and D. J. Ode. 1983. Distribution, production and diversity of C_3 and C_4 dominated communities in a mixed prairie. *Can. J. Bot.* 61: 741–51.

Bazzaz, F. A., and J. A. D. Parrish. 1982. Organization of grassland communities. In *Grasses and grasslands: Systematics and ecology,* ed. J. R. Estes, R. J. Tyrl, and J. N. Brunken, 233–54. Norman, Okla.: University of Oklahoma Press.

Beck, A. M., and R. J. Vogl. 1972. The effects of spring burning on rodent populations in a brush prairie savanna. *J. Mammal.* 53: 336–46.

Belsky, A. J. 1986. Revegetation of artificial disturbances in grasslands of the Serengeti National Park, Tanzania. *J. Ecol.* 74: 937–52.

Biederbeck, V. O., C. A. Campbell, K. E. Bowren, M. Schnitzer, and R. N. McIver. 1980. Effect of burning cereal straw on soil properties and grain yields in Saskatchewan. *Soil Sci. Soc. Am. J.* 44: 103–11.

Blake, A. K. 1935. Viability and germination of seeds and early life history of prairie plants. *Ecol. Monogr.* 5: 405–60.

Blankespoor, G. W. 1987. The effects of prescribed burning on a tall-grass prairie remnant in eastern South Dakota. *Prairie Nat.* 19: 177–88.

Bock, C. E., and J. H. Bock. 1978. Response of birds, small mammals and vegetation to burning sacaton grasslands in southeastern Arizona. *J. Range Manage.* 31: 296–300.

———. 1983. Responses of birds and deer mice to prescribed burning in ponderosa pine. *J. Wildlife Manage.* 47: 836–40.

Bock, J. H., C. E. Bock, and J. R. McKnight. 1976. The study of the effects of grassland fires at the Research Ranch in southeastern Arizona. *Arizona Acad. Sci.* 11: 49–57.

Borchert, J. R. 1950. The climate of the central North American grassland. *Ann. Assoc. Amer. Geog.* 40: 1–39.

Bragg, T. B. 1982. Seasonal variations in fuel and fuel consumption by fires in a bluestem prairie. *Ecology* 63: 7–11.

Bragg, T. B., and L. C. Hulbert. 1976. Woody plant invasion of unburned Kansas bluestem prairie. *J. Range Manage.* 29: 19–23.

Britton, W., and A. Messenger. 1969. Computed soil moisture patterns in and around the prairie peninsula during the great drought of 1933–34. *Trans. Illinois Acad. Sci.* 62: 181–87.

Brown, D. A., and P. J. Gersmehl. 1985. Migration models for grasses in the American midcontinent. *Ann. Assoc. Amer. Geog.* 75: 383–94.

Brown, L. F., and M. J. Trlica. 1977. Interacting effects of soil water, temperature and irradiance on CO_2 exchange of two dominant grasses of the shortgrass steppe. *J. Appl. Ecol.* 14: 197–204.

Cable, D. 1967. Fire effects on semidesert grasses and shrubs. *J. Range Manage.* 20: 170–76.

Callahan, J. M., and C. L. Kucera. 1981. Magnesium flux and storage relationships in Missouri tallgrass prairie. *Amer. Midl. Nat.* 106: 345–51.

Clark, B. K. 1989. Influence of plant litter and habitat structure on small animal assemblages: experimental manipulations and field observations. Ph.D. diss., Kansas State University, Manhattan.

Clark, B. K., D. W. Kaufman, G. A. Kaufman, and E. J. Finck. 1987. Use of tallgrass prairie by *Peromyscus leucopus. J. Mammal.* 68: 158–60.

Clark, O. R. 1940. Interception of rainfall by prairie grasses, weeds, and certain crop plants. *Ecol. Monogr.* 10: 243–77.

Clements, F. E. 1936. Nature and structure of the climax. *J. Ecol.* 24: 552–84.

Clements, F. E., and J. E. Weaver. 1924. *Experimental vegetation.* Carnegie Inst. Washington, Publ. 355. Washington, D.C.

Collins, S. L. 1987. Interaction of disturbances in tallgrass prairie: A field experiment. *Ecology* 68: 1243–50.

————. 1989. Experimental analysis of patch dynamics and community heterogeneity in tallgrass prairie. *Vegetatio* 85: 57–66.

Collins, S. L., and D. E. Adams. 1983. Succession in grasslands: Thirty-two years of change in a central Oklahoma tallgrass prairie. *Vegetatio* 51: 181–90.

Collins, S. L., and S. C. Barber. 1985. Effects of disturbance on diversity in mixed-grass prairie. *Vegetatio* 64: 87–94.

Collins, S. L., and S. M. Glenn. 1988. Disturbance and community structure in North American prairies. In *Diversity and pattern in plant communities*, ed. H. J. During, M. J. A. Werger, and J. H. Willems, 131–43. The Hague: SPB Academic Publ.

Collins, S. L., and G. E. Uno. 1983. The effect of early spring burning on vegetation in buffalo wallows. *Bull. Torrey Bot. Club* 110: 474–81.

Conant, S., and P. G. Risser. 1974. Canopy structure of a tallgrass prairie. *J. Range Manage.* 27: 313–18.

Connell, J. H. 1978. Diversity in tropical rain forests and coral reefs. *Science* 199: 1302–10.

Cook, S. F., Jr. 1959. The effects of fire on a population of small rodents. *Ecology* 40: 102–8.

Coppock, D. L., J. K. Detling, J. E. Ellis, and M. I. Dyer. 1983. Plant-herbivore interactions in a North American mixed-grass prairie. I. Effects of black-tailed prairie dogs on intraseasonal above-ground plant biomass and nutrient dynamics and plant species diversity. *Oecologia* 56: 1–9.

Cottam, G. 1949. The photosociology of an oak woods in southwestern Wisconsin. *Ecology* 30: 271–87.

Cottam, G., and H. C. Wilson. 1966. Community dynamics on an artificial prairie. *Ecology* 47 88–96.

Coupland, R. T. 1950. Ecology of mixed prairie in Canada. *Ecol. Monogr.* 20: 271–315.

Curtis, J. T. 1959. *The vegetation of Wisconsin.* Madison, Wis.: University of Wisconsin Press.

Curtis, J. T., and M. L. Partch. 1948. Effect of fire on the competition between blue grass and certain prairie plants. *Amer. Midl. Nat.* 39: 437–43.

————. 1950. Some factors affecting flower production in *Andropogon gerardii. Ecology* 31: 488–89.

Dahl, B. E., and D. N. Hyder. 1977. Developmental morphology and management implications. In *Rangeland plant physiology*, ed. R. E. Sosebee, 258–90. Range Sci. Ser. No. 4. Denver, Colo.: Soc. Range Manage.

Dahlman, R. C., and C. L. Kucera. 1965. Root productivity and turnover in native prairie. *Ecology* 46: 84–89.

Daubenmire, R. 1959. A canopy coverage method of vegetational analysis. *Northw. Sci.* 33: 43–64.

————. 1968. The ecology of fire in grasslands. *Adv. Ecol. Res.* 5: 209–66.

Davis, M. A., K. L. Lemon, and A. M. Dybvig. 1987. The effect of burning and insect herbivory on seed production of two prairie forbs. *Prairie Nat.* 19: 93–100.

Davis, M. B. 1976. Pleistocene biogeography of temperate deciduous forests. *Geoscience and Man* 13: 13–26.

Delcourt, P., and H. A. Delcourt. 1981. Vegetation maps for eastern North America: 40,000 BP to the present. In *Geobotany II*, ed. R. Romans, 123–65. New York: Plenum.

Deregibus, V. A., R. A. Sanchez, J. J. Casal, and M. J. Trlica. 1985. Tillering responses to enrichment of red light beneath the canopy in a humid natural grassland. *J. Appl. Ecol.* 22: 199–206.

Detling, J. K., and E. L. Painter. 1983. Defoliation responses of western wheatgrass populations with diverse histories of prairie dog grazing. *Oecologia* 57: 65–71.

de Van Booysen, P., and N. M. Tainton, eds. 1984. *Ecological effects of fire in South African ecosystems.* New York: Springer-Verlag.

De Wet, J. M. 1981. Grasses and the cultural history of man. *Ann. Mo. Bot. Gard.* 68: 87–104.

Dhillion, S. S., R. C. Anderson, and A. E. Liberta. 1988. Effect of fire on the mycorrhizal ecology of little bluestem (*Schizachyrium scoparium*). *Can. J. Bot.* 66: 706–13.

Diamond, D. D., and F. E. Smeins. 1988. Gradient analysis of remnant true and upper coastal prairie grasslands of North America. *Can. J. Bot.* 66: 2152–2161.

Dickinson, C. E., and J. L. Dodd. 1976. Phenological pattern in the shortgrass prairie. *Amer. Midl. Nat.* 96: 367–78.

Dickman, L. A., A. E. Liberta, and R. C. Anderson. 1984. Ecological interactions of little bluestem and vesicular-arbuscular mycorrhizal fungi. *Can. J. Bot.* 62: 2272–77.

Dix, R. L. 1960. The effects of burning on the mulch structure and species composition of grasslands in western North Dakota. *Ecology* 41: 49–56.

Dix, R. L., and J. E. Butler. 1954. The effects of fire on a dry, thin soil prairie in Wisconsin. *J. Range Manage.* 7: 265–68.

Dokken, D. A., and L. C. Hulbert. 1978. Effect of standing dead plants on stem density in bluestem prairie. In *Proc. Fifth Midwest Prairie Conference*, ed. D. C. Glenn-Lewin and R. Q. Landers, 78–81. Ames, Iowa: Iowa State University Press.

Dwyer, D. D. 1961. *Activities and grazing preferences of cows with calves in northern Osage County, Oklahoma.* Oklahoma Agric. Expt. Sta. Bull. B-588-61. Stillwater, Okla.: Oklahoma State University.

Dyer, M. I., J. K. Detling, D. C. Coleman, and D. W. Hilbert. 1982. The role of herbivores in grasslands. In *Grasses and grasslands: Systematics and ecology*, ed. J. R. Estes, R. J. Tyrl and J. N. Brunken, 255–95. Norman, Okla.: University of Oklahoma Press.

Ebbers, B. C., R. C. Anderson, and A. E. Liberta. 1987. Aspects of the mycorrhizal ecology of prairie dropseed, *Sporobolus heterolepis* (Poaceae). *Amer. J. Bot.* 74: 564–73.

Ehrenreich, J. H. 1959. Effect of burning and clipping on growth of native prairie in Iowa. *J. Range Manage.* 12: 133–37.

Ehrenreich, J. H., and J. M. Aikman. 1957. Effect of burning on seedstalk production of native prairie grasses. *Proc. Iowa Acad. Sci.* 64: 205–12.

———. 1963. An ecological study of the effect of certain management practices on native prairie in Iowa. *Ecol. Monogr.* 33: 113–30.

Eisele, K. A. 1985. Effects of fire and N and P availability ratio on dinitrogen fixation in the tallgrass prairie. M.S. thesis, Colorado State University, Ft. Collins, Colo.

Eisele, K., D. S. Schimel, L. A. Kapuska, and W. J. Parton. 1989. Fire-simulated N₂ fixation as a result of altered P:N ratios. *Oecologia:* in press.

Ellis, J. E., and M. Travis. 1975. Comparative aspects of foraging behavior of pronghorn antelope and cattle. *J. Appl. Ecol.* 12: 411–20.

England, R. E., and A. DeVos. 1969. Influence of animals on pristine conditions on the Canadian grasslands. *J. Range Manage.* 22: 87–94.

Engle, D. M., and P. M. Bultsma. 1984. Burning of northern mixed prairie during drought. *J. Range Manage.* 37: 398–401.

Erwin, W. J., and R. H. Stasiak. 1979. Vertebrate mortality during the burning of a reestablished prairie in Nebraska. *Amer. Midl. Nat.* 101: 247–49.

Ewing, A. L., and D. M. Engle. 1988. Effects of late summer fire on tallgrass prairie microclimate and community composition. *Amer. Midl. Nat.* 120: 212–23.

Finck, E. J., D. W. Kaufman, G. A. Kaufman, S. K. Gurtz, B. K. Clark, L. J. McLellan, and B. S. Clark. 1986. Mammals of the Konza Prairie Research Natural Area, Kansas. *Prairie Nat.* 18: 153–66.

Forman, R. T. T., and M. Godron. 1986. *Landscape ecology.* New York: John Wiley and Sons.

Fowler, N. L. 1984. Patchiness in patterns of growth and survival of two grasses. *Oecologia* 62: 424–28.

Gartner, F. R., and E. M. White. 1986. Fire in the northern Great Plains and its use in management. In *Proc. Prescribed Fire and Smoke Management Symposium,* 13–21. Denver, Colo.: Soc. Range Manage.

Geluso, K. N., G. D. Scroder, and T. B. Bragg. 1986. Fire-avoidance behavior of meadow voles (*Microtus pennsylvanicus*). *Amer. Midl. Nat.* 116: 202–5.

Gibson, D. J. 1986. Spatial and temporal heterogeneity in soil nutrient supply using *in situ* ion-exchange resin bags. *Plant and Soil* 96: 445–50.

———. 1988. Regeneration and fluctuation in tallgrass prairie vegetation in response to burning frequency. *Bull. Torrey Bot. Club* 115: 1–12.

———. 1989. Effects of animal disturbance on tallgrass prairie vegetation. *Amer. Midl. Nat.* 121: 144–54.

Gibson, D. J., and P. Greig-Smith. 1986. Community pattern analysis: A method for quantifying community mosaic structure. *Vegetatio* 66: 41–47.

Gibson, D. J., and B. A. Hetrick. 1988. Topographic and fire effects on the composition and abundance of VA-mycorrhizal fungi in tallgrass prairie. *Mycologia* 80: 433–41.

Gibson, D. J., and L. C. Hulbert. 1987. Effects of fire, topography and year-to-year climatic variation on species composition in tallgrass prairie. *Vegetatio* 72: 175–85.

Gilliam, F. S. 1987. The chemistry of wet deposition for a tallgrass prairie ecosystem: Inputs and interactions with plant canopies. *Biogeochemistry* 4: 203–18.

Gilliam, F. S., T. R. Seastedt, and A. K. Knapp. 1987. Canopy rainfall interception and throughfall in burned and unburned tallgrass prairie. *Southw. Nat.* 32: 267–71.

Gleason, H. A. 1913. The relation of forest distribution and prairie fires in the Middlewest. *Torreya* 13: 173–81.

———. 1922. Vegetational history of the Middlewest. *Ann. Assoc. Amer. Geog.* 12: 39–86.

Goldberg, D. H., and P. A. Werner. 1983. The effect of size of opening in vegetation and litter cover on seedling establishment of goldenrods (*Solidago* spp.). *Oecologia* 60: 149–55.

Golley, P. M., and F. B. Golley, eds. 1972. *Papers from a symposium on tropical ecology with an emphasis on organic productivity.* Athens, Ga.: Inst. Ecology, University of Georgia.

Gosz, J. R., C. N. Dahm, and P. G. Risser. 1988. Long-path FTIR measurement of atmospheric trace gas concentrations. *Ecology* 69: 1326–30.

Gould, F. W. 1977. *Grasses of the southwestern United States.* Tuscon: University of Arizona Press.

Grimm, E. 1984. Fire and other factors controlling the Big Woods vegetation of Minnesota in the mid-nineteenth century. *Ecol. Monogr.* 54: 291–311.

Hadley, E. B., and B. J. Kieckhefer. 1963. Productivity of two prairie grasses in relation to fire frequency. *Ecology* 44: 389–95.

Hanks, R. J., and K. L. Anderson. 1957. Pasture burning and moisture conservation. *J. Soil Water Conserv.* 12: 228–29.

Hansmire, J. A., D. L. Drawe, D. B. Wester, and C. M. Britton. 1988. Effect of winter burns on forbs and grasses of the Texas coastal prairie. *Southw. Nat.* 33: 333–38.

Hayes, D. C. 1985. Seasonal nitrogen translocation in big bluestem during drought conditions. *J. Range Manage.* 38: 406–10.

———. 1986. Seasonal root biomass and nitrogen dynamics of big bluestem (*Andropogon gerardii* Vitman) under wet and dry conditions. Ph.D. dissertation, Kansas State University, Manhattan, Kan.

Hayes, D. C., and T. R. Seastedt. 1987. Root dynamics of tallgrass prairie in wet and dry years. *Can. J. Bot.* 65: 787–91.

———. 1989. Nitrogen dynamics of soil water in burned and unburned tallgrass prairie. *Soil Biol. Biochem.* 21: in press.

Hays, R., C. P. P. Reid, T. V. St. John, and D. C. Coleman. 1982. Effects of nitrogen and phosphorus on blue grama growth and mycorrhizal infection. *Oecologia* 54: 260–65.

Heil, G. W., M. J. A. Werger, W. de Mol, D. van Dam, and B. Heijne. 1988. Capture of atmospheric ammonium by grassland canopies. *Science* 239: 764–65.

Heitlinger, M. E. 1975. Burning a protected tallgrass prairie to suppress sweet clover, *Melilotus alba* Desc. In *Prairie: A multiple view*, ed. M. K. Wali, 123–31. Grand Forks, N.D.: University of North Dakota Press.

Henderson, R. A., D. L. Lovell, and E. A. Howell. 1983. The flowering responses of 7 grasses to seasonal timing of prescribed burns in remnant Wisconsin prairie. In *Proc. Eighth North American Prairie Conference*, ed. R. Brewer, 7–10. Kalamazoo, Mich.: Western Michigan Univ.

Hetrick, B. A., and J. Bloom. 1983. Vesicular-arbuscular mycorrhizal fungi associated with native tallgrass prairie and cultivated winter wheat. *Can. J. Bot.* 61: 2140–46.

Hill, G. R., and W. J. Platt. 1975. Some effects of fire upon a tallgrass prairie community in northwestern Iowa. In *Prairie: A multiple view*, ed. M. K. Wali, 101–14. Grand Forks, N.D.: University of North Dakota Press.

Hill, M. O. 1973. The intensity of spatial pattern in plant communities. *J. Ecol.* 61: 225–36.

Hill, M. O., and H. G. Gauch, Jr. 1980. Detrended correspondence analysis: An improved ordination technique. *Vegetatio* 42: 47–58.

Holdridge, L. R. 1967. *Life zone ecology.* San Jose, Costa Rica: Tropical Science Center.

Hopkins, H., F. W. Albertson, and A. Riegel. 1948. Some effects of burning upon a prairie in west-central Kansas. *Trans. Kansas Acad. Sci.* 51: 131–41.

Hulbert, L. C. 1969. Fire and litter effects in undisturbed bluestem prairie in Kansas. *Ecology* 50: 874–77.

———. 1973. Management of Konza Prairie to approximate pre-whiteman fire influences. In *Proc. Third Midwest Prairie Conference,* ed. L. C. Hulbert, 14–16. Manhattan, Kan.: Kansas State University.

———. 1978. Controlling experimental bluestem prairie fires. In *Proc. Fifth Midwest Prairie Conference,* ed. D. K. Glenn-Lewin and R. Q. Landers, 169–71. Ames, Iowa: Iowa State University.

———. 1985. History and use of Konza Prairie Research Natural Area. *The Prairie Scout* 5: 63–93.

———. 1986. Fire effects on tallgrass prairie. In *Proc. Ninth North American Prairie Conference,* ed. G. K. Clambey and R. H. Pemble, 138–42. Fargo, N.D.: Tri-College Press.

———. 1988. Causes of fire effects in tallgrass prairie. *Ecology* 69: 46–58.

Hulbert, L. C., and J. K. Wilson. 1980. Fire interval effects on flowering of grasses in Kansas bluestem prairie. In *Proc. Seventh North American Prairie Conference,* ed. C. L. Kucera, 255–57. Columbia, Mo.: University of Missouri.

Humphrey, L. D. 1984. Patterns and mechanisms of plant succession after fire on *Artemisia*-grass sites in southwestern Idaho. *Vegetatio* 57: 91–101.

Humphrey, R. R. 1949. Fire as a means of controlling velvet mesquite, burroweed and cholla on southern Arizona ranges. *J. Range Manage.* 2: 175–82.

———. 1958. The desert grassland. *Bot. Rev.* 14: 195–252.

Ingham, R. E., and J. K. Detling. 1986. Effects of defoliation and nematode consumption on growth and leaf gas exchange in *Bouteloua curtipendula. Oikos* 46: 23–28.

James, S. W. 1982. Effects of fire and soil type on earthworm populations in a tallgrass prairie. *Pedobiologia* 24: 37–40.

———. 1985. An unexpected effect of autumn burning on tallgrass prairie. *Amer. Midl. Nat.* 114: 400–403.

———. 1988. The post-fire environment and earthworm populations in tallgrass prairie. *Ecology* 69: 476–83.

Johnson, L. A. 1987. The effect of fires at different times of the year on vegetative and sexual reproduction of grasses, and on establishment of seedlings. M.S. thesis, Iowa State University, Ames.

Kaufman, D. W., S. K. Gurtz, and G. A. Kaufman. 1988. Movements of *Peromyscus maniculatus* in response to prairie fire. *Prairie Nat.* 20: 225–229.

Kaufman, D. W., G. A. Kaufman, and E. J. Finck. 1983. Effects of fire on rodents in tallgrass prairie of the Flint Hills region of eastern Kansas. *Prairie Nat.* 15: 49–56.

Kaufman, G. A., D. W. Kaufman, and E. J. Finck. 1988. Influence of fire and topography on habitat selection by *Peromyscus maniculatus* and *Reithrodontomys megalotis* in ungrazed tallgrass prairie. *J. Mammal.* 69: 342–52.

Kebart, K., and R. C. Anderson. 1987. Phenological and climatic patterns in three tallgrass prairies. *Southw. Nat.* 29: 29–37.

Keeley, J. E. 1987. Role of fire in seed germination of woody taxa in California chaparral. *Ecology* 68: 434–43.

Kelting, R. W. 1957. Winter burning in central Oklahoma grassland. *Ecology* 38: 520–22.

Kemp, P. R., and G. J. Williams, III. 1980. A physiological basis for niche separation between *Agropyron smithii* (C_3) and *Bouteloua gracilis* (C_4). *Ecology* 61: 846–58.

King, J. E. 1981. Late quaternary vegetational history of Illinois. *Ecol. Monogr.* 51: 43–62.

King, J. E., and W. H. Allen, Jr. 1977. A Holocene vegetation record from the Mississippi River Valley. *Quat. Res.* 8: 307–23.

Kline, V. 1983. Use of oak wilt to control invasion of prairie. In *Proc. Eighth North American Prairie Conference*, ed. R. Brewer, 162–64. Kalamazoo, Mich.: Western Michigan University.

Knapp, A. K. 1984a. Effect of fire in tallgrass prairie on seed production of *Vernonia baldwinii* Torr. (Compositae). *Southw. Nat.* 29: 242–43.

———. 1984b. Post-burn differences in solar radiation, leaf temperature and water stress influencing production in a lowland prairie. *Amer. J. Bot.* 71: 220–27.

———. 1985. Effect of fire and drought on the ecophysiology of *Andropogon gerardii* and *Panicum virgatum* in a tallgrass prairie. *Ecology* 66: 1309–20.

Knapp, A. K., and L. C. Hulbert. 1986. Production, density and height of flowering stalks of three grasses in annually burned and unburned eastern Kansas tallgrass prairie: A four year record. *Southw. Nat.* 31: 235–41.

Knapp, A. K., and T. R. Seastedt. 1986. Detritus accumulation limits productivity of tallgrass prairie. *BioScience* 36: 662–68.

Knight, D. H. 1973. Leaf area dynamics of a shortgrass prairie in Colorado. *Ecology* 54: 891–96.

Koelliker, J. K., M. E. Gurtz, and G. R. Marzolf. 1986. Watershed research at Konza tallgrass prairie. In *Hydraulics and hydrology in the small computer age*, Proc. Spec. Conf. Hydraulics Div. ASCE, 862–67. New York: American Society of Civil Engineers.

Kozlowski, T. T., and C. E. Ahlgren, eds. 1974. *Fire and ecosystems*. New York: Academic Press.

Krueger, K. 1986. Feeding relationships among bison, pronghorn and prairie dogs: An experimental analysis. *Ecology* 67: 760–70.

Kucera, C. L. 1981. Grasslands and fire. In *Fire regimes and ecosystem properties*, ed. H. A. Mooney et al., 90–111. U.S. For. Serv. Gen. Tech. Rep. WO-26.

Kucera, C. L., and R. C. Dahlman. 1968. Root-rhizome relationships in fire-treated stands of big bluestem, *Andropogon gerardii* Vitman. *Amer. Midl. Nat.* 80: 268–71.

Kucera, C. L., R. C. Dahlman, and M. Koelling. 1967. Total net productivity and turnover on an energy basis for tallgrass prairie. *Ecology* 48: 536–41.

Kucera, C. L., and J. H. Ehrenreich. 1962. Some effects of annual burning on central Missouri prairie. *Ecology* 43: 334–36.

Kucera, C. L., and M. Koelling. 1964. The influence of fire on composition of central Missouri prairie. *Amer. Midl. Nat.* 72: 142–47.

Langer, R. H. M. 1963. Tillering in herbage grasses. *Herbage Abstracts* 33: 141–47.

Laude, H. M. 1972. External factors affecting tiller development. In *The biology and utilization of grasses*, ed. V. B. Younger and C. M. McKell, 147–56. New York: Academic Press.

Lauenroth, W. K., and E. M. Preston. 1984. *The Effects of SO₂ on a grassland: A case study in the northern Great Plains of the United States.* New York: Springer-Verlag.

Launchbaugh, J. L., and C. E. Owensby. 1978. *Kansas rangelands: Their management based on a half century of research.* Kansas Agric. Expt. Sta. Bull. 622. Manhattan, Kan.

Leopold, A., and S. E. Jones. 1947. A phenological record for Sauk and Dane counties, Wisconsin, 1935–1945. *Ecol. Monogr.* 17: 81–122.

Leoschke, M. J. 1986. Fire and the life history of shooting star, *Dodecatheon meadii* in Iowa tallgrass prairie. M.S. thesis, Iowa State University, Ames.

Looman, J. 1983. Grassland as natural or semi-natural vegetation. In *Man's impact on vegetation,* ed. W. Holzner, M.J.A. Werger and I. Ikusima, 173–84. The Hague: Junk Publ.

Loucks, O. L. 1970. Evolution of diversity, efficiency and community stability. *Amer. Zool.* 10: 17–25.

Loucks, O. L., M. L. Plumb-Mentjes, and D. Rogers. 1985. Gap processes and large scale disturbances in sand prairies. In *The ecology of natural disturbance and patch dynamics,* ed. S. T. A. Pickett and P. S. White, 71–83. New York: Academic Press.

Lovell, D. L., R. A. Henderson, and E. A. Howell. 1983. The response of forb species to seasonal timing of prescribed burns in remnant Wisconsin prairies. In *Proc. Eighth North American Prairie Conference,* ed. R. Brewer, 11–15. Kalamazoo, Mich.: Western Michigan University.

Lussenhop, J. 1976. Soil arthropod response to prairie burning. *Ecology* 57: 88–98.

———. 1981. Microbial and microarthropod detrital processing in a prairie soil. *Ecology* 62: 694–97.

Martin, R., and C. Cushwa. 1966. Effect of heat and moisture on leguminous seed. *Proc. Tall Timbers Fire Ecol. Conf.* 5: 159–75.

Martin, R., R. Miller, and C. Cushwa. 1975. Germination of legume seeds subjected to moist and dry heat. *Ecology* 56: 1441–45.

McArthur, J. V., M. E. Gurtz, C. M. Tate, and F. S. Gilliam. 1985. The interaction of biological and hydrological phenomena that mediate the qualities of water draining native tallgrass prairie on the Konza Prairie Research Natural Area. In *Perspectives on nonpoint source pollution,* Proc. Nat. EPA Conf. 440/5-85-001, 478–82. Washington, D.C.: U.S. EPA.

McMillan, C. 1959. The role of ecotypic variation in the distribution of the central grassland in North America. *Ecol. Monogr.* 29: 285–308.

McMurphy, W. E., and K. L. Anderson. 1965. Burning Flint Hills range. *J. Range Manage.* 18: 265–69.

McNaughton, S. J. 1979. Grazing as an optimization process: Grass-ungulate relationships in the Serengeti. *Am. Nat.* 113: 691–703.

———. 1985. Ecology of a grazing ecosystem: The Serengeti. *Ecol. Monogr.* 55: 259–94.

McNaughton, S. J., M. B. Coughenour, and L. L. Wallace. 1982. Interactive processes in grassland ecosystems. In *Grasses and grasslands: Systematics and ecology,* ed. J. R. Estes, R. J. Tyrl, and J. N. Brunken, 167–93. Norman, Okla.: University of Oklahoma Press.

Meagher, M. 1973. The bison of Yellowstone National Park. U.S. Natl. Park Serv. Sci Monogr. Ser. 1. Washington, D.C.: U.S. National Park Service.

Mentzer, L. W. 1951. Studies on plant succession in true prairie. *Ecol. Monogr.* 21: 255–67.

Miller, R. M. 1987. The ecology of vesicular-arbuscular mycorrhizae in grass- and shrublands. In *Ecophysiology of VA mycorrhizal plants*, ed. G. R. Safir, 135–70. Boca Raton, Fla.: CRC Press.

Miller, R. M., A. G. Jarstfen, and J. K. Pillai. 1987. Biomass allocation in an *Agropyron smithii–Glomus* symbiosis. *Amer. J. Bot.* 74: 114–22.

Monson, R. K., R. O. Littlejohn, Jr., and G. J. Williams, Ill. 1983. Photosynthetic adaptation to temperature in four species from the Colorado shortgrass steppe: A physiological model for coexistence. *Oecologia* 58: 43–51.

Moreth, L. H., and P. Schramm. 1973. A comparative survey of small mammal populations in various grassland habitats with emphasis on restored prairie. In *Proc. Third Midwest Prairie Conference*, ed. L. C. Hulbert, 79–84. Manhattan, Kan.: Kansas State University.

Netherland, L. 1979. The effect of disturbances in tallgrass prairie sites on an index of diversity and equitability. *Southw. Nat.* 24: 267–74.

Odum, E. P. 1969. The strategy of ecosystem development. *Science* 164: 262–70.

Ojima, D. S. 1987. The short-term and long-term effects of burning on tallgrass prairie ecosystem properties and dynamics. Ph.D. dissertation, Colorado State University, Ft. Collins.

Ojima, D. S., W. J. Parton, D. S. Schimel, and C. E. Owensby. 1988. Simulating the long-term impact of burning on C, N and P cycling in a tallgrass prairie. In *Current perspectives in environmental biogeochemistry*, ed. G. Giovannozzi-Sermanni and P. Hammipieri, 353–70. Rome: C.N.R.-IPRA.

Old, S. M. 1969. Microclimate, fire and plant production in an Illinois prairie. *Ecol. Monogr.* 39: 355–84.

Owensby, C. E., and K. L. Anderson. 1967. Yield response to time of burning in the Kansas Flint Hills. *J. Range Manage.* 20: 12–16.

Owensby, C. E., G. A. Paulsen, and J. D. McKendrick. 1970. Effect of burning and clipping on big bluestem reserve carbohydrates. *J. Range Manage.* 23: 358–62.

Parton, W. J., W. K. Lauenroth, and F. M. Smith. 1981. Water loss from a shortgrass steppe. *Agric. Meteorol.* 24: 97–109.

Parton, W. J., D. S. Schimel, C. V. Cole, and D. S. Ojima. 1987. Analysis of factors controlling soil organic matter levels in Great Plains grasslands. *Soil Sci. Soc. Am. J.* 51: 1173–79.

Parton, W. J., J. W. B. Stewart, and C. V. Cole. 1988. Dynamics of C, N, P and S in grassland soils: A model. *Biogeochemistry* 5: 109–31.

Pastor, J., M. A. Stillwell, and D. Tilman. 1987. Nitrogen mineralization and nitrification in four Minnesota old fields. *Oecologia* 71: 481–85.

Pauly, W. R. 1984. Red pine, shooting star, parsnip: Responses to burning (Wisconsin). *Restor. and Manage. Notes* 2: 28.

Peden, D. G., G. M. van Dyne, R. W. Rice, and R. M. Hansen. 1974. The trophic ecology of *Bison bison* L. on shortgrass plains. *J. Appl. Ecol.* 11: 489–98.

Peet, M., R. Anderson, and M. S. Adams. 1975. Effect of fire on big bluestem production. *Amer. Midl. Nat.* 94: 15–26.

Peet, R. K., D. C. Glenn-Lewin, and J. Walker-Wolf. 1983. Prediction of man's impact on plant species diversity. In *Man's impact on vegetation*, ed. W. Holzner, M. J. A. Werger, and I. Ikusima, 41–54. The Hague: Junk Publ.

Pemble, R. H., G. L. Van Amburg, and L. Mattson. 1981. Interspecific variation in flowering activity following a spring burn on a northwestern Minnesota prairie. In *Proc. Sixth North American Prairie Conference*, ed. R. L. Stuckey and K. J. Reese, 235–40. Ohio Biological Survey Publ. 15. Columbus, Oh.

Penfound, W. T., and R. W. Kelting. 1950. Some effects of winter burning on a moderately grazed pasture. *Ecology* 31: 554–60.

Petersen, N. J. 1983. The effects of fire, litter and ash on flowering in *Andropogon gerardii*. In *Proc. Eighth North American Prairie Conference*, ed. R. Brewer, 21–24. Kalamazoo, Mich.: Western Michigan University.

Peterson, S. K., G. A. Kaufman, and D. W. Kaufman. 1985. Habitat selection by small mammals of the tall-grass prairie: Experimental patch choice. *Prairie Nat.* 17: 65–70.

Petranka, J. W., and J. K. McPherson. 1979. The role of *Rhus copallina* in the dynamics of the forest-prairie ecotone in north-central Oklahoma. *Ecology* 60: 956–65.

Pickett, S. T. A., J. Kolasa, J. J. Armesto, and S. L. Collins. 1989. The ecological concept of disturbance and its expression at various hierarchical levels. *Oikos* 54: 129–36.

Pickett, S. T. A., and P. S. White, eds. 1985. *The ecology of natural disturbance and patch dynamics*. New York: Academic Press.

Platt, W. J. 1975. The colonization and formation of equilibrium plant species associations on badger disturbances in a tall-grass prairie. *Ecol. Monogr.* 45: 285–305.

Power, T. F. 1980. Response of semiarid grassland sites to nitrogen fertilization. I. Plant growth and water use. *Soil Sci. Soc. Am. J.* 44: 545–50.

Pyne, S. J. 1982. *Fire in America: A cultural history of wildland and rural fire.* Princeton, N.J.: Princeton University Press.

———. 1983. Indian fires. *Natural History* 2: 6–11.

———. 1986. "These conflagrated prairies": A cultural fire history of the grasslands. In *Proc. Ninth North American Prairie Conference*, ed. G. K. Clambey and R. H. Pemble, 131–37. Fargo, N.D.: Tri-College University Press.

Rabinowitz, D., and J. K. Rapp. 1985. Colonization and establishment of Missouri prairie plants on artificial soil disturbances. III. Species abundance distributions, survivorship and rarity. *Amer. J. Bot.* 72: 1635–40.

Raison, R. J. 1979. Modification of the soil environment by vegetation fires, with particular reference to nitrogen transformations: A review. *Plant and Soil* 51: 73–108.

Rapp, J. K., and D. Rabinowitz. 1985. Colonization and establishment of Missouri prairie plants on artificial soil disturbances. I. Dynamics of forb and graminoid seedlings and shoots. *Amer. J. Bot.* 72: 1618–28.

Rice, E. L., and R. L. Parenti. 1978. Causes of decreases in productivity in undisturbed tallgrass prairie. *Amer. J. Bot.* 65: 1091–97.

Richards, M. S., and R. Q. Landers. 1973. Responses of species in Kalsow Prairie, Iowa, to an April fire. *Proc. Iowa Acad. Sci.* 80: 159–61.

Ring, C. B., R. A. Nicholson, and J. L. Launchbaugh. 1985. Vegetational traits of patch-grazed rangeland in western central Kansas. *J. Range Manage.* 38: 51–55.

Risser, P. G. 1985. Grasslands. In *Physiological ecology of North American plant communities*, ed. B. F. Chabot and H. A. Mooney, 323–56. London: Chapman and Hall.

———. 1988. Effects of abiotic factors on energetics and nutrient cycles in grasslands and savannas. In *Concepts of ecosystem ecology*, ed. L. R. Pomeroy and J. J. Alberts, 115–29. New York: Springer-Verlag.

Risser, P. G., E. C. Birney, H. D. Blocker, S. W. May, W. J. Parton, and J. A. Wiens. 1981. *The true prairie ecosystem*. Stroudsburg, Pa.: Hutchinson Ross.

Risser, P. G., J. R. Karr, and R. T. T. Forman. 1984. *Landscape ecology: Direction and approaches*. Illinois Nat. Hist. Surv. Special Publ. 2. Champaign, Ill.

Risser, P. G., and W. J. Parton. 1982. Ecosystem analysis of the tallgrass prairie: Nitrogen cycle. *Ecology* 63: 1342–51.

Rodgers, C. S., and R. C. Anderson. 1979. Presettlement vegetation of two prairie peninsula counties. *Bot. Gaz.* 140: 232–40.

Runkle, J. R. 1985. Disturbance regime in temperature forests. In *The ecology of natural disturbance and patch dynamics*, ed. S. T. A. Pickett and P. S. White, 17–33. New York: Academic Press.

Russell, E. W. B. 1983. Indian-set fires in the forests of the northeastern United States. *Ecology* 64: 78–88.

Rykiel, E. J., Jr. 1985. Towards a definition of ecological disturbance. *Aust. J. Ecol.* 10: 361–65.

Sala, O. E., W. K. Lauenroth, W. J. Parton, and M. J. Trlica. 1981. Water status of soil and vegetation in a shortgrass steppe. *Oecologia* 48: 403–5.

Sala, O. E., W. K. Lauenroth, and C. P. P. Reid. 1982. Water relations: a new dimension for niche separation between *Bouteloua gracilis* and *Agropyron smithii* in North American semi-arid grasslands. *J. Appl. Ecol.* 19: 647–57.

Sauer, C. O. 1950. Grassland climax, fire and man. *J. Range. Manage.* 3: 16–21.

Savage, D. A., and L. A. Jacobson. 1935. The killing effect of heat and drought on buffalo grass and blue grama grass at Hays, Kansas. *J. Amer. Soc. Agron.* 27: 566–82.

Schimel, D. S., W. J. Parton, F. J. Adamsen, R. G. Woodmansee, R. L. Senft, and M. A. Stillwell. 1986. The role of cattle in nitrogen budget of a shortgrass steppe. *Biogeochemistry* 2: 39–52.

Schimel, D. S., M. A. Stillwell, and R. G. Woodmansee. 1985. Biogeochemistry of C, N and P in a soil catena of the shortgrass steppe. *Ecology* 66: 276–82.

Schramm, P. 1970. Effects of fire on small mammal populations in a restored tallgrass prairie. In *Proc. Symp. Prairie and Prairie Restoration*, ed. P. Schramm, 39–41. Galesburg, Ill.: Knox College.

Schramm, P., and B. J. Willcutts. 1983. Habitat selection of small mammals in burned and unburned tallgrass prairie. In *Proc. Eighth North American Prairie Conference*, ed. R. Brewer, 49–55. Kalamazoo, Mich.: Western Michigan University.

Schwartz, C. C., and J. E. Ellis. 1981. Feeding ecology and niche separation of some ungulates on the shortgrass prairie. *J. Appl. Ecol.* 18: 343–53.

Schwegman, J. 1973. *Comprehensive plan for the Illinois Nature Preserves system. Part 2. The natural divisions of Illinois*. Rockford, Ill.: Illinois Nature Preserves Commission.

Seastedt, T. R. 1984a. Belowground microarthropods of annually burned and unburned tallgrass prairie. *Amer. Midl. Nat.* 111: 405–40.

———. 1984b. The role of microarthropods in decomposition and mineralization processes. *Ann. Rev. Ent.* 29: 25–46.

———. 1985. Canopy interception of nitrogen in bulk precipitation by annually burned and unburned tallgrass prairie. *Oecologia* 66: 88–92.

————. 1988. Mass, nitrogen and phosporus dynamics of foliage and root detritus of tallgrass prairie. *Ecology* 69: 59–65.

Seastedt, T. R., and D. C. Hayes. 1988. Factors influencing nitrogen concentrations in soil water in a North American tallgrass prairie. *Soil. Biol. Biochem.* 20: 725–30.

Seastedt, T. R., D. C. Hayes, and N. J. Petersen. 1986. Effects of vegetation, burning and mowing on soil arthropods of tallgrass prairie. In *Proc. Ninth North American Prairie Conference*, ed. G. K. Clambey and R. H. Pemble, 99–103. Fargo, N.D.: Tri-College Press.

Seastedt, T. R., D. C. Hayes, and R. A. Ramundo. 1988b. Maximization of belowground consumer densities by removal of foliage: Empirical evidence, graphical and conceptual models. *Oikos* 51: 243–48.

Seastedt, T. R., S. W. James, and T. C. Todd. 1988a. Interactions among invertebrates, microbes and plant growth in tallgrass prairie. *Agric. Ecosys. Environ.* 24: 219–28.

Seastedt, T. R., T. C. Todd, and S. W. James. 1987. Experimental manipulations of arthropod, nematode and earthworm communities in a North American grassland. *Pedobiologia* 30: 9–17.

Senft, R. L., M. B. Coughenour, D. W. Bailey, L. R. Rittenhouse, O. E. Sala, and D. M. Swift. 1987. Large herbivore foraging and ecological hierarchies. *BioScience* 37: 789–99.

Senft, R. L., L. R. Rittenhouse, and R. G. Woodmansee. 1985. Factors influencing patterns of grazing behavior on shortgrass steppe. *J. Range Manage.* 38: 81–87.

Sharrow, S. H., and H. A. Wright. 1977. Effects of fire, ash and litter on soil nitrate, temperature, moisture and tobosagrass production in the Rolling Plains. *J. Range Manage.* 30: 266–70.

Sheedy, J. D., F. L. Johnson, and P. G. Risser. 1973. A model for phosphorus and potassium flux in a tall-grass prairie. *Southw. Nat.* 18: 135–49.

Sims, P. L. 1988. Grasslands. In *North American terrestrial vegetation*, ed. M. G. Barbour and W. D. Billings, 265–86. Cambridge and London: Cambridge University Press.

Singh, J. S., W. K. Lauenroth, and D. G. Milchunas. 1983. Geography of grassland ecosystems. *Prog. Phys. Geog.* 7: 46–79.

Smith, E. F., and C. E. Owensby. 1972. Effects of fire on true prairie grasslands. *Proc. Tall Timbers Fire Ecol. Conf.* 12: 9–22.

Smoliak, S., and J. F. Dormaar. 1985. Productivity of russian wildrye and crested wheatgrass and their effect on prairie soil. *J. Range Manage.* 38: 403–5.

Sorensen, J. T., and D. J. Holden. 1974. Germination of native prairie forb seeds. *J. Range Manage.* 27: 123–26.

Sousa, W. P. 1984. The role of disturbance in natural communities. *Ann. Rev. Ecol. Syst.* 15: 353–92.

————. 1985. Disturbance and patch dynamics on rocky intertidal shores. In *The ecology of natural disturbance and patch dynamics*, ed. S. T. A. Pickett and P. S. White, 101–24. New York: Academic Press.

Springer, J. T., and P. Schramm. 1972. The effects of fire on small mammal populations in a restored prairie with special reference to the short-tailed shrew (*Blarina brevicauda*). In *Proc. Second Midwest Prairie Conference*, ed. J. H. Zimmerman, 91–96. Madison, Wis.: University of Wisconsin.

Stebbins, G. L. 1981. Coevolution of grasses and herbivores. *Ann. Mo. Bot. Gard.* 68: 75–86.

Steiger, T. L. 1930. Structure of prairie vegetation. *Ecology* 11: 170–217.

Steuter, A. A. 1987. C_3/C_4 production shift on seasonal burns—northern mixed prairie. *J. Range Manage.* 40: 27–31.

Stewart, O. C. 1951. Burning and natural vegetation in the United States. *Geog. Rev.* 41: 317–20.

———. 1956. Fire as the first great force employed by man. In *Man's role in changing the face of the earth*, ed. W. L. Thomas, 115–33. Chicago: University of Chicago Press.

Striat, R. A., and M. T. Jackson. 1986. An ecological analysis of the plant communities of Little Bluestem Prairie Nature Preserve: Pre-burning versus post-burning. *Indiana Acad. Sci.* 95: 447–52.

Svejcar, T. J., and J. A. Browning. 1988. Growth and gas exchange of *Andropogon gerardii* as influenced by burning. *J. Range Manage.* 41: 239–44.

Swanson, F. J., T. K. Kratz, N. Caine, and R. G. Woodmansee. 1988. Landform effects on ecosystem patterns and processes. *BioScience* 38: 92–98.

Tainton, N. M. and M. T. Mentis. 1984. Fire in grassland. In *Ecological effects of fire in South African ecosystems*, ed. P. de Van Booysen and N. Tainton, 117–47. New York: Springer-Verlag.

Tate, C. M. 1985. A study of temporal and spatial variation in nitrogen concentrations in a tallgrass prairie stream. Ph.D. dissertation, Kansas State University, Manhattan, Kan.

Tester, J. R. 1965. Effects of a controlled burn on small mammals in a Minnesota oak-savanna. *Amer. Midl. Nat.* 74: 240–43.

Tester, J. R., and W. H. Marshall. 1961. A study of certain plant and animal interrelations on a native prairie in northwestern Minnesota. *Occasional Papers Mus. Nat. Hist., Univ. Minnesota* 8: 1–51.

Tilman, D. 1985. The resource ratio hypothesis of plant succession. *Am. Nat.* 125: 827–52.

Tobey, R. 1981. *Saving the prairies: The life cycle of the founding school of American plant ecology, 1895–1955.* Berkeley: University of California Press.

Towne, G., and C. Owensby. 1984. Long-term effects of annual burning at different dates in ungrazed Kansas tallgrass prairie. *J. Range Manage.* 37: 392–97.

Trabaud, L., ed. 1987. *The role of fire in ecological systems.* The Hague: SPB Academic Publ.

Transeau, E. 1935. The prairie peninsula. *Ecology* 16: 423–27.

Ueckert, D. N. 1979. Impact of a white grub (*Phyllophaga crinita*) on a shortgrass community and evaluation of selected rehabilitation practices. *J. Range Manage.* 32: 445–48.

Urban, D. L., R. V. O'Neill, and H. H. Shugart. 1987. Landscape ecology. *BioScience* 37: 119–27.

Vacanti, P. L., and K. N. Geluso. 1985. Recolonization of a burned prairie by meadow voles (*Microtus pennsylvanicus*). *Prairie Nat.* 17: 15–22.

Vogl, R. J. 1964. Vegetational history of Crex Meadows, a prairie savannah in northwestern Wisconsin. *Amer. Midl. Nat.* 78: 487–95.

———. 1974. Effects of fire on grasslands. In *Fire and ecosystems*, ed. T. T. Kozlowski and C. E. Ahlgren, 139–94. New York: Academic Press.

Walker, J., and R. K. Peet. 1983. Composition and species diversity of pine-wiregrass savannas of the Green Swamp, North Carolina. *Vegetatio* 55: 163–79.

Wallace, L. L. 1987. Effects of clipping and soil compaction on growth, morphology and mycorrhizal colonization of *Schizachyrium scoparium*, a C_4 bunchgrass. *Oecologia* 72: 423–28.

Wallace, L. L., and T. J. Svejcar. 1987. Mycorrhizal and clipping effects on *Andropogon gerardii* photosynthesis. *Amer. J. Bot.* 74: 1138–42.

Warner, N. J., M. F. Allen, and J. A. MacMahon. 1987. Dispersal agents of vesicular-arbuscular mycorrhizal fungi in a disturbed arid ecosystem. *Mycologia* 79: 721–30.

Warren, S. D., C. J. Scifres, and P. D. Teel. 1987. Response of grassland arthropods to burning: A review. *Agric. Ecosys. Environ.* 19: 105–30.

Weaver, J. E. 1954. *North American prairie*. Lincoln, Neb.: University of Nebraska Press.

———. 1961. The living network in prairie soils. *Bot. Gaz.* 123: 16–28.

———. 1968. *Prairie plants and their environment*. Lincoln, Neb.: University of Nebraska Press.

Weaver, J. E., and F. W. Albertson. 1936. Effects of the great drought on the prairies of Iowa, Nebraska and Kansas. *Ecology* 17: 567–639.

———. 1956. Grasslands of the Great Plains. Lincoln, Neb.: Johnsen.

Weaver, J. E., and W. E. Bruner. 1954. Nature and place of transition from true prairie to mixed prairie. *Ecology* 35: 117–26.

Weaver, J. E., and T. J. Fitzpatrick. 1934. The prairie. *Ecol. Monogr.* 4: 109–295.

Weaver, J. E., and N. W. Rowland. 1952. Effects of excessive natural mulch on development, yield and structure of native grassland. *Bot. Gaz.* 114: 1–19.

Wells, P. V. 1970a. Historical factors controlling vegetation patterns and floristic distribution in the central plains region of North America. In *Pleistocene and recent environments of the central Great Plains*, ed. W. Dort and J. Jones 211–21. Spec. Publ. 3. Lawrence, Kan.: University of Kansas Press.

———. 1970b. Postglacial vegetational history of the Great Plains. *Science* 167: 1574–82.

White, J. A., and D. C. Glenn-Lewin. 1984. Regional and local variation in tallgrass prairie remnants of Iowa and eastern Nebraska. *Vegetatio* 57: 65–78.

Whittaker, R. H. 1977. Evolution of species diversity in land communities. *Evol. Biol.* 10: 1–67.

Wiens, J. A., C. S. Crawford, and J. R. Gosz. 1985. Boundary dynamics: a conceptual framework for studying landscape ecosystems. *Oikos* 45: 421–27.

Woodmansee, R. G. 1978. Additions and losses of nitrogen in grassland ecosystems. *BioScience* 28: 448–53.

Woodmansee, R. G., and F. J. Adamsen. 1983. Biogeochemical cycles and ecological hierarchies. In *Nutrient cycling in agricultural ecosystems*, ed. R. R. Lowrance, R. L. Todd, L. Asmussen, and R. A. Leonard, 497–516. College Agric. Expt. Sta. Spec. Publ. No. 23. Athens, Ga.: University of Georgia.

Woodmansee, R. G., and L. S. Wallach. 1981. Effects of fire regimes on biogeochemical cycles. In *Fire regimes and ecosystem properties*, ed. H. A. Mooney et al., 379–400. U.S.D.A. For. Serv. Gen. Tech. Rep. WO-26.

Wright, H. A. 1974. Range burning. *J. Range Manage.* 27: 5–11.

———. 1980. *The role and use of fire in the semidesert grass-shrub type*. U.S.D.A. For. Serv. Gen. Tech. Rep. INT-85.

Wright, H. A., and A. W. Bailey. 1980. *Fire ecology and prescribed burning in the Great Plains: A research review*. U.S.D.A. For. Serv. Gen. Tech. Rep INT-77.

————. 1982. *Fire ecology.* New York: John Wiley and Sons.

Zar, J. H. 1974. *Biostatistical analysis.* Englewood Cliffs, N.J.: Prentice Hall.

Zedler, J., and O. L. Loucks. 1969. Differential burning of *Poa pratensis* fields and *Andropogon scoparius* prairies in central Wisconsin. *Amer. Midl. Nat.* 81: 341–52.

The Contributors

Ann Akey, Department of Botany, Iowa State University, Ames, Iowa 50011.

Roger C. Anderson, Department of Biology, Illinois State University, Normal, Illinois 61761.

Scott L. Collins, Department of Botany and Microbiology, University of Oklahoma, Norman, Oklahoma 73019.

Elmer J. Finck, Division of Biology, Kansas State University, Manhattan, Kansas 66506. Present address: Division of Biological Sciences, Emporia State University, Emporia, Kansas 66801.

David J. Gibson, Division of Biology, Kansas State University, Manhattan, Kansas 66506. Present address: Department of Biology, University of West Florida, Pensacola, Florida 32514.

David C. Glenn-Lewin, Department of Botany, Iowa State University, Ames, Iowa 50011.

Louise A. Johnson, Department of Botany, Iowa State University, Ames, Iowa 50011.

Thomas W. Jurik, Department of Botany, Iowa State University, Ames, Iowa 50011.

Donald W. Kaufman, Division of Biology, Kansas State University, Manhattan, Kansas 66506.

Glennis A. Kaufman, Division of Biology, Kansas State University, Manhattan, Kansas 66506.

Mark Leoschke, Department of Botany, Iowa State University, Ames, Iowa 50011.

Dennis Ojima, Natural Resource Ecology Laboratory, Colorado State University, Fort Collins, Colorado 80523.

Clinton E. Owensby, Department of Agronomy, Kansas State University, Manhattan, Kansas 66506.

William J. Parton, Natural Resource Ecology Laboratory, Colorado State University, Fort Collins, Colorado 80523.

Rosemary A. Ramundo, Division of Biology, Kansas State University, Manhattan, Kansas 66506.

Paul G. Risser, Vice President for Research, University of New Mexico, Albuquerque, New Mexico 87131.

Tom Rosburg, Department of Botany, Iowa State University, Ames, Iowa 50011.

David S. Schimel, Natural Resource Ecology Laboratory, Colorado State University, Fort Collins, Colorado 80523.

Tim R. Seastedt, Division of Biology, Kansas State University, Manhattan, Kansas 66506.

Tony J. Svejcar, U.S. Department of Agriculture, Agricultural Research Service, 920 Valley Road, Reno, Nevada 89512.

Linda L. Wallace, Department of Botany and Microbiology, University of Oklahoma, Norman, Oklahoma 73019.

Index

Acidification: 144
Agropyron smithii: 134, 138–39, 141
Agrostis stolonifera: 32
Alberta: 85, 88
Aldous sites: 119–24
Ambrosia psilostachya: 22, 83
American Indians: 3, 10, 14, 17
Andropogon gerardii: 4, 19–27, 32, 33, 36, 39, 40, 83, 94–96, 119, 134, 147
Andropogon scoparius: 22, 32, 83, 108, 119, 134, 141
Anemone cylindrica: 33
Annuals: 90
Arizona: 52, 87
Artemisia ludoviciana: 22, 83
Ash: 104
Aster ericoides: 33
Aster laevis: 33
Aster azureus: 38

Badgers: 94
Belowground system: 101–102
Biomass: 21–22; belowground, 23, 106–109, 120, 123; aboveground, 1–4, 120, 123
Bison: 83, 135
Bouteloua curtipendula: 30, 32
Bouteloua gracilis: 134, 138–39, 141
Buchloe dactyloides: 134, 138–39
Buffalo wallows: 92, 136

C_3 grasses: 29, 85, 88, 103, 138–39
C_4 grasses: 4, 85, 88, 89, 103, 138–39
Calamagrostis inexpansa: 32
California: 49, 69
California vole: 49, 69
Carbon: 23, 25
CENTURY model: 119, 124–30
Cirsium spp.: 38
Clements, F. E.: 3, 83
Climate: 8–18, 77; climatic change, 138–41, 146
Colorado: 140

Community heterogeneity: 90, 92, 94, 116
Community pattern: 90
Conyza canadensis: 83

Daucus carota: 38
Decomposition: 111–12
Deer mouse: 49, 50, 51, 52, 53, 56, 57, 58, 59, 61, 67, 68, 71, 72–75, 77–78
Disturbance: 4, 5
Disturbance regime: 4, 5, 73–77, 82–83
Dodecatheon meadii: 33, 36
Drought: 3, 8–9, 11, 12, 16, 17, 77, 134, 138–39, 142

Earthworms: 109
Elliot's short-tailed shrew: 56, 59, 63, 64, 68, 71, 72–75

Fire-negative species: 47–61
Fire-neutral species: 47–61
Fire-positive species: 47–61
Flowering: grasses, 29–33; forbs, 33–35
Forbs: 29, 33–35, 87–88, 89, 90, 103, 134
Fuel: 3, 15, 16

Galium boreale: 33
Gradient: 141, 142
Grazing: 3, 8, 9, 10, 17, 78, 92, 94, 116, 136–37, 138–39, 140, 142, 143
Great Britain: 145

Helianthus maxmilliana: 33
Hispid cotton rat: 52
Hispid pocket mouse: 52, 53
Hypoxis hirsuta: 33

Illinois: 22, 50, 51, 52, 106, 141–42
Iowa: 29, 32, 33, 37, 39, 88

Kansas: 22, 26, 32, 33, 52, 56–65, 66–68, 71–78, 88, 90, 94
Konza Prairie: 53, 56–65, 66–68, 71–78, 85, 90, 96–97, 103–17, 119–24

Lactuca seriola: 38
LAI: see Leaf area index
Landscape ecology: 133–46
Leaching: 123
Leaf area index: 25, 26
Litter: 85, 89, 105, 106, 148, 149, 151

Macroarthropods: 109–10
Masked shrew: 50
Meadow jumping mouse: 51, 52
Meadow vole: 49, 50, 51, 52, 53, 56,
  65–66, 67, 71
Medicago lupulina: 33, 38
Melilotus alba: 38, 88
Merriam's kangaroo rat: 52
Methodological problems: 42–44
Microarthropods: 109–10
Microbes in soil: 104, 105, 112–13, 114,
  122, 129–30
Mineralization: 121, 122, 123, 129
Minnesota: 29, 30, 32, 33, 36, 49, 50
Miocene: 8
Missouri: 22, 100
Monarda fistulosa: 36
Mortality of small mammals: 65–67
Mycorrhizae: 108–109, 140–41

Nebraska: 53, 66, 67
Nematodes: 109–10
Netherlands: 145
Net primary production: 9, 104, 112
Nitrogen: in soil, 21, 104, 105, 110–16,
  122–23, 125–30; in plants, 120–21
Nitrogen fixation: 123–24, 129–30
Nitrogen use efficiency: 114, 120, 123
Northern short-tailed shrew: 51, 52
NPP: see Net primary production
NUE: see Nitrogen use efficiency
Nutrient cycling: 101, 103, 104, 114,
  121–22, 129

Oklahoma: 22, 23, 25, 26, 87, 88, 90, 94,
  141–42
Oxalis stricta: 38, 83

Panicum scribnerianum: 38
Panicum virgatum: 134, 147
PAR: see Photosynthetically active
  radiation
Pastinaca sativa: 38
Patch: dynamics, 5, 94; structure, 82, 83,
  90, 149, 150
Petalostemon purpureum: 33
Phenotype: 141–42
Phlox pilosa: 29

Phosphorus: in soil, 104, 111, 122, 123–24,
  125–30; in plant, 120–21
Photosynthetically active radiation: 21, 23
Plains pocket gopher: 94
Poa pratensis: 32, 33, 36, 38, 41
Pollutants: 144–45
Population dynamics of small mammals:
  67–68
Prairie dogs: 94
Prairie peninsula: 12–14
Prairie vole: 50, 52, 56, 59, 60, 61, 65–66,
  67, 68, 71, 78
Precipitation: 8, 11, 14, 106, 114
Prenanthes racemosa: 33
Pronghorn: 135
Psoralea argophylla: 33
Pycanthemum virginianum: 33

Ratibida pinnata: 29, 36
Reproduction: 28–45; asexual, 148; sexual,
  148
Rudbeckia hirta: 29

Scale: 90, 137–38, 141, 145, 148–51
Season of burning: 14, 17, 22–23, 30–35,
  41, 88, 103
Seed: production, 36–37; pool, 85, 94, 97
Seedling establishment: 37–40
Senecio plattensis: 83
Shortgrass steppe: 136, 138–39, 140, 142
Sisyrinchium angustifolium: 33
Small mammals: 46–80, 148
Soils: 8; moisture, 14, 26, 121; tempera-
  ture, 21, 121; carbon, 120–21, 125–30;
  organic matter, 122–24, 125–30
Solidago canadensis: 33, 83
Sorghastrum nutans: 22, 32, 33, 36, 41, 83,
  119, 134
South Dakota: 22, 53
Southern bog lemming: 56, 59, 60, 68
Southern grasshopper mouse: 52
Species diversity: 5, 61, 82, 83, 88–89,
  92–94; richness, 61–65, 82, 85–88, 89,
  92–94, 95–97; evenness, 82, 89
Sporobolus heterolepis: 32, 141
Sporobolus asper: 83
Standing dead biomass: 105, 106
Stipa spp.: 134
Succession: small mammals, 69–73; plants,
  85, 89, 95–97, 147–48

Tawny cotton rat: 52
Thirteen-lined ground squirrel: 51, 56, 59,
  61
Throughfall: 105

Tillering: 4, 19–21, 40–42
Topography: 8, 10, 14, 17, 77, 140
Trifolium repens: 38
Turnover: roots, 107–108; soil organic matter, 122–123

Ungulates: 149, 150, 151

Verbena hastata: 33
Verbena stricta: 38
Vernonia baldwinii: 33, 36, 83
Vernonia fasciculata: 33
Viola peditifida: 38

Weaver, J. E.: 3, 99–100
Western harvest mouse: 49, 53, 56, 59, 63, 66, 68, 69, 71, 72–75, 77–78
White-footed mouse: 50, 51, 52, 56, 60–61, 71
White-throated woodrat: 52
Wisconsin: 30, 32, 39, 51, 141–42
Wyoming: 140, 147

Yellowstone National Park: 147